ALSO BY DR. REUVEN BAR-LEVAV

Thinking in the Shadow of Feelings
Published by Simon and Schuster

EVERY FAMILY NEEDS A C.E.O.

What Mothers and Fathers Can Do
About Our
Deteriorating Families
and Values

REUVEN BAR-LEVAV, M.D.

NEW YORK / WASHINGTON / DETROIT / JERUSALEM

FATHERING, INC. PRESS is a registered trademark
of Fathering, Inc.

Cover Design by Robert Aulicino
Manufactured in the United States of America

1   3   5   7   9   10   8   6   4   2

Library of Congress Cataloging in Publication Data

Bar-Levav, Reuven, date.
Every Family Needs a C.E.O.

Includes index.
1. Values—Social aspects.   2. Mental health—Children.
3. Critical thinking—Social aspects.   4. Character education.
5. Parenting—Mothering.   6. Parenting—Fathering.
7. Authority—Family.   8. Authority—Social aspects.   I. Title.
HQ769.B46   1995   649.7   94-61637
ISBN 0-9644177-0-7

I would like to thank the following writers, publishers, and copyright holders for permission to reprint the quoted material listed below.

"Growing Up is Hard to Do" by Travis Simpkins, Newsweek, Inc., June 21, 1993.

"Wild in the Streets" by Barbara Kantrowitz, Newsweek, Inc., August 2, 1993. All rights reserved.

"Wilding in the Night" by Nancy Gibbs, Copyright ©1989, Time Inc. Reprinted by permission.

Native Stranger, by Eddy L. Harris, Copyright ©1992. Reprinted by permission of Simon and Schuster, Inc.

CONTENTS

DEDICATION   9

INTRODUCTION   11

FIRST SECTION
THE DIFFICULT JOB OF FATHERING
CHAPTER   1.   What is Fathering? And a Brief
               Introduction to Mothering   19
          2.   Fathers are even More Important than Dads   26
          3.   Life without Good Fathering: A Few
               Extreme Examples and Lessons   30
          4.   Where Have All the Fathers Gone? And the
               Story of Mothers Stuck with the
               Job of Fathering   37
          5.   More about Mothering. No Fathering is
               Possible without it. And a Note about
               Children who Suicide   43
          6.   A Few Suggestions to Improve the Ability
               to Father   48
          7.   How *Not* to Father   57

SECOND SECTION
THE HOPE, JOY AND SILENT PAIN OF FATHERS,
MOTHERS, SONS AND DAUGHTERS
          8.   A Rare Christmas Tale of a Father-Son
               Reconciliation   69
          9.   Larry and Friends: Too Little Fathering   74

10. Black Youngsters and their Heroes. And
    More about Z   78
11. The Missing Father: A Special Tragedy
    of Blacks   85
12. Roger and the Walleye   92
13. Fathering Children of Divorced Parents: A
    Nearly Impossible Task. And more
    about Larry   97
14. The Silent Loneliness of a Father: Dr. Gene   105
15. The Sad Tale of Daughters who Lose
    their Daddies at Adolescence. And more
    about Marie   113
16. Homosexual Men and their Fathers
    and Mothers   122
17. A Story of Four Generations   130
18. Growing Up is Hard to Do   134
19. A Page from Father's Diary   137
20. Fathers Running Away in Panic after
    their Child is Born   141

THIRD SECTION
THE MANY TASKS OF GOOD FATHERING: A MANUAL

21. A Simplified Formula for Raising Healthy
    Children   151
22. Push Sons to Leave Mother's Apron Strings
    and Help them Stand Tall as Men   157
23. Make Room for Expressions of Anger
    Yet Control Impulsive Acts   171
24. No Disdain in the Fight Against Authority   179
25. Set Limits and Instill Self-Restraint   185

26.   Battle Self-Indulgence and Instill
      Self-Discipline   194
27.   Help the Child Express Hurt but Don't
      Overprotect   202
28.   Challenge the Child's False Claims of
      Competence and Incompetence   207
29.   Force the Child to Think and to Live
      Thoughtfully   220
30.   Teach the Child to be Sensitive
      and Empathetic   230
31.   Encourage, Support and Teach Self-
      Mothering   241
32.   Demand Excellence, Instill Values and
      Develop Respect for Learning   254

A PERSONAL NOTE FROM THE AUTHOR   263

ACKNOWLEDGEMENTS   267

BIBLIOGRAPHY   269

INDEX   273

AN INVITATION TO THE READER   286

TO DAVID BEN-GURION
WHO INSPIRED ME

TO LOTTE LEAH HEILMANN-TUCHMANN
MY FATHERING MOTHER

TO AVRAHAM TUCHMANN
MY SENSITIVE MOTHERING FATHER AND

TO DORON, ILANA AND LEORA BAR-LEVAV
WHO WOULD HAVE HAD AN EVEN BETTER FATHER
HAD I KNOWN WHAT I KNOW NOW

INTRODUCTION

Here, finally, is a book that not only describes the widely recognized need for character education and the teaching of values, but which also shows specifically how to do it.

Fathering is in short supply. Permissiveness is widespread. Youngsters are often unruly, rebellious and irresponsible. A large and increasing minority of our population now has such attitudes. This is how the lack of enough fathering in the family is endangering the future of our society.

Some estimates claim that 70% of black babies are born to single mothers out of wedlock. But the white community is having trouble too. Teachers report from various parts of the country that the majority of white children in many elementary schools go home to a one-parent family. That parent is often at work when the child comes home to an empty house. It makes no sense merely to condemn such situations. They are a fact of life. All these children are the citizens and voters of tomorrow. Whatever our personal attitudes, we must see to it that all these children become solid citizens so that our society survives and all of us live safely wherever we are. As chapter 3 and many others will show, we are all in this together. No one is exempt.

The logo of our publisher, Fathering, Inc. Press, shows a picture of an intact family unit, but even here fatherlessness is common. We have by far more daddies than we have fathers, as chapter 2 shows. It is easier to father children when a mother and a father are both on the scene, but this arrangement alone does not guarantee that the job will be done. Millions of kids everywhere from intact families such as these are fuzzy about right and wrong. This book should help.

It is easy to explain the causes of fatherlessness, and easier yet to blame. But this does not change anything. Many powerful trends have combined to bring us here, and no sudden reversal of the situation is likely. But a lot can be done to improve things. Citizens are the building blocks of society, and we can start by seeing to it that the child or children under our own care end up better off. This is an important first step towards constructing safe and law-abiding societies. Our democracy and affluence are unique blessings that deserve to be saved. We are the only ones who can save them.

So here is a book with practical ideas to help married as well as single mothers and fathers learn to father their children better. Fathering is not a gender-related job. As we shall see in chapter 4 and elsewhere, mothers can and often must do it. The Manual (Third Section) is full of specific suggestions and recommendations, but no easy or quick solutions exist. Raising youngsters well requires persistence and patience. It also demands that we change the expectations we have of ourselves, of our children, and of others. This is not easy, but it can be done. The reader will discover here many ways to do it.

Over the years we have made many mistakes in public policy that helped create our present conditions. With time some of these will have to be undone. Children don't grow up in a vacuum. They, and adults too, are strongly affected by the prevailing mores around them. It's time to change course, and we really have no choice but to do it. But we humans usually change only when the rewards are big enough or when not changing becomes too costly and painful. More and more people begin to see now that with good fathering success is possible, and without it tragedies and broken lives are common. With consistent efforts over time even divorced or single parents can raise sensible and responsible adults. Therefore there is hope.

We have reached a low point. In our great eagerness to be just, fair and compassionate to everyone we have become much too permissive. We excuse too much. A judge in Hamburg, Germany freed a fan who stabbed tennis star Monica Seles in April, 1993. The defendant, an East German who attacked Seles out of an obsessive love for her rival, Steffi Graf, received only a suspended sentence. The judge said that the defendant's mental state played a role in the decision to not punish him more severely.

It is not really surprising therefore that within a few months a Tonya Harding could be involved in a vicious attack on her Olympic ice-skating rival, Nancy Kerrigan. Worse yet, friends and many others stood by and supported Harding, and they did not condemn with horror even such a deed. The post office delivered huge boxes of supportive letters to her, and people in her entourage worried mostly about the loss of millions of dollars in potential product endorsements. We have created an atmosphere where almost anything can be explained away and forgiven. Greed and violence are increasingly invading our lives, including the sports arenas, and crime has become our number one concern.

But the affairs of men and women run in cycles, and we are due for an upswing. More and more people see that individually and as a society we are facing a very dangerous and growing crisis. This has created momentum for change. There is widespread interest in character education and a growing recognition that basic values of civilized living must be instilled. This is becoming a powerful force for good. Many alarmed voices are being heard on the political Left and on the Right, among nonbelievers and believers alike. They all remind us that civilizations can die, just as individuals do. There is still a little time left for us to change course. But not much.

$$\bullet \; \bullet \; \bullet$$

The book consists of three Sections: The First is an introduction to fathering and it shows what happens to individuals and to societies without enough of it. Here the reader is also introduced to mothering, the all-important experience that every baby and young child must have to feel safe. Fathering is not possible except on the basis of enough good mothering. The first few practical suggestions to improve the ability to father are given in chapter 6, and chapter 7 spells out how not to father. Authoritarian and unjust fathering is not only a bad way to raise children, but it also is dangerous.

We quickly see here that many of our social ills are the result of a widespread lack of good or enough fathering. Fatherlessness is everywhere these days. With the collapse of many of the traditional values that sustained us, instant self-gratification is in. Antiauthority, antifathering attitudes now support kids in doing whatever they feel like, as seen in chapter 13 and elsewhere. Besides, it is objectively very hard to father, especially when the people who must do it had little or no fathering themselves. But it is learnable.

This First Section thus prepares the reader for the touching examples and stories that follow. In the Second Section we find fathers, mothers, sons and daughters, all trying to live with each other the best they can. This often turns out poorly. These are all recognizable struggles that most people have, or have had, sometime in their lives. We have a chance here to get a close look into normally hidden private experiences and to learn from them. It becomes clear that usually no one is to blame, even when the hurt and the pain are extreme.

The real culprits in these stories are misunderstanding, insensitivity, deep disappointment and clumsiness in speech and in human interactions. And also an almost universal lack of skills in fathering. This is why so many youngsters end up spoiled and irresponsible, disrespectful to themselves and to others, without enough self-restraint and self-discipline, indulgent, thoughtless or lacking in compassion. Many of these traits are reversible. The parents of such kids are not bad people, even though their children often turn out to be destructive. Those who must father and those who need fathering are often equally at a loss.

Most readers will find themselves in these stories, either as the child or as the parent, and sometimes as both.

The Third Section is the Manual, a treasure of practical ideas about good fathering and how to do it. Although each chapter is devoted to a different subject, many points are overlapping. It would be best to read this entire Third Section as a whole, even if one subject stands out as most important. The Manual contains many useful insights and suggestions that the reader will want to come back to again and again.

Many parents have used this as a workbook for their children. They read sections out loud to start openhearted discussions in the family. Children yield more easily to unpleasant demands that interfere with their fun when they understand that the demands make sense. They are often surprisingly willing to change their behavior. Even young kids can understand many of these points when parents take the time to explain them patiently on the child's level.

This book is intended for parents-to-be concerned with raising emotionally healthy children who will be able to resist the street culture, and for single and married parents who recognize a need to improve their parenting skills. It also is for grandparents, other relatives, and friends of families with rebellious, withdrawn or otherwise difficult children.

Thoughtful men and women who are concerned with the welfare of our societies and the survival of our way of life will find here much to agree with. By now practically everyone is concerned with the widespread presence of crime, drugs, alcoholism and suicide among us. There obviously is an urgent need for character education and for learning and teaching the basic values of decency and civility.

It is hard to grow up. Relatively few adults have had enough good guidance for themselves. This book offers the down-to-earth practical answers that many have been searching for. Use it often.

FIRST SECTION

...

THE DIFFICULT JOB OF FATHERING

1

What is Fathering?
And a Brief Introduction
to Mothering

Growing children do not become self-disciplined
unless they have been disciplined
first by consistent fathering   p.22

Values are not learned merely by listening
to sermons. Reasonable pressure to do the right
thing and to not do wrong is usually needed   p.23

Here is a hard-to-find outline for a job description of fathering. Every "he" also applies to "she," since mother is often the fathering parent. Neither fathering nor mothering are necessarily gender related. Many men are better in mothering than they are in fathering, and many women excel as fathers.

The job of fathering revolves mainly around five overlapping areas:

1. **Protecting and Providing (but not Nurturing).** *Being consistently present near the growing child as a strong, calm, firm and steady presence.*

Young children are small creatures in a big world that is pretty scary and often unsafe. Once out of infancy, they need and want a strong father to stand next to. In his shadow they feel protected and safer. He shields them from bigger "bad" kids, from being taken advantage of, and even from ghosts. That he appears to have all the answers and to never be scared is the most reassuring quality of all. It does not matter whether father is really so powerful. He may in fact be filled with self-doubt. The young child feels safe either way, as long as he or she does not notice father's real shortcomings.

Without such a father young children become hardened much too soon. They act as if they were tough to hide their vulnerability, hurt and fear. The more energy they spend hiding, the less energy is left to learn how to really be safe.

Young plants are nursed in greenhouses to help them grow up well. Within these walls they are protected from winds. From insects and birds. From too much sun. From drying and from extreme temperatures. Here they can be watered and fed carefully. And monitored. Children need no less. A good fathering parent provides these conditions for the young child.

Father used to hunt for bear while mother tended to the hearth. Now both parents commonly work outside the home. Both provide. Father's role as the provider has become less important but the fathering parent's role as protector is still essential.

2. Serving as a Reasonable and Fair Authority.

When little children quarrel and disagree they immediately seek someone to confirm their view of the world. "My daddy is bigger than your daddy, he's a fireman," is what kids used to say to each other at such moments. Our society is much more sophisticated than others in the past. Even young children usually know too much to make such naive statements. They grow up more exposed. Father is no longer the ultimate authority, but a fathering parent is still needed to confirm their discoveries about the world.

Father explains. He confirms. He teaches what is right and what is wrong. Children need a fathering voice to do this more now than ever. Many kids are truly overwhelmed by TV and by the mass culture that invades the home. They learn a lot from TV, good and bad. They need guidance to distinguish one from the other. They have intimate relationships with computers and video games. Many lose their innocence (and their virginity) much too early.

Fathers do not appear so big or powerful anymore. Their authority is diminished. Our homes are therefore not as well protected against outside influences as they used to be. TV not only teaches but it also sells. Products. And modes of behavior. Values and fashions. It molds loyalties. It defines what is humorous, clever, proper and wise. Without a father children mimic what they see. TV now often sets the standards for public and private behavior.

Fathers who serve as the authority at home regulate this invasion from the outside. They scrutinize, supervise and limit its influence. They contradict its lessons when necessary. They insist that their children not become intoxicated by passive watching of the "tube." They demand that the children examine what they see and hear, and teach them how to do it. They thus slowly teach the children to think independently. And critically. To reason. To remain objective. To render judgments thoughtfully.

Such fathering still exists in some ethnic groups that maintain solid families with desirable values such as a strong work ethic. Japanese, Korean and other Far Eastern immigrants are a good example. So are Orthodox Jews, black converts to Islam and others with a clear sense of mission. Their families are still shielded enough.

For the stability of young children the fathering parent must serve as the final arbiter in the family. As a yardstick of right and wrong. The spokesperson and interpreter of a clear, reasonable and just value system. The one who allows and disallows. He or she defines priorities and preferences. This protects the children from being swayed, lured, bribed and sold by advertising and by the street culture.

The fathering parent is the one most responsible for molding the child's character. He or she determines, for instance, that reading is still in, the number and types of movies to be watched, and the time spent on the phone.

3. **Making and Enforcing Rules.** *Setting limits on unacceptable behavior.*

We all are born uncivilized. Babies loudly demand what they want without any regard for others. Every newborn is not only a fragile creature, but it also acts as an undisciplined, unrestrained and impulsive dictator. The powerful primitive urges that we are born with do not yield to reason. Even later in life. They must gently but firmly be curbed from the time the baby is rather young.

The baby's will must not be crushed and his or her curiosity must be allowed to soar. But impulsivity and unreasonableness must slowly be lessened. Many, many painful struggles are involved.

On one side of the battle is the forceful, willful, headstrong and impulse-ridden organism called the growing child. The forces of reason and moderation also need a commander in chief and a strategist. Or the battle will be lost. This is the fathering parent's role even if commanding does not come easily.

Babies and young children are in many ways like animals who have to be housebroken. Their resistance and rebelliousness must be overcome so that they can live with and among thoughtful and reasonable people. Impulsivity, irresponsibility and unreason otherwise continue to plague them. Growing children do not become self-disciplined unless they have been disciplined first by consistent fathering. No one becomes civilized without it.

4. **Serving as a Representative of Reality.** *Pushing the child forward and towards excellence.*

By nature most children get discouraged too easily. We humans tend to seek the path of least resistance. Effort is hard. Witness the lure of a free lunch, of lotteries, sweepstakes, gambling and other fast-buck schemes.

Children and adults prefer activities in which they can succeed easily. They will devote more energy to these and become good at them, neglecting others. They tend to put aside difficult projects that do not provide immediate gratification. "I can't" soon becomes a self-fulfilling prophecy.

It is a father's job to push the child beyond this point. Children then discover that they can go much further and achieve much more. This applies to all areas of endeavor, physical, emotional and intellectual.

Father must also be the uncompromising spokesperson of reality, which often is unpleasant and painful. But living by its dictates minimizes pain and confusion. It maximizes the chances of living peacefully and joyously. Wishful thinking is easier, but only in the short run. Reality always wins in spite of our most fervent wishes to have it otherwise. Reality always comes first. We waste time, energy, resources and segments of life when we try to circumvent it. But we are ahead if we base all our considerations of everything on it. Yet all young children and many adults do the opposite.

The fathering parent must teach the children to see distant consequences. He or she must block the avenues for delusional living.

5. Serving as a Model.

Values are not learned merely by listening to sermons. Reasonable pressure to do the right thing and to not do wrong is usually needed. And this pressure is most effective when it comes from parents and teachers who serve as models of rectitude, love and justice. Children will emulate those whom they respect, look up to, and admire.

Father is the one who must sometimes forbid and set limits. Children are therefore tempted at times to reject him and what he stands for. Sometimes they become very angry at him, hurt and disappointed. To remain effective the fathering parent must continue to be respected even when the child is angry. The parent must live in a way that commands respect. It requires first and foremost that he respect and like himself. This is always critical, but even more so when the male parent is fathering his sons. Chapter 22 explains why this is so.

Fathers who settle for less than the best they are capable of cannot succeed in demanding excellence from their children. What people are and what they do speaks louder than what they say. Those who drink cannot keep their children from using alcohol. Those who typically cut corners and take the easy way out cannot expect their children to do better. This is why the job of fathering is so difficult and so demanding.

• • •

It is not surprising that there is a critical and tragic shortage of fathers.

But the common misunderstanding of what fathering is makes the situation even worse. Contrary to the current popular fads and contrary even to the opinion of many "experts," fathering is essentially not nurturing. This is the essence of mothering.

Mothering consists of feeding. Of giving, nurturing and allowing. Of assuring, holding and welcoming. As we shall see in chapter 5, no fathering will take except on the basis of sufficient good mothering, which is all-important. Children literally die without mothering. Without fathering we can survive, though not well. We lack self-discipline and self-restraint. We never develop our potential. We are against all rules. But we remain alive.

Good mothering provides an inner sense of safety and physiologic stability. This is all any newborn needs. But within a few short months fathering must also begin. Practically always, mother is the first to do this fathering. Remember, fathering is not mothering done by a male. It is not being a buddy to the child, even though fathers and mothers ought to be trusted friends. And fathering is much, much more than taking a daughter on a trip or pitching balls to a son.

For reasons we shall see in chapter 4 and elsewhere, it is generally much less confusing both for sons and daughters if father does most of fathering, and mother—the mothering. This is the optimal division of labor. Either parent should support the other's reasonable decisions in relation to the child. Even so, youngsters can still go for momentary solace to the "good" parent when they are angry at the fathering one. A "good cop, bad cop" combination is useful in any conflict situation.

But ever more families consist of only a single mother or father. One person must then run the entire show. In such situations fathering is much more difficult, especially if the mother or father is young and did not have much fathering as a child. But even so, the children in such homes also need and deserve a firm hand to guide them in the process of growing up. This book, and especially the Manual, can serve such single and inexperienced parents as their missing partner in fathering their young.

2

Fathers are even More Important than Dads

Since daddies do not force issues, fathers must   p.28

Everyone is ahead when a headstrong child loses and a reasonable father wins   p. 29

Most children are fortunate enough to have a dad. His shoulders are always experienced as broad. His knowledge is infinite. His power is magical. His smile, approval and acceptance banish dread. They bring contentment and joy. He even heals with a kiss. We trust him, so we are only a little scared when he throws us up playfully into space. We feel safe with him. He stands by us, plays with us and takes us to exciting places. Like the zoo.

Dad is the idealized, powerful and protecting parent of every little child. This is why children love their dads. But they do not always love their fathers. Quite often they are very angry at them. Sometimes they even hate them.

So it is not surprising that every man prefers to remain a daddy for as long as possible. Many men never become fathers. If they are ever questioned they say that it is unnecessary to change. Practically everyone thinks being a dad is enough. This is "in" now. There is less conflict without fathering, they say.

And indeed, is it not better to win a child's cooperation with playfulness and humor rather than with discipline? Why disappoint a child? Why hurt his or her feelings? Why not just reason with children? Why not reward their compliance and even convince them that it is fun to do what dad says. Why say "No"?

Because reasoning does not work with young children. And not very well with older ones. Especially when children become stubborn or when they have temper tantrums. Irrationality never yields to reason, not in children and not in adults either, as we all know. Also, it is not true that doing what dad expects is always fun.

The reward for attending to one's responsibilities should be inner satisfaction, not a bribe that the kid is eager to have. Otherwise children only learn to do what's right when they have to. And they shoplift or steal when nobody watches.

Besides, lying and bribing are dishonest. They should never be used. A right lesson can't be taught by using a wrong tool.

Children may complain when they are not allowed to watch TV before their homework is done. Or when they are prevented from just "taking" what is not theirs. But beyond the anger they begin to accept the unpleasant fact that they cannot always get their way. They also discover that they can survive without always having fun. And that stealing even a small thing is against the law. Even more importantly: it is wrong. Other human beings also have rights. And their property is theirs, not ours to take.

Even little children can understand this. And generally they agree with such lessons when somebody takes the time to teach them. Learning to live in a civilized way is a very slow process. This is one reason it must begin early, well before the child is two. And many of these lessons are learned only with the help of fathering pressure. Since daddies do not force issues, fathers must.

Dads often sense the heat of the necessary battles and they do all they can to stay away from them. These are unpleasant and painful situations at best. The anger of sons and daughters can be frightening. Possible rejection by a hurt child is often scary to a parent.

But children who do not learn to live according to reality do poorly in life. We will see some extreme examples of this in the next chapter. We cannot even afford to postpone teaching our children that they must yield to reality even when it's unpleasant. A two-year-old learns it much faster, more easily and much more thoroughly than a six-year-old.

Fathers and mothers generally mean well. Mostly they want to do their parenting job responsibly. But daddy was himself a little boy only a few short years before. Often he himself still pines to be loved by everyone. And to be taken care of. Sometimes he actually believes that he needs this to survive. Such a man would not dare to chance alienating anyone. Not even his own child.

Confusion from the not-so-distant past of childhood frequently persists throughout life. Fathers are not exempt. But with or without outside help they must overcome this difficulty if they are to father their children. Otherwise they will fail those whom they love.

Dads compromise. They always rationalize. They yield. Appease. Please. Retreat. Give in. They refuse a child's demands only when there is absolutely no other choice. And then they apologize for having to do so. Daddies can be manipulated, usually easily. Even though they generally are good and well-meaning people, they do harm. It is self-serving to remain a daddy when a father is needed. And the child is the one who will pay the price later in life. His or her future will be harder, not easier.

The children of daddies indeed do not resent them for awhile. But when they are old enough to know better they often despise them. Weakness and vacillation in fathers are bad for children. They grow up without firm yardsticks. With fuzzy values. Confused about how to be and how to behave in the world.

Such children often end up as anxious and self-doubting adults. Or as self-indulgent quitters without guts. They have trouble tolerating the normal pressures of living. Typically they have a frustration tolerance that is too low. They are impulsive. So again and again they get into trouble. They always demand and always expect to have their way. They complain of being victimized and cannot understand why people reject them. But such people have really been victimized. They have been shortchanged by inadequate fathering.

No thoughtful father or mother wants to produce such crippled offspring. But dads cannot help it. Only fathers can do better. They take charge. They direct the battles against irrationality in its many forms. It may not be obvious in the midst of a confrontation, but everyone is ahead when a headstrong child loses and a reasonable father wins. The child's feelings will be hurt but the ability to live sensibly is improved. The hurt feelings will pass quickly but the lessons learned will serve the child well throughout life.

3
___

Life without Good Fathering: A Few Extreme Examples and Lessons

In the absence of consistent fathering children often fail to become civilized beings p.32

A basic sense of compassion does not come in mother's milk p.33

What happens to youngsters raised without enough fathering? They frequently lack built-in standards of right and wrong. They remain impulsive. They don't learn to think. They often damage or even destroy lives. Their own and those of others. Here's one extreme example:

Andrew DeYoung, 19, lived with his parents, brother and sister in a quiet, heavily wooded, middle-class enclave at the end of a cul-de-sac in Cobb, Georgia. His was a decent, God-fearing, typical American family. His grandparents had adopted a black boy and two Korean girls after their three natural-born children grew up. Grandmother was a homemaker who used to quilt a lot. And buy a dozen loaves of day-old bread at a time. And clothes at the resale shop. She would always explain with a soft voice and a smile that sharing was God's command. Grandfather was a bemused professor. He was entertained by his children but hardly ever did he discipline them.

Andrew's father, Gary, became a nuclear engineer. He fathered his three children as he himself was fathered: mildly and by reasoning with them, avoiding all confrontations. Even when Andrew, at age 17, got involved with witchcraft and Satanic worship. The family was devoutly Christian. Gary finally insisted that Andrew at least attend church every Sunday as a condition of his living at home. Too late. Andy refused and offered to move out. But the parents were overcome by compassion and guilt. They told him to stay at home anyway, to "work it out." Gary also wrote to friends asking for their prayers on Andy's behalf. He was a good and very intelligent kid and they were sometimes proud of his achievements. For instance, he was so good at Nintendo playing that he qualified to participate in national championships.

The bodies of Gary and Kathy DeYoung, both 41, and of their daughter, Sarah, 14, were found on the floor of their bedrooms after the other son, Nathan, 16, escaped through a basement window and called the police. All three were in nightclothes. The telephone lines had been cut. They had all been brutally killed by being stabbed repeatedly. They bled to death. Andrew was arrested for carefully planning the massacre, down to drawing a detailed map of the route between his family's home and that of his accomplice.

Most youngsters are not so disturbed and they do not murder. But without enough good fathering their confusion about right and wrong is massive anyway. Many live by the rule of law only because they are afraid of being caught. Not because it is right to do so. Even good kids often speed dangerously in traffic. They cheat on exams. They shoplift. They take or even push drugs. And increasingly there is a casual attitude towards physical violence.

Six teenagers from stable families who provided baseball coaching and music lessons were indicted in Manhattan for a gang rape. They attacked a 28-year-old investment banker who was jogging in Central Park. Two other youths were indicted for assaulting a male jogger on the same night. They were just "wilding" in the night, they said. Why? How did these apparently normal youngsters become involved in "one of the most vicious and brutal crimes in the history of New York"? What causes supposedly decent kids to bash a five-foot, 100-pound, defenseless woman with a rock, a brick and a metal pipe, badly fracturing her skull? And then still gang-rape her? How do humans become so savage and so merciless?

In the absence of consistent fathering children often fail to become civilized beings. Our nature is such that we can end up being kind or cruel. Unlike animals in the wild, we humans kill for many other reasons than merely to satisfy our hunger for food. Humans kill out of jealousy and anger. For "fun" which really means to relieve anxiety. To demonstrate power. To banish the sense of being small, insignificant and powerless.

Time, in its May 9, 1989 issue, describes some details of the brutal attack in Manhattan and wonders about the causes:

> Looking, they said, for something to do, [the teenagers] roamed the park's northern reaches, splintering into smaller groups and...assaulting one hapless victim after another. Finally, one pack came upon...[the] 28-year-old woman jogging alone past a grove of sycamore trees....When she was found three hours later, she had lost three-quarters of her blood and had lapsed into a coma.
>
> By last week the attack had escalated from a local tragedy into a morbid national obsession. Perhaps the story resonated across the country because the victim was a wealthy, white financier with degrees from Wellesley and Yale....
>
> According to investigators, these were not crimes of drugs or race or robbery....The youths, some barely into their teens, may not have been altar boys, but they hardly seemed like candidates for a rampage. One was known for helping elderly neighbors at his middle-income Harlem apartment complex. Another was a born-again Christian who had persuaded his mother to join his church. Only one had ever been in trouble with the police.
>
> If children so seemingly normal went so horribly wrong, the obvious question is Why? The youths, described by police as smug and remorseless, have offered only one motive: escape from boredom...."It was something to do."
>
> The evidence that youthful offenders are becoming more violent is everywhere....At a Los Angeles Greyhound station, a 15-year-old girl was kidnapped at knifepoint by two men, held captive

for five days and repeatedly raped. She managed to escape and flagged down a passing car. "Get me out of here!" she begged the three teenagers inside. They did, and took her to a park in East Los Angeles, where the eldest of the boys, 18, allegedly raped her again....

"Blaming society, parents, poverty, racism, school systems and neighborhoods for teenage violence is too easy," said Dr. Edward Shaw, director of mental health for the New York State division of youth. "It does not answer the question why do some teenagers in the same environment get into trouble and others do not?"

But there is an answer: the absence of fathering. A basic sense of compassion does not come in mother's milk. It must be learned. And kids usually incorporate it only after they win many struggles against their cruel urges. We'll see in chapter 19 one example of how this may be done. Many tears are usually involved, and many disappointments. Explanations alone are not enough. Children naturally want to avoid such confrontations, which is why committed parents who are able to father must pressure them, even against their will. And it makes good sense for parents to join these battles willingly, since horrible tragedies might thus be prevented.

Youth violence is so common now that it represents the norm. The Justice Department estimates that each year nearly a million young people between 12 and 19 are raped, robbed or assaulted in the U.S., often by their peers. Other estimates are much higher. According to Newsweek of August 3, 1993:

> That's the official count. The true number of injuries from teen violence could be even higher. When emergency medical technicians in Boston recently addressed a class of fifth graders, they were astonished to find that nearly three quarters of the children knew someone who had been shot or stabbed. "A lot of violence goes unmeasured...."
>
> The statistics are shocking—and so is the way some teenagers react when they're caught and accused of brutal crimes. "Hey, great! We've hit the big time," 17-year-old defendant Raul Omar Villareal allegedly boasted to another boy after hearing that they

might be charged with murder. Villareal was one of six Houston teens arrested and charged last month in the brutal rape and strangulation of two young girls who made the fatal mistake of taking a shortcut through a wooded area where, police say, the boys were initiating two new members into their gang....

Growing children are better off when their parents supervise and regulate their friendships and their activities. Troubled, disturbed, confused or unruly friends can easily mislead a youngster whose character is still in formation. They do not have to be out and out "bad" kids. And too much fantasy input can similarly be confusing and damaging. For instance, too much TV violence or video games.

One February evening, after a day of skipping classes to play Nintendo, watch "Die Hard 2" and take target practice, Forsyth Central High School senior David Wright and a friend went to a secluded house at Lake Lanier and waited for David's family to come home, police said. As his mother, adoptive father and half-brother returned, one by one, they were shot to death.

"You just could not expect this," said a classmate. "You'd expect this from a headbanger who did drugs and alcohol and had green hair." But David "was quiet but not withdrawn, he excelled in classes, lettered on the tennis team and looked forward to enrolling at Georgia Tech," said his principal. So what happened?

He was not controlled enough. Not fathered properly, or enough. How can we know this? Because well-fathered youngsters do not skip school to play computer games, watch movies and shoot a gun. These are either a clear sign of an authority vacuum or extreme acts of authority defiance. Well-fathered children fight their battles on lesser battlegrounds. The confrontations happen much earlier too. When the kids are still toddlers. When they try to play with matches or torture a fly. Even experts often fail to see that children may feel overcontrolled when in fact they have not been controlled enough, and early enough.

Both Andy DeYoung and David Wright were addicted to Nintendo. There you can kill, mutilate and destroy your enemies without restraint. And the more the better. But not in reality. Why was Andy's involvement with Nintendo not limited, or even stopped altogether? Gary DeYoung knew about his son's confusion. The freedom of youngsters to engage in fantasies must always be limited by their parents to fit the children's ability to know what is real. Overload here is extremely dangerous. This is why it must never be allowed to happen.

Young children at first have no idea that others can also have real pain. Or that they have rights too. They must be taught these things till they know them very well. Reasoning with a young child has only limited value. Such lessons, like all important ones, must be taught by example and by an uncompromising intolerance of even innocent cruelty and brutality. To father is to civilize the child. It requires years of effort. Many painful struggles. And lots of patience.

The Central Park rapists, Andy DeYoung and David Wright did not have enough of such fathering. Music lessons and baseball coaching are no substitute. Neither is fear of the law, or even the fear of God. Beyond fear, children must learn that some things are wrong in and of themselves. Even if no one is watching. Even without a policeman around. They must begin to accept this while they still are very young.

Children develop self-discipline slowly from being disciplined fairly and consistently by others. Self-restraint is also born out of an intimate relationship with a just parent who demonstrates reasonable restraint. Personal example is all-important. No easy or quick solutions exist.

Many children learn to behave in more or less acceptable ways when they are afraid to be caught doing otherwise. But this obviously is not enough. Humans can become worse than wild beasts if they have not learned to discipline and to control themselves from within. With consistent fathering this can be achieved.

• • •

Most youngsters are not so disturbed, and they do not rape, kill or mutilate even when they have been fathered only a little. But often they are destructive to themselves and to others in lesser ways. Many are only sullen, stubborn, lazy or self-indulgent, without enough of a sense of responsibility or respect for anyone. Millions live like children throughout life, financially supported by parents or by government without ever working steadily. Fatherlessness is damaging to the young even when it does not extract as high a price as that in the extreme examples given here.

4

Where Have All the Fathers Gone? And the Story of Mothers Stuck with the Job of Fathering

*Much fathering is done by
mothers. They are the ones who
must deal with their young children
whenever father is away from home   p. 37*

*A good father is often seen as "the bad
one." A fathering parent must therefore
be able to cope with anger and conflict   p. 41*

We have already noted that much fathering is done by mothers. They are the ones who must deal with their young children whenever father is away from home. And many fathers are away a lot. Some are absent altogether. More and more children don't even know their father.

But even if father is only away at work, mother can often not wait for him to come home when the children become unruly and difficult to manage. This can happen at any time. With or without father around, children become rebellious and defiant or they have their temper tantrums. Kids are cute and lovable, but not always. Someone has to impose rules then. Mother usually does.

But it is easier for the parents and better for the children when the fathering is done by fathers, and the mothering by mothers. This is especially important for growing boys. Mothers can father them successfully only while they are relatively small. Before puberty. Before they have much to do with other boys. But not later on. To become men, boys need to be closely involved with good male models. Otherwise they remain boys and they never dare to stand tall enough. But even so, we face a tragic shortage of good fathers and a severe absence of good fathering. Where have all the fathers gone?

Father used to be the provider, but this is less true nowadays. Mothers often work outside the home now and they are providers too. Besides, our affluent societies spread wide safety nets to catch the ones who fail and fall. Families can thus exist pretty well even without a father, at least financially. Males are also no longer really needed to defend the female or the young. The phony chivalry of the 19th century appears ridiculous now. Women no longer need the protective club of the caveman. With his diminished value father has also lost much of his authority.

Such developments have been with us for a very long time. As a result, many boys everywhere have grown up with fathers who were not strong enough to do much good fathering. In most families mother is clearly the dominant parent. In the not-so-distant past she would often prop father up in a way that still enabled him to look good. But this is much less common now. So, many men have grown up lacking good male models, and they remained boys. And as boys they become the fathers of the next generation.

Many fathers are thus ill-equipped for their task. Intellectually and emotionally they are not ready. They lack the necessary know-how. They also lack the guts to stand firm. This cannot usually be learned except in an apprenticeship with a good teacher who serves as a model. Such young men are usually unsure of themselves when they try to father their children. They vacillate too often. They give up when they meet with resistance. The vicious cycle of insufficient fathering often repeats itself in one generation after another, in a worsening spiral.

By now even many of our teachers, political leaders and opinion makers are the products of insufficient fathering. Consequently, what children are taught and what adults commonly hear, read and see all around them is often grossly incorrect. Even God's commandments are sometimes presented merely as recommendations. By now our collective knowledge of fathering has been diluted to the point that it often is defined as mothering by a father. And in the process even our values and many of our institutions have basically changed. And so have our mores. We have become much too permissive. Almost anything goes. In language. In dress. In behavior. Religion and the law used to speak with a clear and unequivocal moral voice. People did not always do the right thing, but they knew what it was. No more. Now we tend to excuse even the inexcusable.

• • •

Father's job is very demanding even when he is ideally prepared for his task. It requires one fine adjustment after another. Above all, father must be involved and loving. He must also be sensitive and thoughtful, fair, consistent and firm. And he must be comfortable with power and able to function as a just authority. Such a combination of qualities is not common. It requires more wisdom and more emotional maturity than most young men or women possess.

So, many fathers get discouraged and bitter sooner or later, even if they try at first to do the job right. One day they tire of the effort and withdraw from the battle and into themselves. Then they console themselves behind the daily paper. Or they gamble, golf, use alcohol or overwork for distraction. Typically they become silent in resignation. They do not see much anymore, hear only a little, and speak hardly at all. They may well sense that their children, and especially their sons, need them. But they are convinced that they cannot be but ineffective. Many will admit defeat openly, with a broken spirit and with much pain.

Fathers often see in their sons the same rebellious attitude and behavior that they themselves had a generation earlier, and which helped them defeat their own fathers. By then they usually know the cost. And they can see the coming tragic consequences of yielding to self-indulgence. But though they warn their sons and daughters and desperately try to stop them, their words usually fall on deaf ears.

Losing this battle to shape the character of their children is often the crucial turning point in the lives of fathers. It sometimes precipitates midlife crises. More commonly, a veil of pained silence covers their eyes from then on. Not only have they failed to be heard by their headstrong and obstinate offspring, but they are often also blamed by the children's mother for pushing too hard, or for not trying hard enough. Having been a child herself not so long ago, she may even side with the youngster who fights against father. She may still resent not getting what she wanted as a girl. Or what she still wants now. Father is then all alone. Everyone is against him. No wonder that he withdraws.

Such sad dramas are very common in families. Father, the one traditionally thought of as the head of his household, is in fact the outcast. The target of hidden and open hostility by everyone around. Knowingly or not, mother may be competing for the children's affection and loyalty, and for control of the family.

• • •

Mothers are generally better educated now, more independent and less docile than generations ago. They are not only homemakers any more. They compete with men successfully in the marketplace and in the political arena. This erodes the shaky position and self-image of many fathers even further. More than ever they feel battered both at home and at work. Eventually many retreat in discouragement. Mothers then understandably resent having so little help with the children. Without support they are often really unable to hold everything together and in check, and unwilling to try harder. Many families fall apart.

And when a mother must raise a son mostly by herself he often ends up very confused, seeing the world through her eyes. From a woman's perspective. His identity as a male is then often shaky. Some escape into homosexuality. More typically such sons become compulsive pleasers, especially of women. Such oppressive inner slavery is very tiring, and anger is often associated with it also. Many of these men blame women for "doing it" to them, but this is usually untrue. Such an outlook is the almost inevitable result of boys growing up without a strong enough male influence.

A day comes in the lives of many such men when they cannot take it any more. Perhaps at midlife. Or later. Then something gives, or breaks. The marriage. His health. His career. Or the will to live. Almost everyone knows such tragic figures. Or we knew them before they somehow destroyed themselves.

Happier endings exist, but not a happy end. Boys remain boys forever without enough good fathering from a man. This always turns out to be an ongoing source of agony and loneliness for them, for their wives and for their children. Such "boys" become self-respecting and self-disciplined men only rarely.

Girls have it easier. They can grow up to become good women even without a male influence. Mothers can father them, though even girls do much better with a good fathering father. Daughters also pay a price when they don't have one. Often they end up spoiled, or too sweet. They tend to continue seeing themselves as little girls and they speak and behave accordingly. Or they become hysterical. This may work well in their relationships with men, but it obviously limits them otherwise. Some fatherless girls become too efficient and too hard, as we shall see in chapter 15. Even for girls there is less confusion if their fathering was done by a competent and loving father, rather than by mother.

But since at least in the short run fathering is a thankless job, it has relatively few applicants and fewer takers yet. Children resist his interventions. These cramp their style and limit their freedom. Fathers must insist on self-discipline. Occasionally they impose hardships. Who wants that? A good father is often seen as "the bad one." A fathering parent must therefore be able to cope with anger and conflict. Fathers are therefore not usually eager to take on this job of fathering, though it obviously needs to be done.

The pool of good fathers has been dwindling, and it continues to shrink. Everywhere we look we can see the dangerous consequences. Too much is at stake. Wherever the fathers have gone, we must find ways to bring them back.

5

More about Mothering.
No Fathering is Possible
without it.
And a Note about Children
who Suicide

*No fathering will ever take except
on a bedrock of good mothering   p. 43*

*We demand a license to drive and to
marry, but not to bear children   p. 46*

Fathering civilizes the young, but mothering is even more important. It makes life possible by providing at least minimal safety. Without enough fathering life is characterized by impulsivity, irrational urges, headstrong stubbornness and sometimes by almost total self-preoccupation. But no fathering will ever take except on a bedrock of good mothering.

Since the mothering parent nurtures, gives and reassures, she or he provides the bond that holds the child. Fathering tightens this hold till the child's personality is molded into a compassionate and thoughtful humane shape. But without at least minimal good mothering the child remains too anxious to be fathered. The hold can be tightened only when it already exists.

Mother not only gives birth to the newborn but she also cares for it when it is most fragile. Her bosom is a lifeline, her lap the source of security. This is why mothers are and often remain central in importance, even for many grownups. The effects of both good and bad mothering are profound. Both have lasting consequences. Those who have been mothered well are ahead in life and their struggles are easier. The damage done by bad mothering is repairable, but only with much effort over a long period of time. This happens only rarely.

In nature not all mothers love their young. Some fish even eat their offspring. And among us humans too, the natural instinct of mothers to protect and to care for their babies varies in intensity. It depends on the mother's emotional health and maturity. Very young mothers are often too anxious to really give much to their young. And they are often angry at having to do so. The same for mothers of any age who have themselves not been mothered well enough. The children of such mothers never know real inner peace. They are generally anxious and jumpy. Some become hyperactive or ad- dicted. Many are typically dissatisfied. Or socially irresponsible. Depressed.

Babies and young kids find reassurance in physical closeness and contentment in the warm embrace of a contented mother. They also must have the freedom to explore their surroundings away from her. Hardly anyone, ever, has had enough of these in exactly the right proportions. Having the right dosage of mothering at exactly the right times is rare. So it is not surprising that most adults still crave physical closeness. And being lovingly touched. Or held. Those who were held in a choking grip are the exception. They get more anxious with intimacy.

But all people always welcome and even seek more of what gives them a sense of safety and warmth. Even adults feel fulfilled when they are filled. This is why people normally fill themselves. With food. With alcohol. With knowledge. With sex. With material possessions. With belief systems. Without these they feel more anxious. Detached. Raw. Vulnerable. Lonely even when not alone. In short, scared.

Most people do not really feel secure at the core. Rejection shakes them deeply. The wish to be loved, welcomed and cared for by others usually lingers. It is at the bottom of what people seek in marriages. Parents often have children to satisfy this wish, at least secretly hoping or expecting that their kids will look after them when they are old and feeble. Holding an infant close to her body sometimes calms the mother more than she calms her baby. Even a devoted pet fills this need. Although often unknowingly, people expect others to add stability to their lives and seek to be repeatedly reassured that they are lovable.

Without good early mothering some anxiety "for no reason at all" is an almost constant companion. Such anxiety may only be mild, but it can be so intense that it interferes with the ability to work and to enjoy life. It can seriously disturb concentration and even sleep. And the ability to study and to think clearly. Above all, it interferes with the capacity to form trusting, close relationships. Anxious individuals often cling to others but they cannot really be involved in sensible and lasting relationships. Loneliness results. Hurt and anger, sadness and pain are commonly present. Bitterness and despair are usually not far behind. The push away from anxiety and dread explains much of human behavior.

Some anxious people become stimulus freaks, others numb themselves. In the first group are the devotees of slam- or break-dancing and those who find solace in the distracting beat of loud rock music. Some pursue sex or money compulsively or they become endlessly involved in sports. This is why people risk their lives in bungee jumping, why they drive too fast or gamble. To numb themselves people drink, smoke or get "high" on drugs. All these offer temporary relief or at least distracting busyness. Short-term escape claimed as pleasure. All at a very high cost. Some people withdraw from all social contact into a silent, lonely and cold shell.

But when none of these devices works well enough, anxiety, hurt and pain can become subjectively unbearable. Some people suicide then. For parents, the suicide of a child is often the most painful of all experiences. Mothers suffer terribly, but fathers often break, especially if they tried to father their offspring. They often blame themselves for having made demands. Underneath the hard exterior, many fathers are very soft. They invest many of their dreams and hopes in their children and, since they usually are less involved in their care than mothers, they tend to be more unrealistic about them. Some fathers even follow a suiciding child at a later date.

The confusion of fathers is often especially severe if the suiciding child was a son. Fathers are usually harder on boys than they are on girls. Perhaps they should not have imposed such strict limits, they say to themselves. Perhaps they should not have insisted. If only they had been more permissive, more lenient, more "reasonable." If only...

But the despair that leads to suicide is more commonly the result of insufficient mothering or fathering, not of excessive fathering. Bad fathering can be grossly harsh. It sometimes is authoritarian and unjust. Even cruel. Such treatment will provoke rage. Perhaps even murder in extreme cases. But not suicide. This always results from overwhelming anxiety and depression. Not from rage at an oppressor.

In fact fathers err more often by allowing and giving too much. They may try to be the mothering parent. But males have no breasts and they can mother only up to a point. At best they can understand the child exquisitely. They can be compassionate. And kind. But a mother's body is generally softer. It more readily provides the warmth and the physical reassurance that youngsters need and crave. Nature determined that males and females are different. These differences limit the mothering ability of fathers.

Neither fathers nor mothers are generally guilty of their child's suicide, though poor mothering can be literally fatal. Even the most inadequate mothers do their best. They may feel guilty but they are not. Our society is.

We demand a license to drive and to marry, but not to bear children. Hardly anybody even advocates compulsory training in the basic principles of mothering and fathering as a prerequisite for childbearing. Practically everyone is allowed to have and to raise children without restriction. We only interfere after child abuse is discovered.

Even so, many fathers collapse under the unbearable weight of their irrational shame and guilt when their child suicides. As if they were responsible and had taken that life. As if it were their fault. As if they deserved to be punished.

6

A Few Suggestions to Improve
the Ability to Father

You cannot always please your child
without causing serious harm in the long run   p. 49

Nature abhors the existence of a vacuum.
This holds true for an authority
vacuum as well. Someone always fills it.
If reason doesn't, unreason does   p. 54

Miracles happen in fairy tales. But not often in real life. Fathers and mothers who themselves have not been fathered well often fail in fathering their children. They try, but they don't know how. Often they make up for what they lack by showering the children with material things. With gifts. With trips. With cars. With money. And with much too much freedom. This only makes a bad situation worse.

Good fathering often requires the opposite. The fathering parent must somehow learn to also give less and to say "no" at times. He or she must sometimes restrict children and curb their wishes.

But many fathers simply cannot stomach the conflicts that inevitably follow. They get anxious when they precipitate a confrontation. They get very hurt when the frustrated child screams in anger that he or she hates them. So they yield when they shouldn't. They try to reason with temper tantrums. They love their children and mean very well, but they fail them nonetheless.

If fathers and mothers want to have emotionally healthy children they must learn to overcome this built-in obstacle. There is no other choice.

Many parents sense or even know that what they are doing is not getting the desired results. But even so they do not know how to change the situation for the better. Naturally they worry. They need help to do the job more effectively. So here are a few hints and general guidelines that can be put into practice by anyone who tries.

• • •

A. **For fathering parents who are typically too mild, too nice, too lenient and too helpful.** *For those who smile too often and give too much:*

1. Remember that being a good dad is not the same as being a good father. Review chapter 2.

2. Try to be more firm. Since this goes against your grain you will at first be a poor judge as to when you are firm enough. In general, assume that you yield too much and too soon.

3. Remember that you cannot always please your child without causing serious harm in the long run. Since you want to do no harm, remember not to please so much. Pleasing comes naturally to you, so beware and be aware.

4. Children get angry when they are refused. Or they get hurt. Some become quiet and withdraw. Others will raise their voice in protest, perhaps disrespectfully. Remember that anger and hurt are feelings, and they pass quickly. Especially if you stand firm. Feelings should not be hidden but expressed openly, yet always respectfully. This will be made clearer in the Manual.

Do not let your own anxiety or hurt change a decision that is right for the child. *Your* anxiety and hurt will also pass quickly. The knowledge that you are helping your child in a difficult battle should help. It is hard to gain self-sufficiency, self-restraint and self-discipline. You are giving your child much more by sometimes refusing to give than by giving in.

5. Verbal expressions of hurt and anger are necessary to clear the air. They should be allowed. In fact, help your children to express their disappointment, hurt and anger. Encourage them to do so actively. Even extremely strong reactions are safe as long as they are only verbal. But acts based on any of these feelings should never be tolerated. No throwing of things. No withdrawing from the relationship with you. No silent pouting. No disrespectful loudness. No hate. No disdain. These are all either dangerous or ruinous to relationships. Or both. More about this in chapters 23, 24 and 27.

6. Insist that your child and you talk as soon as a storm of feelings is over. Help the child talk at an age-appropriate level. By doing so you are also helping your son or daughter learn to think. Listen carefully and consider the arguments. But do not yield if you are right. Explain. Explain again and then leave it. Some explanations only begin to make sense after some time has passed. Confrontations will get easier with time. Both for you and for your child. Reconciliations will come faster. Ideally they should leave no residue of bitterness.

7. Learn (from this book and from other sources) what are reasonable expectations and limits for children at various ages. These are not all the same for every child. But there is an acceptable and reasonable range of expectations. To demand and to expect too little is to infantilize and thus to damage your child. Children treated this way will not develop their full potential. To demand and to expect too much is to set them up to fail. It will discourage and dishearten them, and it will make it more difficult for them to try again.

8. You will make mistakes. It is impossible to always gauge things exactly and accurately. It is not wrong to correct yourself and to change your original decision if it was wrong. Admit an error openly. But never change your mind because of the pressure of protest and anger. Never let your children charm you into changing. Never change your mind because you feel guilty, scared, hurt or angry. Whatever makes sense must prevail, regardless of your own feelings. Or your child's.

. . .

Always be guided by what makes sense in reality. Do not be guided by feelings. This is easier said than done. Most people do not live by this principle because they cannot. Many do not even understand what it means. Or that it is possible. But everyone can slowly learn to live this way.

Our feelings are usually distorted by past personal experience. And feelings usually lead to the wrong conclusions. This is even true when we "fall" in love. Cupid is blind. Help your children feel whatever they feel openly, and help them to express it. But you and they must always act rationally. Reason and thinking must always prevail.

Since your children's welfare, and sometimes their very lives, depend on them being fathered well and enough, it makes sense that you practice and learn to follow these principles. Seek help if mastering them proves to be impossibly difficult.

. . .

B.   For fathers and mothers who are typically authoritarian, too hard and too demanding. *For those who know that unruly kids should be put in their place. For fathers who often hear that they punish too much, too quickly or too severely:*

1. Remember that being firm is not the same as being harsh. Firm means holding the line even under pressure. Harsh is needlessly hard. It lacks compassion and love. It contains anger and is often unjust. The tendency to be harsh is rarely related to the current situation and usually reflects personal experiences from long ago.

2. From time to time you may have an "unexplainable" urge to get even with anyone breaking the "rules." Do not act according to this urge. Almost always this is to give *you* relief from inner pressure of old, hidden anger. Remember that your stubborn child may only be experimenting with being assertive. All healthy children want and need to test their strength and see how it is to use it. Do not break your child's will. Be intolerant of unreasonable stubbornness by standing firm, not harshly.

3. Remember that you are much bigger and much more powerful than your child. When a nuclear power reacts militarily in an international crisis it must be a restrained reaction. Much more so than the reaction of a weak, underdeveloped country. Those with power must be much more careful. And more responsible.

Use your power sparingly and appropriately. Just enough to achieve the necessary goal. Anything more comes from another agenda. It is therefore wrong. It also damages your standing with your child. And it hinders your child's ability to stand tall.

Firmness and harshness are often experienced by others as one and the same. Initially both are equally resented. But children and adults can usually recognize quickly (after they're done with protesting) that firmness is based on reason. And on sound principles. It is fair. It cannot be rejected out of hand. Harshness on the other hand is counterproductive. It is unnecessarily rough. It produces the opposite of what it intends to achieve. Since harshness serves the needs of the one who is harsh, not the needs of the child, it also is unjust. Harshness should always be avoided. It is never justified.

4. Many people are quick to anger and slow to regain their composure. You may be one of them. Since punishing in the midst of anger is dangerous, it is always wrong. Be sure you are fully calm and fully composed and reasonable if you ever hit or strike your child. A firm arm squeeze will get the child's attention equally well. And cause less bitterness and no shame. Never be cruel or excessive in punishment. Never beat your child. To father well you must monitor your actions and decisions carefully at all times. Only the child's needs should be considered.

Always allow for a long enough cooling off period whenever you get angry at anyone. Be especially careful when you're very angry at a child. Anger often has deep roots that go way back. Children can easily provoke parents by what they do, or fail to do, but excessively strong angry reactions are not justified even then. Allow enough time for your anger to subside completely. This may even take as long as 48 hours. Only then decide on any punishment, unless it is objectively unsafe to wait.

5. Remember that character habits do not change easily or quickly. The power of the will is rather limited. This is true for everyone, including both you and your child.

Learning is a slow process. Character change is even slower. You may have told the youngster the same thing many times before, but even so all children forget, even if they pay attention to what they're told. Feelings are so powerful that they even distort our memory. And our thinking.

Remember that people often claim that they thought something over when they really were just ruminating. Such people are not liars. They tell the truth as they see it. Rationalizing is automatic. All this is especially true for children. They fabricate innocently when they are little.

6. You cannot teach any lesson which contradicts what you are. And how you behave. Remember this especially when you are about to react too quickly because you feel something too strongly.

7. Don't trust yourself without double-checking your reactions and decisions. Especially in important and big matters. Beware of becoming arbitrary or high-handed. Avoid harming your children out of excessive worry and concern about their future.

C. For fathers who are essentially uninvolved, distant and removed from their children:

1. Nature abhors the existence of a vacuum. This holds true for an authority vacuum as well. Someone always fills it. If reason doesn't, unreason does. Without rules, children remain unruly. They become adults who lack self-discipline and self-respect. They do not become self-reliant. Your children need you.

2. Remember that what must be done today cannot always be postponed for tomorrow. It is much easier to guide the growth of a young sapling by supporting it soon after it is planted than to bend back a misshapen grown tree. The same with children.

3. Children who are insufficiently fathered are obviously de-prived. But the fathers of such children are also deprived. They are deprived of the joy of seeing their young become productive and healthy adults. They are also deprived of the friendship of sane and loving family members. And of their loyalty and support. You may wish these things much more than you realize. More perhaps than anything else in life. Most people want them very badly. Be sure not to deprive yourself.

4. Many fathers are deeply hurt by being misunderstood by their children. This is one reason they withdraw from them. They give up and leave the scene emotionally, even if they remain physically at home. You may be one such father. Remember that being so deeply hurt for being misunderstood usually has deep roots in one's past, and it is not necessarily all your child's doing. Reverse course. Seek help if you can't do it alone.

5. Fathers withdraw to minimize their pain, but being a silent nonobserver does not really protect you. The pain usually continues and sometimes it even gets worse. Troubling things happen in every family. And remember that your withdrawal is very damaging to your children. So look again. With or without outside help find enough of your strength to try again. Do not remain on the sidelines. The returns you will get are always worth the hard effort. Sometimes a child's very life depends on a father's continued involvement.

6. Fathering is indeed an extremely difficult task. And often a painful one too. Fathers who father actively are regularly blamed unjustly by their young. Sometimes they are also judged wrongly and accused by their spouses. It is a lonely spot. But all the alternatives are more painful. And besides, few things in life are more satisfying than seeing your child grow up well to become a good, effective and decent human being. The job is doable.

• • •

The inability to father is always rooted in the father's own upbringing and character. It cannot suddenly change in any major way. But everyone has the ability to change slowly and gradually. This requires many, many reminders. We tend to repeat our mistakes automatically. Changing also requires a willingness to endure the embarrassment involved in admitting errors and in correcting ourselves. It therefore requires courage. But so much is at stake that many fathers will try. And try again.

Determine carefully in which of these three categories you fit best. This in itself should prove to be of enormous value. Do not claim that you fit in none of the three. Then take small steps in a new and different direction. Refer to these suggestions frequently. Some may appear strange at first. And wrong. Those may be the most important ones for you to consider and to reconsider. With time, you may discover that what you disagreed with the most may well have been the most useful. It is hard to get used to new attitudes and approaches. They sometimes begin to make sense only much later.

7

How *Not* to Father

Being harsh is always wrong.
Being firm is almost always right   p. 59

Good fathering aims at helping the child
stand tall and appropriately proud   p. 60

P arents have arbitrary power over their children. This power is not always used wisely. Even well-meaning fathers and mothers abuse it at times, and not everyone always means well. Some parents are not well-balanced emotionally, or mature enough to handle their job responsibly. And besides, it takes lots of wisdom to rule properly, and most parents have even less know-how in this area than politicians.

As a result, many grownups have on occasion known at least some mild mistreatment during childhood. No wonder that many people are suspicious of anyone in power, and with power. Power indeed tends to corrupt, and absolute power can corrupt absolutely. Many people know this to be true from their own flesh.

Randy's story is simple and not very unusual. Now that he is in his 50's he can finally talk about it without choking. And without fury. Here it is:

I was an average kid. Not particularly good nor bad. Like all my sisters and brothers I knew that our father worked hard and that my mother was emotionally very sick. We tried somehow to survive. We helped around the house. But sometimes we forgot.

Sometimes we didn't finish all our homework. None of us was the best student in class. But then, neither did any of us ever flunk out. We were decent kids.

Even so, mother would have angry outbursts at one of us quite often. I seemed to have been the one she targeted the most. I was the oldest. It began in earnest when I was seven. She would scream at the top of her lungs because of something minor. Eventually she would angrily dispatch me to my room. There I was to wait till father came home. Sometimes it was for many long hours. I used to sit there quietly, biting my fingernails and worrying about what father would do to me.

He was a very big man. His life was hard. And he was an impatient person. He too was quick to anger. When he came home after a long day of driving his truck he was very tired. He would close the door behind him very deliberately, face me and recite the list of accusations. Is this what happened?

I always remained silent. No, this wasn't what happened, I wanted to shout. But I did so only once. And I remember him exploding and screaming back at me on that occasion. He demanded to know whether I claimed that mother was lying. I didn't answer. He would beat me mercilessly if I said yes. And he would beat me even harder if I had said no. So I agreed, mother wasn't lying and all the accusations were true. There really was no way of convincing him. I could not tell him that she was a sick and confused woman. He didn't want to know. He needed her. She kept the house for us. He always sided with her.

The beatings were terrible. He used a belt and sometimes I literally couldn't sit down for days. But the humiliation was worse. And worst of all was the fact that the whole thing was unjust. Most of the time I was really accused wrongly. Mother was very troubled. She was hospitalized in one psychiatric hospital or another at least every two years. In between she could be very sweet. And then, without any provocation or any apparent reason she would sink into deep moods of despair. These would be interrupted with outbursts of extreme rage. One of the kids would always get it.

Father either didn't know about these episodes or he didn't know what to do about them. To placate her he always went along. I wanted to scream. To hit him back when he beat me. To run away. To kill her. But she was my mother. He was my father. And I was only 7 or 8 or 9 years old.

Authoritarian rule is always harsh. Arbitrary and high-handed.

Unjust. Cruel and often violent. It always tries to wear the mask of justice, but in fact it is the opposite of the rule of law, the opposite of legitimate authority. Those who don't have what it takes to become authoritative tend to become authoritarian. The first is absolutely essential in the raising of children and in orderly living, the second is poisonous. And many people confuse the two and regard them both as one and the same. Fathering should never be authoritarian. Such fathers are bound to fail.

All generals command troops. Some command mostly by instilling fear. Other generals are respected. Even loved. In battle, troops in the second category do much better. They follow their commanders more loyally. They act more courageously. Under fire they don't turn back so quickly. Those ruled by fear crumble under pressure. The others who follow a respected leader often prevail in similar circumstances.

The same is true in the family. Fathers must also command. But their authority should not be based on fear. Like the more successful generals, they must earn respect. They must also keep it to be effective. It is best if fathers hardly ever need to use their power or position to command. A look, a gentle but firm tap on the shoulder, a verbal reminder or a stern voice ought to be enough. Ideally a father should hold the child very tightly with a wide open hand.

Fathers sometimes have no choice but to impose their will by force. But even then, this must not necessarily be physical force. Withdrawing approval, privileges or something else that the growing child badly wants are also interventions that force an issue. Hitting or striking the child is best reserved for the most rare occasions only. And then it should be used sparingly and sadly. Never in anger. Never to hurt the child physically. Never to shame. Only to get through. Only after all other reasonable methods of persuasion have failed.

Being harsh is always wrong. Being firm is almost always right. Harshness lacks flexibility. It is based on insensitivity. It contains anger or even hate, unlike firmness which is based on love. Good fathering always tries to elicit the willing cooperation of those being fathered. Poor fathering is satisfied with compliance.

Randy's authoritarian father demanded unquestioning obedience. It left no room for doubt, for discussion or for an open expression of Randy's point of view. Authoritarian rule always aims at crushing the spirit. This is the very opposite of what fathers should do. Authoritarian regimes prevail by inducing fear. The more the better. And they use shame. They mean to diminish the power of their opponents. To decrease their stature. To destroy them and their resistance by any means.

By contrast, good fathering aims at helping the child stand tall and appropriately proud. Self-assured. Successful fathers love their children and want them to become powerful men and women who gain their full stature. This is why fear should hardly ever be used, although it is occasionally needed in restraining very young kids such as toddlers. They do not yet understand enough. A loud voice that scares them usually stops them from innocently running into traffic.

Many kids with Randy's background grow up with seething fury. They hate. Some become criminals. Others merely end up having knee-jerk reactions against every authority. They automatically become furious when anyone takes a firm stand. As parents they are too permissive. Being allergic to authority, they are unable to exercise it. They hardly ever assert themselves even when their children badly need a strong guiding hand and firm limits. Chapter 17 is one example.

But Randy was different. He became a sheriff. Married and divorced four times, he became a heavy drinker. Twelve beers a night. And sometimes more. In charge of a small city prison, he would let a stubborn prisoner have a taste of his fists from time to time. When no one watched. They were lawbreakers, he told himself. Thieves. Drug-dealers. Murderers. They deserved no better. He merely got even. In a way he did, but the prisoners were not his father.

Here are a few recommendations about how *not* to father:

1. Do not use fear to enforce your rules, except as a last resort and in extreme circumstances. For instance, to stop a dangerous situation from developing. Fear can stop, but it does not teach. This is why it is not a good basis for raising emotionally healthy children. It is almost always damaging. No child will learn the things that were forced down its throat. In France they force-feed geese to fatten them, but then they kill them. To incorporate our lessons children must be at least somewhat willing to follow our teachings. This requires that they respect the integrity and good intentions of the teacher. Do not become an ominous presence in your child's life.

2. Children will always rebel against fathers who use force harshly to do their job. Harsh treatment usually produces the opposite of what it means to achieve. Remember that even an obnoxious child is not an enemy, and should not be treated as such. Incorrigible kids are emotionally troubled and often very hurt and furious. This is their "badness." Their sickness is *not* an excuse. Even they cannot be allowed to do the wrong thing. Violent kids must be stopped by any means, but they cannot be corrected by extra severity. And even they are sometimes reachable by fairness and by reason. It is very hard to love such youngsters. But they can sometimes respond to it when nothing else works.

3. Violence tends to beget violence. Do not spank your child routinely even if this was done to you. Never spank with anything but an open hand. And never in anger nor in public. Never hit your child in the face. This is meant to shame. Teenagers cannot be spanked anymore, even if they are way out of line. Grossly disobedient, disrespectful or violent youngsters must be forced to move out unless they control themselves, but spanking no longer corrects such tragic and dangerous situations.

4. Do not use shame to enforce your demands. Or guilt. These two are virulent variants of fear, and they are therefore especially dangerous. They cause lasting damage. Youngsters who are often shamed or made to feel guilty tend to become emotionally crippled. Guilt and shame become part of their character. And also at least hidden fury mixed with hate. People raised this way eventually produce their own shame and guilt automatically. They never stop punishing themselves and sometimes others too.

5. Obviously, never use your children to get pleasure at their expense. You may enjoy them but not use them. Their welfare must always be considered. You have no right to expect benefits from them that ignore their well-being. They are human beings, not property. You do not own them even though you brought them into this world and paid for their upbringing. It used to be different in the distant past when people lived as peasants in poverty and in slavery. Some parents forget that in the present this no longer applies. It is not only illegal to use or abuse your child but also morally wrong to do so.

6. Stay physically away from your children when you fear getting out of control. When you are too tired to know exactly what you're doing. Or when you drink too much. Or use drugs. Or are too angry. Or scared. Or very hurt. In protecting your children from yourself you're also treating yourself better. Horrible things can happen when people are under the influence of anything that lessens their good judgment.

7. Do not punish arbitrarily. Or excessively. Do not punish too soon or out of your own frustration. Punish only for something very specific. No cruelty is ever justified.

8. Do not be wishy-washy and then rage when you are not understood. Make your expectations very clear. Children often don't get it the first time. Especially when they are scared, hurt or angry. Be patient. Always try to earn the child's cooperation before you become the "heavy." Nobody can know what you expect unless you spell it out. Speak coherently.

9. Inconsistency is damaging. Change your mind and your decisions as soon as possible and as often as needed when you realize you're wrong. But not because of outside or inside pressure. Changing your mind when your position is right is not a sign of love but of weakness. It is not a good way to make up for past mistakes.

10. Don't insist that you're always right. Both you and your child know that this cannot be true. Admit your errors openly. You cannot be taken seriously for long when you claim that you're right because you said it. Such statements weaken your authority in general.

11. Never stop a child's reasonable protests unless they are clearly used as a provocation and are grossly excessive. Disallowing protest often results in the development of hate. Stopping the child from expressing his or her protests also breeds disrespect and scorn. Open protest should be encouraged, even if you must limit its length. In itself protest is not disrespectful, even when loud and powerful.

• • •

Margaret remembers loving to sit in her father's lap. It was so welcoming and safe. She would sit there every day after school and tell him what she learned in her second grade class. She felt very scared as a little girl, especially when she had to go to school, away from home. But being held by her daddy's strong arms made up for it. Margaret would tell him everything. All she remembered. But he was not satisfied.

She recalls with tears the sentence he spoke to her softly hundreds of times: "But the little angel told me that there were more things that happened to you in school today." This is how she slowly discovered that something was wrong with her. She didn't remember anything else. She hid nothing. But can an angel be wrong?

So she began to make up things. They didn't always fit the stories she made up previously. That's when she was accused of being a liar. And punished. And punished more severely for "lying" again. Eventually she would linger in class after school, dreading to go home. She was punished for being late. And for causing her daddy and mommy so many worries. Now she knew she was really bad. She tried to be a good girl but she could never satisfy them.

Father meant well. He only wanted to protect her from bad influences. To keep her away from hanging around with bad friends. But she ended up an angry, bitchy and rebellious woman. Furious and moody. She trusted neither men nor women. And she stubbornly refused to attend her father's funeral.

Power corrupts mainly those who feel powerless. To feel "one-up," such people tend to put others down. And being a parent is the most common position in which a grownup has power over others.

Even so, most parents do not grossly abuse their children. It is rare for parents to burn their child with cigarette butts. It also is relatively rare for parents to use their children for sex. But lesser forms of abuse are practically universal. At least on a rare occasion almost every parent has told his or her child to do, or not to do, something mostly because they had the power to decide. Without malice parents get a little pleasure sometimes from exercising this power. Children somehow know when this happens. They notice things. Even when they're quite small they are not easily fooled. Such mini-abuse can also breed distrust of authority if it happens more than on rare occasions. A vague but real expectation develops that the power to rule is tied up with injustice. This overdetermines the political and social attitudes of many people. For life.

By now the number of people who have been fathered harshly is legion. Add to these the ones who suffered at the hands of harsh nuns and other teachers with the old attitudes of an earlier age. In 1900 practically all teachers used rulers to rule. Teaching was overly strict, often harsh. As a reaction, an antiauthority "value" has found its way into educational psychology. And into value systems and the mass media. Proper, correct and necessary authority is widely confused with authoritarian rule.

It's high time that we make an urgently needed correction.

SECOND SECTION

...

THE HOPE, JOY
AND SILENT PAIN
OF FATHERS, MOTHERS,
SONS AND DAUGHTERS

8

—

A Rare Christmas Tale of a Father-Son Reconciliation

Reconciliations between fathers and sons
are rare. More often fathers die before
their sons find them and greet them   p. 69

Reconciliations between fathers and sons are rare. More often fathers die before their sons find them and greet them. And then the same tragedy repeats itself when the sons become old. Daughters usually renew contact with their aging fathers more easily.

Here's an unusual note written by a 47-year-old man. There was no reconciliation here. This son is still emotionally disconnected from his father. And also geographically distant. Hundreds of miles separate them, and all their meetings so far have been too short. They never found a language to reach each other. But the son could at least imagine what his father might tell him, if only he knew the words:

> I always wanted a son and got lucky the third time out. I was sailing when you were born. Donna already acted like she owned you when she showed you to me that first time. I was young and didn't know what to do, so I was reluctant to hold you. I went to the tavern to lift a few with my friends but couldn't talk about my joy for the sadness.
>
> Later on I was embarrassed by your girlishness. I told Donna she was poisoning your mind against me. I wish now I had stood my ground.
>
> The first time I took you hunting you were four. I sat you on

69

a stump and told you to be quiet, I would be right back. I was tracking a deer towards you when I heard shrieking and saw flailing arms. You told me you did it to warn the deer. I was so goddam mad, but when I told Donna and the girls I was smiling.

I don't see you much anymore. You're forty-seven years old and live far away. You call every so often but we don't talk about much but the weather. I don't know how you live. It doesn't surprise me that you never married; you couldn't have helped but sense my disappointment. Wishing you were different or that we were different doesn't make it so.

I never talked to my dad either. Now the wheel of time is coming full circle, as if the secrets of a hidden tale are finally being revealed to me. It's a very sad story.

Those scissortails from the lower peninsula come up here to abuse our land, hunt our woods, bleed us dry, and then return below. My son, you're one of them now, but for you I'd happily make an exception.

But this man's father does not yet know such words. And the son can do no more than write them. He still becomes tongue-tied when he meets his old dad in person. And soon it will be too late.

But Bob was much more fortunate. He was almost 50 and his father was nearing 75 when at long last the son found the father he had always missed. And always yearned for. It also is the happy tale of a father who finally discovered a loving son, taking the place of a disdainful one. Such stories are not common.

They lived together or near each other all those years, but their contacts were infrequent. Neither had liked the other. From the start, mother came in between them. She meant no harm but she expropriated the son for herself. Fussing over him. Spoiling him. Always siding with him and against her husband, the boy's father. Thus she gained the boy's loyalty and his endless devotion. Father was excluded and he was angry at them both.

Suffering from massive anxiety even as a child, mother needed something, or someone, to reassure her at all times. Her husband was not always available. He also tired of her endless demands for reassurance. So, she simply took the newly born child unto herself, as if he were her property. With him by her side she felt less anxious. More calm. Better.

She did not let go for almost thirty years. Finally Bob somehow escaped her clutches. Afraid of and hating all women by then, he was a compulsive yes-man who hated to say yes. So he hated himself. And mother. But he did not even hate his father. Bob tolerated him. Father remained a stranger, a distant and neutral outsider. To Bob he was a decent but ineffective creature, not really a man. A weakling unable to stand up for himself. Bob's face usually betrayed some disdain when they were together, even though he strongly wished to hide it. The son could not respect the father. As a boy, Bob never hesitated in rejecting the occasional invitations to go fishing or hunting together. Eventually he was no longer invited.

Bob was handsome, tall and physically strong. But emotionally he was distorted. Childlike. Too easily hurt. Shy. Suspicious. Extremely sensitive. All this he tried to hide under a mantle of impatience and a faraway look. He saw all men as weak, dominated by their women. Or as insensitive. With only a few exceptions he saw them as pathetic clowns trying to look powerful. Often boorish clowns. Being a man, he also disliked himself.

The rejected and hurt father grew to despise Bob and his aloof softness. Both were glad to stay away from each other. Each was carrying a heavy weight of solitary pain.

And then came Bob's midlife crisis. It packed an unusual punch. For the first time Bob experienced the emptiness in his life and the absence of meaning. This emptiness was not only emotional. He had very few human relationships, except at work. Essentially he lived without people. Without many contacts. In silent isolation that was interrupted by occasional storms of anger and jealousy. But now something had snapped inside him. He sought professional help. The lifelong fog that clouded his vision began to slowly lift in psychotherapy. New images of both father and mother began to jell within him.

Bob's father was seriously debilitated by diabetes by then. He had lost both feet and part of one leg. Totally confined to his wheelchair, he always needed the help of others. Bob now sought opportunities to check this man out afresh. He would visit frequently and began to notice mother's many insecurities. And father's courage.

To his great surprise, Bob began to admire the old man's indomitable spirit. His will to live. His sense of humor. The many enduring friendships that he cultivated and maintained. The father turned out to be very resourceful. An enjoyable character. Very different from the father of his childhood. Bob increasingly also began to like himself as a man. He did not want to be known as Bob anymore, insisting that his name was Robert. With much trepidation he began to date. Sadly he discovered that women can be a little boring and immature, but he noticed joyously that they were not dangerous. Life was full of surprises.

Three generations of Robert's family gathered one evening to welcome the Christmas season. They did so every year but this was different. It was not the usual routine. This time there really was friendliness and merriment. A fat Santa was hired for the evening and many eager little children were running around. Every child sat in Santa's ample lap during the evening, presenting him with their wish list. But Bob's greatest wish had already been fulfilled: he had found his long-lost dad.

Tears were rolling down Robert's cheeks as he recalled the events of that evening. Tears of sadness and joy. It was such a very long wait. Five decades. But at long last Robert was able to see his old father as a man deserving of respect. A real man. With disappointments. And dreams. With fear, and pain. And joy. Like himself. And he was finally able to experience love for this father. And for himself.

The old man looked at his son longingly. Finally he found the courage to whisper a strange request into his left ear: he too wanted to sit in Santa's lap. "All my life I wanted to do this, but I never dared. And I never had the chance. I know it is silly. I remember crying about it as a little boy," he said. "It's now or never."

Robert picked his father up and placed him gently in Santa's lap. The white-haired man sat there contentedly, stumps dangling and eyes glistening. These too were tears of joy. He was surprised when told later that everyone in the room was applauding loudly. He heard nothing. He was with his Santa. And with his son. A 75-year-old dream was coming true. It almost didn't happen.

9

Larry and Friends:
Too Little Fathering

*Z never felt any remorse about the two
guys killed the previous year. It was a
necessary shootout with the other gang.
One's territory must be defended p. 76*

*Giving the impression of being a cover girl is
obviously very helpful in earning a good living
as an escort. She is very popular with men p. 76*

Here are a few sketches of young people, recognizable
because we all know others like them:

LARRY

Life would have been better if the professor wouldn't have been
such an ass. Larry had to enroll in that course to fulfill a requirement.
But he resents it. And he needs a decent grade to get into graduate
school. What can he do? He does not have enough time to attend
classes. Even so, he sits there half-bored 60% of the time. Well,
maybe only 50%. The professor refused to promise Larry the "B"
that he asked for. The man is unreasonable. He expects everyone to
actually pass his stupid tests.

But with his hockey schedule and his new girlfriend, he really
can't get everything done. It's also very hard to get up on time. The

class is held the first thing in the morning. And his two former girlfriends also make demands upon his time, even though he doesn't sleep with them regularly anymore. And he does crack a book every once in a while. There is just too much to do.

It is obvious that he is trying. After all, he earned 35 points out of 100 on the last test. The prof is obviously old-fashioned and out of it. He is expecting Larry to do all that reading. Besides, his car must be traded in. He can't postpone it anymore. This too takes time.

He had a bunch of kids over the other day. All neighbors. All from good families. They all agreed. Learning is just too hard. They had plenty of beer and ended up in a topless bar. Everybody needs to relax a little.

Z

Like everyone else, he too was given a first and last name. But everyone knows him only as Z. Even at the police station he is known that way. They have no trouble finding his full legal name when they book him, as they do from time to time. Like everyone else, he also has an address. But he doesn't live there. He just hangs out. He has a territory. No one challenges him there. Z and his gang see to it.

He does not know his father. Never met him. Each of his six brothers and sisters has a different father. Mother raised him for a while and then his grandparents took care of him. But mostly he grew up on the streets. He was in and out of several foster homes and is proud that he was never inside a prison. He knows that he is too smart for that.

Nobody challenges him inside the gang either. He is also too smart for this. And too tough. Unlike most others around him, he can read reasonably well. He is also pretty good with numbers. He can add, subtract, multiply and divide in his head rather quickly. And very accurately. He often uses cunning. He can outsmart everyone around him.

Z never felt any remorse about the two guys killed the previous year. It was a necessary shootout with the other gang. One's territory must be defended. Although it's no secret that he was involved, nobody ever charged him. He helps keep the place in order. The policemen seem to respect him. At the very least they leave him alone most of the time. Even the sister of one of the dead guys doesn't blame him. She slips into his pad once in awhile and spends the night there. They would kill her if they knew, but this is not his business.

MARIE

Long-legged with high cheek bones, beautifully proportioned and well-dressed, she is secretly the envy of other women. Giving the impression of being a cover girl is obviously very helpful in earning a good living as an escort. She is very popular with men.

Marie likes it. There is plenty of money even if there is no glamour. She even enjoys being touched and tries to do a good job. She is careful not to get any disease and says that she has a sixth sense that protects her. She knows to avoid kooks and dangerous crack-pots. But she is 26 and worries about the future. She hasn't saved enough money yet.

Her parents know about her work. Her mother even appears to be proud of her at times. Her father never says much, but at least he's glad that he doesn't have to worry about her financially.

Although she aims to please them, she secretly despises men. They are such little boys. Pathetic. Each of them wants to come across as a great lover. She always has to pretend that they over-whelm her and turn her on. That makes them feel important and big.

What's wrong with this kind of life anyway? Everyone is ahead by what she does. She is not making trouble like those hate-filled feminists. She is pleased and so are her customers. She does the most with what she has. Isn't this what one is supposed to do?

But every once in awhile she is overcome by storms of rage that she doesn't understand. Like the time when that older john had a heart attack. She just left him there. She didn't even take the money that was hers by right. She never found out what happened to him. She still doesn't care.

And she is often miserable. It makes no sense. That's the only reason she takes drugs from time to time. Not hard drugs. This is the only way to find a little peace. Away from everyone. And that's why, when she needs some release, she masturbates.

• • •

Although so very different from each other, Larry, Z, and Marie have a lot in common. They all have had either no father or too little fathering. They have no roots. No direction. They are confused about values and about life. They are all very anxious. Like wild weeds in a barren field, they were all tough enough to survive. But not very well.

They probably were never mothered well enough either. People pay such a high price in distorted living mostly to find a little safety inside, enough to settle down a bit. All three appear to have been always somewhat jumpy, restless, tense. This is the real root of trouble like this. But later, when they could have used some guidance, there was no firm hand of support either. No encouragement. Nobody to push them beyond their fears. No one tall to stand next to. No one to counsel them and to stop them when they acted stupidly. No father to be protected by.

And there are so many frightening pressures and tensions in the adult world, so much confusion.

10

Black Youngsters and their Heroes.
And More about Z

*They learned the wrong lessons. That one can
do well with a minimum of self-discipline.
Without much self-respect. With little
self-restraint.... Without regular work every day   p. 81*

*Even now many black kids and some adults too still
see civilized behavior as an attempt to "act
white." They look down not only on white people
but also on the black middle class   p. 82*

Z was fortunate. On one of his many forced visits to the police station Hunter, an older officer, spent a little extra time with him and got to like him. Hunter was not fooled by Z's arrogant manner or by his attempts to look menacing. Z was strapping and handsome, a 6'2" boy on the way to becoming a man. He always carried some sort of weapon on his body. It was not safe for him to be anywhere without it. His dress, haircut and general demeanor were also designed to scare others. It's not surprising that people made sure that their car door was locked when they had to stop at a traffic light and his car happened to be next to theirs. They instinctively would raise their car's windows all the way up.

Z liked the effect he was having on others, but even so he was a good kid. Underneath the tough facade he was sensitive, like many of his friends. But very few people saw through it, though toughness was but a thin cover. Hunter was one of them. In a way he adopted Z.

The first time Hunter asked Z to come over to the house both felt somewhat strange about it. But from then on Z would join the family for a meal on occasion. They would barbecue together in the summer. Once in a while they went to a baseball game. And on one occasion Hunter even took Z to a police picnic.

Z was at first hesitant. He did not want to endanger his credentials and standing with the gang by socializing with the enemy. But then he reasoned that it was good to have a special relationship with the cops. To have contacts. It would help them all.

Z didn't even notice at the beginning that his life was slowly changing, but he liked it anyway. Hunter was a good role model. His family came from Alabama. Great-grandfather was just one generation away from slavery, but he was a truly free man. Self-respecting. Modest in his tastes and wants. Very responsible and grateful for what he had. God-fearing. But he feared no man. And though he resented white discrimination and was quietly angry every time it affected him, he was never bitter. Because he wouldn't put up with this kind of life, he moved north. A younger brother came along. Great-grandpa also took his responsibilities as a father very seriously: every one of his many children were raised to be hardworking and honest, like himself.

Hunter's grandfather had fewer children but he respected himself no less. He was raised to be responsible and to take care of himself, and he did. This grandfather still speaks proudly of the fact that none of his children or grandchildren have ever received a welfare or unemployment check. None of his descendants has ever been on Aid to Families with Dependent Children. He is active in his church. Even at his age he still strongly supports the NAACP. But he's often loudly critical of the leadership. They are shortsighted and self-serving.

Grandfather also made sure that all his children finished high school. The girls too. His own slave grandmother was the solid pillar who provided stability to the entire family. And to the neighbors too. Her husband was a big and physically powerful man, but he leaned on his wife for support and guidance. Her daughter came from the same mold. She would sternly admonish youngsters who didn't mind her. Hunter's grandfather knew that his girls might also have to hold families together. He wanted them to be educated.

It was Hunter's father who was the first in the large family to go to college. But he did not finish his schooling. World War II intervened. He served in the Army and then stayed on for 28 years. It was much more than a career. The army also was a home and a good family.

He was patriotic and proud to be an American, a man who really cared about his country. Though he understood that it was somehow legal to burn the flag, he could not accept it. It infuriated him. Something was wrong with a system that allowed such a thing. He knew about Constitutional rights, but the fact that Congress did nothing to prohibit such a craze only proved to him once again that politicians are not to be trusted. They don't really represent the people. He had no respect for any of them. If they're not corrupt then they are self-serving. He made that clear at the dinner table on many occasions. It is not surprising that two of the sons became policemen. Hunter is the younger of the two.

Z absorbed the family culture eagerly and before long became one of them. But his brothers and sisters were not so lucky. Like millions of other black youngsters they were caught up in the vicious cycle of poverty, crime and despair. Without a hand to lift them onto new ground, none of them made it out of the ghetto. It is hard for everyone to grow up, but it is practically an impossible task for sons without fathers and without good fatherlike models.

The role models of Z's siblings were superstar athletes and entertainers. Magic Johnson and Michael Jordan. And Wilt Chamberlain. Even Michael Jackson and others. They admired such men, imitated them and incorporated their styles and many of their manners. It was obvious that having lots of money opened all doors. Becoming rich was therefore a most cherished dream. These role models also spent lavishly on fancy limos and fast cars, and the athletes got all the women they ever wanted. And then some. They fit the stereotype video image of young black males being tough and obsessed with sex. They all were on the fast track. They all became VIP's. They kowtowed to nobody. Everyone looks up to them. Even whites. Their shortcomings were overlooked. Gambling in the big leagues and being high rollers and big spenders only increased their clout. Their money gave them enough power to be contemptuous and disdainful, and to get away with it.

And these guys also proved that being famous was all-important. It didn't work for Mike Tyson but this was the exception that proved the rule. Having AIDS only made Magic into a more celebrated celebrity. Z's brothers, like many other kids, also wanted to make it the same way but they didn't have the talent. And they ignored the fact that it takes years of training to succeed even in sports. An athletic career also takes brains, discipline and hard work. Without fathering they remained dreamers. They washed out. They gave up. Two of the boys now make their money dealing drugs. One of the two girls sells her body. They have no place to go.

They learned the wrong lessons. That one can do well with a minimum of self-discipline. Without much self-respect. With little self-restraint. Without thoughtfulness. Without compassion. Without regular work every day.

And how does Michael Jackson qualify as a model? He himself is obviously confused, prissy and someone reputed to have strange sexual interests. Light-footed with one white glove. Very sweet. Delicate features. Almost a girl. Nothing that ghetto kids can identify with. But even so, Michael Jackson was invited to the White House. The President welcomed him and took much time to show him around and to be with him. He is a star, a millionaire many times over, on the cover of news magazines. Envied. Welcomed in Russia.

Imitated in China. What does all this mean?

That if you have lots of money and lots of fame everything else does not matter. With money and fame everything else is forgiven and overlooked. Money and fame are all that matters. That's why getting them is all-important. Any way one can. Legally and illegally. In the pursuit of momentary notoriety people put syringes into their own Coke cans and then report their "find" to the police. Fame means that one is finally seen. Noticed. Mentioned on national TV. At least once. Andy Warhol was wrong: fame is not 15 minutes in the limelight, it is 15 seconds.

But why didn't Arthur Ashe, Hank Aaron, Willie Mays and other black athletes become the heroes of more black youngsters? Because the positive values that they projected didn't fit the ghetto mores and conditions. They were models of individual responsibility and nonbragging moderation. They were neither flashy nor abrasive nor cool. They were part of the Establishment. Their lives were not marred by explosive anger.

Z's brothers, on the other hand, still lived by the confused ideas of the Black Power movement of the 1960's. The Marxist and revolutionary clichés of Huey Newton, Eldrige Cleaver and Angela Davis made it respectable to see every antisocial act by blacks as an expression of justified anger at the wrongdoings of white society. Lawbreakers were made out to look like hero-victims, the most authentic of all black people. Even now many black kids and some adults too still see civilized behavior as an attempt to "act white." They look down not only on white people but also on the black middle class.

"Quit trying to eat white" is the chant that one youngster had to endure from his classmates because he made the mistake of cutting up his chicken with a knife in the school's lunchroom, instead of eating it with his fingers. "If they prefer reading books to slam-dunking basketballs...[or] if they don't talk like the people in music videos [they worry that] they're going to be accused of [acting or] talking white," says Betty DeRamus in a 1993 column in the *Detroit News*.

"This is a terrible thing because it implies that you have to fail in life...to be truly black." Dennis Archer who was elected mayor of Detroit was "slammed" by his black opponent for allegedly earning $500,000.00 a year as a lawyer.

Less than 1% of black youths commit murders and other major crimes, while the rest are terrorized and killed by the thugs. But nothing can change as long as the confusion about the self-image of blacks continues to exist. The criminal occupation of our cities will not stop until many more Hunters father many more kids like Z.

In their hopeless despair, Z's siblings also cannot identify with Colin Powell, Thurgood Marshall, Clarence Thomas, Barbara Jordan, Jesse Jackson, Sidney Poitier, Spencer Christian or Bryant Gumble. They can't serve as role models because they are too far removed from the value systems of black ghetto kids. Generals and judges even speak differently: they "talk proper," grammatically correct English. They are well-educated and sophisticated. They are models of striving, responsibility, excellence and achievement. And they all adhere to the work ethic. They have a capacity for critical thinking. They are self-respecting.

Such qualities of character do not catch the imagination of youngsters who have no economic stake in the system and who also were never really fathered. And since these qualities have all been discounted in the U.S. for the last three decades they are in extremely short supply now. Even among whites. But not among immigrants from Korea and other Asian countries. Here the values of hard work and family loyalty have not yet been eroded. And self-responsibility still counts. This is why they succeed.

Slavery in America and dependency on Colonial rule in Africa robbed blacks of a chance to develop a tradition of being self-starters. Not only kids and lower classes are involved. The number of minority scholars who earned doctorates increased substantially between 1982 and 1992, according to the American Council on Education. Asians had an 83% gain, Hispanics a 41% gain and native Americans nearly doubled their doctorates. But blacks saw a 9.2% decline.

Eddy Harris, in his book *Native Stranger: A Black American's Journey Into the Heart of Africa,* quotes Denis, a successful Ivory Coast businessman as follows:

> If others could do what I have done, all of Africa would not be headed for...a disaster. It takes only a little hard work and initiative, you see. But we have become a lazy people. We have forgotten how to work. When the French owned us, they did everything and we learned to rely on them. Now we wait for someone else to do what we could do for ourselves.

This inner state of mind needs to be altered before outside conditions will change for the better. And states of mind change only with good fathering.

11

The Missing Father:
A Special Tragedy of Blacks

*Many slaves succeeded in maintaining their
inner human dignity. Even extreme provocation,
degradation and abuse did not cause them
to feel or to behave like slaves   p. 86*

*We lead the industrialized world in murder,
rape and violent crime. To finally stop the
killings we must all begin to regard those
who terrorize and murder as criminals first
and foremost. Race is only a secondary and
incidental finding. Rosa Parks...was
herself recently beaten and robbed by a black
youth who even knew her identity   p. 90*

*All of us, white and black, are in this together.
No one is safe in unsafe societies   p. 91*

Why is fatherlessness so common especially among blacks? Three main factors are at the root of this tragedy:

1. Disfigured remnants of slavery,
2. Misunderstanding of the African heritage, and

3. The well-meaning laws proposed, promoted and enacted by guilty whites.

The cumulative effect has been destructive to the black family. And to black pride. These factors have all perpetuated the fatherlessness and sometimes they even intensify it.

1. Many slaves succeeded in maintaining their inner human dignity. Even extreme provocation, degradation and abuse did not cause them to feel or to behave like slaves. The same was also true for poor Jews in the ghettos of Europe during the Middle Ages. Degrading poverty, endless toil and repeated acts of gross injustice only hardened their resolve: they would not lose their self-respect.

But many more slaves were inwardly damaged by the repeated put-downs. They became bitter. Hateful. Hopeless. Resigned. Above all, they learned to endure anything without protest. Not surprisingly, their spirit eventually broke. Not only that but their families were also broken up and destroyed. Parents were separated from each other, and from their children. Fathers were arbitrarily taken away and sold. They were the strongest and the most valuable workers. In their absence, children had to be raised by mothers and by grandparents. This became the familiar pattern. Black kids are often still raised this way. We humans tend to repeat what we know. We even reproduce our own tragedies.

Slavery and discrimination are legally gone. But their long-term effects of bitterness, hopelessness, hate and apathy often remain. And so does the old pattern of fatherlessness.

2. Monogamy was never total in Africa. Even now many African men have more than one wife, and they have children with more than one woman. But at least in the past those who fathered children typically also supported them. These fathers usually were men of wealth. In fact, having children with several women was a sign of wealth. Like big cars and big houses in the U.S. But even there, fathers spread themselves too thinly over several households that often were at great distances from each other. Many African children grew up without a constant and regularly present father. Relative fatherlessness is an old African tradition.

These fathers were generally not irresponsible men. The practice may have been unfair to the women who had to share their men with others, but this is how it was. And how it often still is. This is how African societies sometimes organized themselves. And it is not altogether different here. Men often have children with several women. But here and now they often don't support them. Men find it easier in a welfare state to just enjoy sex and leave. Someone will surely do something to take care of the rest. So here fatherlessness is a much more damaging condition. We have no tribal support networks to help children grow up. An old African saying confirms that "it takes a village to raise a child." Social workers and school counselors are not the same.

3. Compassion for children and for life prompts civilized and affluent societies to support fatherless babies. Our heart goes out to them. We want to make sure that they will at least have food and a home. Ours is a decent society and we mean well. So we Aid Families with Dependent Children. And see to it that every child gets immunized and has good medical care. We even provide prescriptions without co-pay. And food stamps. Public housing. Summer camps. Educational facilities and even extra tutoring for youngsters who fail. And more.

Most of these are worthwhile programs. But they all infantilize their recipients. They keep the mothers and their children in an on-going state of dependency, living on handouts and expecting them as a birthright. This corrupts the will to work and to be productive. It builds a beggar mentality into the character of the young. New Jersey welfare mothers have actually sued to overturn a provision in a 1992 state law that prohibits increasing the grants for women who have additional babies.

To make things worse, many of these programs have built-in

disincentives for keeping the fathers at home. They make it easy for fathers to avoid personal responsibility. They make fatherlessness pay off.

In this way many of these programs have been ruinous to the black family. They perpetuate a tragedy. This is slowly becoming clear even to some of the recipients. The National Urban League now recognizes that "Washington can't cure every African-American problem." Its 1994 annual report says that "African-Americans have to help themselves, not wait for government to halt the rise of poverty, crime and unemployment in their communities." In the past the League took the opposite tack: it pressed hard for the expansion of social welfare programs.

Many of these programs were initiated and promoted by well-to-do whites who felt guilty about their good fortune and wished to do something to set things right. They felt better when they did "good." But in fact many of these brainchildren of white social planners ended up crippling those they meant to help. They raised false expectations, deepened the despair and legitimized outbursts of mass rage.

We would have fewer fatherless children if welfare programs had strong incentives to work. Subsidies would decrease and eventually vanish with increased irresponsibility. At the beginning even some children would suffer more, but the message would eventually get through and sink in. In the long run fewer people would suffer and die. More blacks and more whites would have a chance to live with dignity.

But most Americans are not yet ready to make such hard choices. It would require the rest of us to accept the fact that our real choices are not between good and bad, but between bad and less bad. It takes courage and fortitude to stand firm when we see others in pain, but it helps to remember that less harm would be done in the name of good. Now we indirectly encourage the birth of children who will never have a fair chance in life. It probably is more humane and kinder to clamp down on teenage pregnancies and to pressure fathers to stick around by making it too expensive for them to leave.

Teenage pregnancies are a disaster from a societal point of view: children give birth to children. Then the young mothers raise them without a father, often incompetently. Such pregnancies are also a tragedy from the child's point of view: it is born into conditions from which usually there is no escape. Such youngsters are generally condemned to repeat the same pattern a generation later.

But from the mother's point of view, becoming pregnant is not all bad. Caught in a hopeless trap without exits, this provides at least a tiny ray of hope, a little relief. With society's aid such young girls can at least leave their mothers and have a place of their own. A little privacy and independence. A way to survive. It is not a good way to live but a far better one than getting caught up and perhaps killed in gang wars. It is better than a life of criminality. Better than prostitution. Better than drug dealing. Unfortunately teenage mothers sometimes practice these too on the side. Cocaine-addicted mothers have been known to leave their infants in crack houses while pursuing such activities.

Sometimes teenage mothers are not even interested in having the father around. He may be a relative stranger, an occasional sex partner who is also being used for the production of a baby. Someone enjoying himself while helping a lost girl find a way to survive. And many of these fathers are themselves emotionally lost little boys. They are not the wealthy men of substance who used to father children in Africa.

• • •

Raising sons and daughters is a labor-intensive effort. Hunter spent many days as an active role model. It called upon him to be patient, wise, loving and consistent. It worked. These efforts bore fruit because one man was deeply committed to saving one life. Schools alone cannot do it. Societies also cannot do it. They can only help by legislating better. To claim otherwise is to pass the buck and to encourage false hope. The work of raising children is up to individuals and families.

Fathers and role models do not have to be generals or Supreme Court judges to be seen as heroes by their sons and daughters. Simple decency is enough. Children need fair-minded, present and involved parents who can be counted on, even during and after angry confrontations. They need basic acceptance. Nonrejection. Someone they can talk to who will hear them. Youngsters must simply be exposed to years of predictable and sensible behavior to become emotionally healthy adults and solid citizens. And they also need firm fathering that sets clear limits, teaches right and wrong, and demands excellence and responsibility. This is what happened with Z. As always, this kind of work was done without fanfare or press releases. At home. Quietly. Steadily. Slowly.

To save many more kids like Z it is urgently necessary to extract and to remove from the streets the hardened criminals who terrorize everyone else, especially the good kids. A huge majority of black youngsters suffers because a tiny minority makes them all appear as dangerous. Even responsible black youngsters from stable families are commonly subject to the outrage of being stopped and frisked by the police. Only because of the color of their skin. A leading black politician once admitted publicly that he was relieved when he realized that the footsteps behind him were those of white kids.

A basic change in the attitudes of the black community is needed before we can enforce much tougher penalties on criminals. This will happen only if ideas such as these are not interpreted as indicating hatred of black people or hidden racism.

The 1994 Children's Defense Fund report estimates that 50,000 children, mostly black, were killed by gunfire between 1979 and 1991, almost matching the number of Americans killed in the Korean War. One child is shot dead every two hours around the clock. Children not only give birth to other children now, but in the absence of fathering they also kill each other regularly.

We lead the industrialized world in murder, rape and violent crime. To finally stop the killings we must all begin to regard those who terrorize and murder as criminals first and foremost. Race is only a secondary and incidental finding. Rosa Parks, who refused to give up her bus seat to a white man in 1955 and thus was the catalyst that triggered the civil rights movement, was herself recently beaten and robbed by a black youth who even knew her identity. It makes no sense to automatically rise to the defense of black criminals just because they are black.

How many black youngsters will be saved from the quicksand of hopelessness, prostitution, drugs, crime and gang wars? Only time will tell. Their number is still much too small. All of us, white and black, are in this together. No one is safe in unsafe societies. All our achievements may be lost unless many, many more come in from the cold.

Many responsible black men and women from all social classes are needed to do what Hunter did. People who give a damn. Whites can help. But they can't do this job. Whites cannot help develop black pride. White mentors are confusing to black identification.

Hard-core gang members and other street kids have nowhere to go. Many will not make it. But tens of thousands of well-educated black men willing to get involved can make a big difference for the others. Committed and mature black women able to father as well as to mother can do the same for lost teenage girls. This is an unpleasant, demanding, and difficult job, full of disappointments. It tests endurance and it requires much time and courage. But there are no shortcuts. And often there is the satisfaction of knowing that lives have literally been saved.

In the meantime, black grandmothers come to the rescue. They father. On occasion even black grandfathers do. Many successful black men and women have escaped poverty and the ghetto because of the steady support of hardworking grandmothers. They devoted their lives to fathering their grandchildren. Without them the dimensions of the tragedy would have been multiplied.

Z vowed to pull a few kids out of the abyss. As soon as he's ready.

12

Roger and the Walleye

*Fathers and sons commonly grope and try
to reach each other throughout life.
And commonly they fail to find what
they are so eagerly looking for   p. 92*

Fathers and sons commonly grope and try to reach each other throughout life. And commonly they fail to find what they are so eagerly looking for. If at first they miss, they often try again. Harder. And then again. Until they are disappointed. But this hardly stops them. At least one of the two usually continues to try. Again. Once more. Only to again be disappointed. This time more deeply. And so it often goes for many years.

Finally something breaks within. Both give up. A gap remains. It often is deep, wide and unbridgeable, filled with loneliness and pain. With dashed dreams. And with lots of anger and hurt. Sometimes, if they are lucky, they manage to have a long, meaningful handshake just before father dies. And with teary eyes each can then finally see into the other's heart. The story is never finished before one of the two shuts his eyes forever. Even death is not necessarily the end. The pain and yearnings often continue.

Here is how this sad scenario of misunderstandings played itself out in one family:

John very much wanted a family. He was the only child of hardworking parents who had but meager emotional supplies. John was also hardworking. Straightforward and easygoing. But he was always envious of his schoolmates who had brothers and sisters. They would go home "to do things" with the family. This was worth living for, he had told himself since he was very young.

Such thoughts sustained him in his isolated existence. This was the recurrent theme of many day- and night-dreams: having a family of his own. A home full of laughter with happy children running around. He knew exactly what he wanted from life.

Then he married his high school sweetheart and all seemed well. But Judy contracted polio. And besides, she turned out not to be so sweet. The illness brought out a previously hidden bitterness. Like her own mother, she was angry at men. As a daughter she was disappointed in her father and as a wife she was always critical of John. He wasn't there enough, she complained daily. Self-pity became her solace. The more Judy complained the more John ran for cover.

By then he was financially well off. He had bought a boat. It was his escape. He provided his wife with the usual comforts and all the physical help she needed, but he was often absent. He deserved a little peace after a long day's work, he said to himself. A rest period. Sometimes he played golf with the "boys." At other times he played cards in the evening. He was not interested in other women but he stayed away a lot. This embittered Judy even more.

At first she would join him on the boat on weekends. But being partly paralyzed this was difficult for her. Besides she didn't like the water. He would fish for hours, content to just sit there. She was bored and it was really hard to take care of a baby on board. So she nagged, and he became increasingly uncommunicative. Eventually she just stayed home more and more frequently. He spent many weekends on the boat all alone.

So it is easy to see why he was waiting eagerly for the children to grow up. They would join him! The son at least, if not the daughter. The third child, also a boy, was only a little baby. But one day the sons would fish with him. His dream was still alive.

But, as often happens, the children became the battleground

between the parents. Mother raised them most of the time, as mothers usually do, while John was away either making a living or spending his time on the boat or on the golf course. All that time the children saw the hard life of their crippled mother and eventually came to believe her many complaints about father. He was the cause of her deep pain and the reason behind her loneliness. They could never see the deeper roots of her resentment, dissatisfaction and disappointment. Instead, they identified with her and became embittered too. The older son especially saw his father as she did. As insensitive and selfish. And as thoughtless. He treated him as if he were almost evil and was openly disrespectful, even when only five years old. Eventually he avoided John and stayed away from him completely. His rejection of his father was soon blatant and unrestrained.

John didn't know what to do about it. He knew very little about fathering, not having had much of a relationship with his own dad. Instead he got very hurt. And angry. He became gruff and punished the son too often. Unreasonably. This only alienated the boy more. But the son did not like his crippled and demanding mother either. So he left home after quitting school at age 16. Now he's in jail for having pushed drugs as an adult.

The daughter protected herself from both parents by becoming a shy, diffident and self-effacing, sweet girl. She always helped out. But she was neither close to her mother nor a buddy to her father. She remained a good daughter, never a friend. Eventually she married and had her own children. John and Judy see them on holidays. The two families have few other contacts.

But with Roger, the baby, it would be different, John still hoped. His dream was not dead. With Roger he tried the hardest and the longest. But he could not really reach him either.

Roger was an unusually sensitive child. As such he also protected mother and sided with her. She was obviously suffering. He would help her in the kitchen and always fetched things for her eagerly. But he was not very good at sports. As a male he was clumsy.

He loved poetry instead. Boating and fishing interested him only a little, though he tried. But he loved his dad in spite of everything that happened in the family.

With Roger, John was tolerant. Patient. Eager to help. But secretly he was disappointed that the boy was not more masculine. Even so, he was determined: this son, finally, would be his companion. And indeed, Roger would accompany his father to the boat regularly, in spite of mother's many objections and her not-so-hidden sabotage of their growing closeness.

John was an accomplished sailor and taught his son how to compete and win. They enjoyed trimming the sails and grilling hamburgers together. But even then, they did not talk very much. John was not the talking kind and Roger didn't know how to. It was not what John had hoped for. A pall of heaviness often fell over them both, like the black clouds on the horizon.

And besides, Roger did not have a knack for fishing. Over the years, again and again, father's line would come up with a big and impressive fish, while Roger would bring in tiny ones. He did not understand, nor could father explain why or how this happened. John tried to conceal his disappointment, but traces of it showed anyway. And Roger, being very sensitive, always noticed it and always was hurt. Not only were the fish he caught small, but he also experienced himself as not measuring up. So he tried ever harder.

One day at age 15 he decided to take the boat out on his own to try again. It was a beautiful summer evening. Everything was golden in the light of the setting sun. Peaceful. Tranquil. Perfect. And then it happened. Roger felt an unusually strong pull on his line. His heart pounded as hard as the fish fought to free itself. And after a long struggle he brought in an eight-pound walleye. Finally Roger netted it. He was excited and overjoyed. He could hardly wait to see his father's reaction.

But John was not happy. He simply didn't believe the story. It was too good to be true. He wanted to know who really caught the fish. Where did Roger get it?

Roger did not respond. He just stood there for a long time in numbed silence. It was the last time Roger went fishing with his father. It also was the end of John's dream.

Only many years later did the grown son notice that he had overreacted. Like the other children in the family, he too had seen father from mother's perspective. He could have protested father's insensitivity, but he did not. Instead, he used it to get away.

13

Fathering Children of Divorced Parents: A Nearly Impossible Task. And more about Larry

*The judicial system is thus inadvertently
supporting uncivil behavior and even crass
lawlessness. And the open flaunting of
legitimate authority p. 101*

*With or without a divorce, children should
never become pawns in the battles
between their parents p. 101*

*Willful irrational acts were sanctioned
by courts of law. And aided by the police p. 104*

We have already seen that fathering requires pressure. Conflict is not always avoidable. Naturally, it elicits hurt and anger and these usually are aimed directly at the one who fathers. Such anger can easily turn into hate when scorn and disdain are not nipped in the bud.

We have also seen that mothering is soothing. It consists of giving, of allowing, of reassuring. Everyone wants more of these. Children usually love the ones who mother them, but they do not always like the ones who father.

And when parents divorce at least some bitterness is commonly present. Often, father and mother are both hurt and angry at each other. Sometimes they also are scared by the breakup. Each parent then normally tries to win the children to his or her side. To be vindicated. And to gain support during such a difficult period. Backing by the children also makes the other parent look bad. The children become part of the battleground.

So it is not surprising that both parents usually mother too much at such a time and nobody fathers. Both repeatedly up the ante. They give and permit more and more. Restrict and demand less and less. Above all, don't antagonize the children!

Such bribing, even if unintentional, is nonetheless harmful. But in the midst of such a crisis parents forget. Or they don't care. They too have to survive. They fight for their dignity, for property and for the loyalty of friends and children. And they both try to maintain their self-image as worthwhile human beings. All is fair in love and war. Each parent claims that he or she is the better one for the children and that the other is obviously much worse.

Jodie was 12 years old when her parents separated. Father was a prominent physician, mother a minor celebrity on the charity circuit. Neither was a good parent: father was busy seeing patients and making money while mother was exercising, shopping and driving the children to school and to their many activities. This and her volunteer work kept her busy. Neither took much time nor showed a genuine interest in the three children. They were raised by a series of nannies and spent time with their friends. Meaningful contacts with the parents were rare and they occurred mostly during vacations.

The legal battles were long and ugly but at the end the parents were given joint custody. The condominium in Florida was awarded to mother. She was going to use it for herself and for the kids during their vacations, including the upcoming Christmas vacation. But Jodie refused to go. She was the oldest, the most stubborn and the most spoiled of the kids. Nobody had fathered her much even before the divorce. She wanted to go to the mountains instead. Skiing. And she insisted on having her own suite. This is what father sometimes provided. All along he gave the children too much. To make up for his absences. And later he bribed them to win their loyalty.

Jodie paid a high price for such bribes. She was crafty and old enough to manipulate. And very good at it. From early on she played one parent against the other. Now she reigned supreme. She became an obnoxious and unabashedly capricious dictator. She fully expected to always get her way.

She might agree to go to Florida, Jodie said, and then she might not. She "suggested" that mother prepare a "back-up" for her flight ticket, just in case. But she would consent to go on a cruise. As long as she got her own cabin. "Father would surely have given it to me, and you can afford it too," she mumbled self-righteously. She was "too old" to share quarters with her family.

Mother finally woke up. She had a social monster on her hands. Up to this point the family was always run like a democracy. Neither father nor mother ever dictated and never asserted themselves. Everything was decided by consensus. The kids were used to getting whatever they wanted. In everything. Mother suddenly realized that this had to change, but it was too late.

Father was more interested in defeating mother than in helping Jodie straighten out. He refused to intervene. And mother was unsuccessful in confronting her daughter. The brat always found ways to sneak away. Yet the departure day to Florida was fast approaching.

Finally mother decided to engineer a confrontation. Time to nail down the arrangements. The son was sent to visit a friend and she insisted that Jodie sit down with her to talk. Jodie refused. "You're smoking," she said haughtily, "and I don't sit in the same room with a smoker."

It was another provocation. Jodie herself was a smoker. Up to two packs a day. Neither parent had ever even tried to stop her. She was allowed to be disrespectful and to get away with temper tantrums. Now they came back to haunt mother. Now she was the one to be mistreated.

Mother demanded that Jodie go to her room "until you're ready to discuss this properly and respectfully." Looking mother straight in the eye, the 12-year-old simply shrugged and mumbled a "No." Mother could no longer avoid the challenge. She grabbed the girl by an arm and a leg and began dragging her towards her room. Kicking, screaming and swearing, Jodie almost knocked mother down. Still, she was unwilling to proceed on her own. Using her greater strength, mother turned her over to one side and in exasperation smacked her a few times on one of her buttocks. Then on the other. When the daughter refused to budge she continued dragging her, finally pushing her into her room. Huffing and puffing mother then slammed the door shut.

With father's help Jodie contacted Protective Services the same day. Mother was sued. Charged with assault and battery. The girl did not claim to have suffered any damage, only that she was mistreated and physically abused by being dragged and spanked.

Expensive lawyers got involved. They tried to negotiate a "compromise": everybody would admit to having been wrong. Mother refused. This would be harmful to Jodie. It would harden her insolent and haughty attitude. But under pressure she yielded.

Not so Jodie. She did nothing wrong. She would not apologize. But she would perhaps be agreeable to dropping the suit if mother apologized to her publicly.

This was the last time the two met. Jodie always refused to talk to her mother. No reconciliation was ever possible. Mother eventually mourned for her as if she were dead.

It was only a little over ten years later that Jodie really died. Her irrationality and arrogant disdain of others ruined all her relationships. She married and divorced twice in quick succession. It was always someone else's fault. She was glacial in her bitchy, biting and bitter manner. Full of righteous indignation. Then she met Larry, the young man from chapter 9. They lived together and did cocaine. One night they overdid it. They were found side by side the next morning near an empty vodka bottle. Jodie was 23.

And what if a father had tried to discipline a rebellious and contemptuous daughter like Jodie? He would probably also have been accused of sexual assault. His daughter was almost a woman! To drag her and to slap her as mother did could easily be portrayed these days as a sexual attack. Self-obsessed and unscrupulous daughters have been known to threaten their fathers with such suits in attempts to extort and to pressure them.

The atmosphere is so charged nowadays that a sexual accusation, in itself, is often regarded as a guilty verdict. Juries and public opinion quickly condemn men who cannot prove that such accusations are groundless. Fathers are not exempt. With daughters as out of control as Jodie it actually is dangerous to father these days. Unruly youngsters often get away with anything. On occasion even with murder. The Menendez brothers are a probable example.

The judicial system is thus inadvertently supporting uncivil behavior and even crass lawlessness. And the open flaunting of legitimate authority. Judges were also children once, and many males on the bench are emotionally still the loyal servants of their mothers. They went to a college and graduated from a law school but even so they have not individuated enough. They tend therefore to over-identify with female litigants who succeed in portraying themselves as fragile. Or as having been abused and victimized. Such judges fail to see the steely hate that is often hidden just beneath the surface. They are usually honest, but nevertheless responsible for many miscarriages of justice. They cause harm to children like Jodie. And they often badly wound those who try to father, like Jodie's mother.

Children of divorcing parents are often troubled not only because they lack a stable home after the separation. They usually also had insufficient or poor mothering and fathering for years before. A divorce can sometimes even help the children by removing them from an intolerably bad situation. But with or without a divorce, children should never become pawns in the battles between their parents.

Children in divorce situations normally side with mother because kids are more strongly attached to her than to father. Mother is the giver of life and the one who nurtured. And they tend to stand by her even more steadfastly if they also see her as the abused party. Mother's hard work is obvious. She must clean and shop and cook, often after she finishes her job away from home. She is usually also the parent most involved in raising the children and in charge of the family finances, perhaps even without much help from her husband. It is not surprising that children tend to side with her. It is easy to paint her as a martyr.

Father, on the other hand, is usually away at work. Or on business trips. He's absent a lot. This can be used as proof that he does not care much about the family. In addition, he often is the one who wants out of the marriage. It is easy to portray him as a philanderer. As irresponsible. Or at least as insensitive. His loneliness, hurt and pain usually remain hidden.

But marital conflict is hardly ever so black and white. Such a stark picture of a totally good mother and a grossly defective father is not often accurate. And it causes severe damage to the self-image and identity of sons. It also harms daughters. All men become somewhat tainted if their own father has no redeeming qualities. All men are from then on always under a cloud of suspicion. They too might turn out to be irresponsible, insensitive or cruel.

Jerry was really an inadequate father. It was inevitable: he was inadequate as a person. A nice guy but ineffective. Very insecure inside, and it showed outside. He always smiled. And stuttered slightly. But he had a good heart and went out of his way to help others. And he was generous. As a boy he felt so unsure of himself that he dated only rarely. He always expected to be rejected by everyone. His hardworking mother raised him without help since his father had died when he was four.

So mother and friends were surprised and delighted when he finally married at 36. His bride was an attractive teacher. How very lucky he was, they commented. They did not know that Andrea had never dated. She too was very scared. And angry at men. Her father, an alcoholic, deserted the family. Condemning him and all men was the recurring theme at dinner time. Those men were no good. Losers. Andrea was taught not to trust even the best of them. But she coolly decided one day that her biologic clock left her very little time. She wanted to have children. She had to find a man to help her in this project.

Jerry was no threat. Nice and ineffectual. She was completely dominant in that relationship. He was overjoyed with the arrival of each of the two children. And he was a model of a devoted father and slavish husband. He never even noticed that Andrea was emotionally uninvolved and distant. How could he? He had never even dreamt of a better relationship.

When he was served with divorce papers it came as a bolt out of the blue. He was literally speechless for many hours. Something broke inside. Not knowing what had hit him, he drove around aimlessly for a long time. Then he ended up at his mother's house. He was no fighter and did not know what else to do. He even lost the battle for joint custody. Andrea painted him in the darkest of colors. Any complaint that the children ever had about him was embellished and used to make him look bad. The children would be raised by Andrea alone.

Eventually the kids even refused to visit father. And mother wouldn't force them. Week after week Jerry went to visit them at his ex-wife's house. The children were polite but standoffish. He would beg them to join him, but could not demand. Or insist. Each time he returned home in his empty car he looked and felt like a whipped dog. He did not know what to do. The light that went out of his eyes that awful day when he was served with the papers never came on again.

In the midst of his massive anxiety and hurt Jerry could also not organize his thoughts. This too was used against him. Mother petitioned and the court granted permission for the children not to associate with father. Except when they wanted to. They didn't. All contact between them soon ceased.

But Jerry did not give up. The children were the dearest thing he had ever had. He loved them in spite of their many rejections. So he decided to continue trying. That year he brought them birthday and Christmas gifts. Mother didn't let him into the house. They wouldn't even open the door. So he left the gifts outside. A few days later they came back by mail. Unopened. The same with all the letters and cards he sent over the years. When the son got married many years later Jerry was not invited. He read about it in the newspaper. He was regarded by his children as a nonperson. As if he didn't exist.

What happens to such children? What are their human qualities and values as adults? They grow up confused and selfish. Hard and insensitive. Often with immense rage. Also deeply hurt. The boys are usually awkward as males. The girls have trouble with men. And with women. They are spoiled, with a perpetual sense of having been wronged. They are nongiving and incapable of having an open and loving relationship with anyone.

The system helped cripple them. These children prevailed even when they were wrong. Willful irrational acts were sanctioned by courts of law. And aided by the police. In Jodie's case, she went one day to pick up her belongings from mother's house, escorted by a police car so she wouldn't be "abused again." As she looked at her mother, the daughter sneered victoriously.

But there are no victors in such tragic dramas. Parents have no children. Sons and daughters grow up with hate. An increasing segment of the population accepts brutality and cruelty as part of daily life. Respect for all proper authority is diminishing. Everyone loses.

14

The Silent Loneliness of a Father: Dr. Gene

Father never asked for much.
And expected less. They got used to it.
He couldn't change it now p. 108

In the U.S., 23 million more telephone
calls were made on a recent Mother's Day
than on Father's Day p. 110

Inside, in secret and in hiding, many fathers
basically are hurt, scared and lonely boys.
They are not really in charge enough. Everyone
suffers from this authority vacuum. Wives are lonely
and must carry too much of the burden p. 111

Here is another tale about a father and his silent pain, a tale in which there are no villains. Normal circumstances have come together here to create an epic tragedy. Perhaps this is why this true story can touch us again and again.

Gene was a Depression baby. Father was laid off. He was a simple man, hardworking. So was his wife. She kept a neat house and was very frugal. She had to be. They were raising six children and although there was always bread on the table, not always was there much more. Gene was the oldest and the only boy. Life was spartan. Decent. Everyone helped.

When father could no longer keep up the payments for his Model

T Ford he worried that the bank would repossess it. But the family needed the car. To look for work and to drive to the bakery outlet where they could buy day-old bread. It was long before the days of unemployment checks and food stamps.

So Gene was sent to sleep in the car. Father reasoned that they would not take a car with a seven-year-old child in it. His instructions were simple: Do not open the locked car doors for anyone. And scream loudly if anyone tries to tow it away. Gene slept several nights in the car. Alone. Cold and always very scared. He had no choice. He also "understood" why it had to be done.

By then he already knew the hard life. Even as a five-year-old he had carried coal from the curb where it was dumped to the opening of the bin. It was a man's job, not a boy's. But father was still working at the factory then, and there was no one else to do it. Mother was busy with the little girls. And with the house. And with the cooking and the cleaning. So he slaved. For very long hours. In the snow. His back used to ache beyond hurt before he became numb to pain. His hands were raw. Sometimes he actually wished that he had died as a baby from the attack of scarlet fever. But such thoughts did not slow his work. He didn't even complain or protest. There was no other way, there really was no choice.

Years later he went to college, the first child in the entire family to do so. To cover his expenses he worked. There were very few scholarships and no student loans then either, but still he considered himself very fortunate. He had become hardened long before. No one in his family had ever mentioned any feelings. This was a luxury reserved for the rich. Everything that was not essential for survival was ignored.

But inside his outer shell he remained a very sensitive boy. Secretly he would scribble short poems into his notebook. This was the only way to express his dreams, his hopes and his pain. No one ever saw his writings. He wrote for himself, to make room for his heart. His mouth never spoke such words out loud, nor had he ever heard them spoken by anyone else. All the words used at home were about practical matters.

Gene's mother, a God-fearing woman, always had the meals ready on time. Modest but adequate. The clothes were always well-mended. But like father she also didn't hug much. Open expressions of her love were not known here. Mother herself came from a large family with many children and many needs. She couldn't offer what she herself never had. As a child she didn't receive much, and as a mother she simply didn't know how to give more. But both parents were obviously well-meaning. Quiet, simple folk.

Like many other lonely boys and girls and like John in chapter 12, Gene also dreamt of having a family of his own. He craved warmth. A welcoming home. Children. He loved music and imagined owning a piano one day. Perhaps he would play it and one of his children would sing. Such hopes sustained him. They gave him the strength to persist and to do well at school. Eventually he became a doctor of medicine. It was a tough and long road but he made it. All on his own.

Gene turned out to be a reasonably handsome fellow, but not worldly. He was never very talkative. A little shy. So he did not date much. A young, lonely man with a strong body, powerful arms and legs and a big chest. Perhaps to contain the deep, dull and nebulous sadness and hurt which were always part of him. He assumed that everyone else was similarly weighed down. That this was the normal condition of human beings. But even so, some days it was hard for him to get up in the morning, difficult to find the strength to take care of his patients. He needed a home. He was hungry for contact. Like a plant, limp for want of water, so Gene was shriveling in the absence of love.

So he married the first girl who really welcomed him. She was nice but also a little quiet. Withdrawn and a little suspicious. But like him, she also wanted children. This attracted him. He was beginning to see his dreams come true.

They eventually had three sons and a daughter. He worked long hours since it was very important for him to provide well for his wife Ruthie and for the four children. A conscientious and attentive family doctor, his practice grew quickly. He was often on call but didn't resent being so busy. He liked his patients and he liked being needed. He missed Ruthie and the kids when he had to remain in the hospital overnight but was at peace knowing that mother took good care of everyone. He loved them all very much.

And indeed Ruthie was a meticulous homemaker, even more than Gene's mother. No one was allowed into the house with their shoes on. Everyone was always expected to leave them at the side door. Ruthie was compulsive in the pursuit of order and cleanliness. Unforgiving when anyone forgot the rules. So everyone learned to comply and was careful not to anger her. Otherwise she would be sullen and uncommunicative for hours. She was not the explosive type.

Ruthie would mumble a few angry words when disappointed and just cry quietly. This would frighten the children. And the husband. So everyone worked extra hard to please her. At all times. Everyone tiptoed around her. No one noticed that the home had become an oppressive place to live in. Well-run like a tight ship, but without laughter and without music. Without joy. Gene never got his piano. It took years before he realized that he was very, very lonely. And that he had failed to protect the children from becoming slaves to mother's shifting moods. Or that his life's dream was not to be.

Suddenly he was 50 years old. And suddenly he noticed that his children were all strangers to him. He did not know when they grew up. He had pushed them all to go to college and paid all their expenses, but they were hardly grateful. And they hardly knew him. They would all still go to sporting events together from time to time as they had for years, and they would still travel together sometimes. As always, he continued to attend his daughter's ballet performances at high school but, even so, the family members were all merely acquaintances. And unfriendly to him. Everyone in the family seemed to avoid him. They fully expected him to provide for them but offered nothing in return. And he never asked for much. And expected less. They got used to it. He couldn't change it now.

All four children sided with Ruthie when he finally sought a divorce. He could take the situation no longer. The grown children even stopped talking to him, blaming him both in their hearts and in words. He tried hard to reason with them and to explain. But it was too late. His telephone calls were often not returned. Even some old college friends did not understand. Why was he divorcing now? They had all seemed like such a happy and harmonious family. He was shunned. And thinking of suicide.

Gene's daughter did not let him lead her to the altar when she got married. But at least she invited him to her wedding as a guest. A son excluded him from the christening of Gene's first grandchild. He did not want the grandfather to "spoil" the happy occasion with his presence, he said, since the baby's mother, Gene's daughter-in-law, "hates" him. The son did not want to annoy his wife. From childhood he had been well-trained to comply and to obey. He never openly disagreed with his wife. Like father, like son.

For years Gene continued to try reaching each of his children. He worried about them and blamed himself for his contributions to the tragedy. But this only pained him more. Two of the sons were repeating the same destructive pattern in their own families. He wanted to save them and desperately wished to explain, to warn and to show them before it was too late. But they could not see and would not listen.

Three of the four grown children finally came around. They made peace with their father. Gene's loving devotion to them over the years was too much to ignore. At first they only accepted his birthday cards, Christmas gifts and phone calls. Then they began to visit him on rare occasions, mostly when Gene initiated it. Slowly they began to appreciate their father. He was a good man, they discovered.

Gene sobbed for a long time when his daughter unexpectedly showed up in the hospital where he was being treated for cancer. And his eyes were wet when the three joined his friends to celebrate his 65th birthday. But these were tears of joy. Finally. The missing son did not even send a card.

• • •

This story is unusual only because it is unusually tragic in its dimensions. But lesser loneliness and hurt are quite common in fathers, as anger is in their offspring. Mothers generally remain of central importance and many adults remain emotionally attached to them. Even grown children tend to side with their mothers and worry about them. They are less understanding and often openly insensitive to their fathers.

More telephone calls are made on Mother's Day than on any other day of the year. More than on Thanksgiving. More than on Christmas. In the U.S., 23 million more telephone calls were made on a recent Mother's Day than on Father's Day. Not only that: more collect calls are made on Father's Day than on any other day of the year. These strange statistics are not really so strange. They make sad sense.

Mothers are more important because the role assigned them by nature is to give birth and nourish. And all living things form their strongest attachments with those who care for them when they are most vulnerable, most scared, most fragile and most needy. Saviors are always hallowed, worshipped and protected. We feel safer when their status is not questioned by anyone.

Fathers are hardly ever members of the inner circle that consists of mother and of the favorite child or children. Often they are the outsiders, even when they are the designated "head" of the family, and even when formally they maintain control of the purse strings. Children are usually most afraid of their fathers, but below the surface mothers usually have more power. At least they tend to be the power behind the throne, which is where real power often resides.

And why are children so often afraid of their fathers? Because they were designated by nature as the enforcers of the social order. This is more obvious among lions and apes and in the animal kingdom in general, but it also holds true among us humans. By nature, males are usually larger in size and louder in their roar. This makes fathers more intimidating. In addition, mothers often threaten the children with punishment by father. And to make matters worse, fathers sometimes try to appear bigger and more powerful than they really are to hide their inner doubts about themselves and to succeed in enforcing the rules.

But inside, in secret and in hiding, many fathers basically are hurt, scared and lonely boys. They are not really in charge enough. Everyone suffers from this authority vacuum. Wives are lonely and must carry too much of the burden. And while the situation was always this way, now it is much worse. In large part this is the existential tragedy of our age.

Many older men and women eventually discover these things by themselves, sometimes after they have weathered a midlife crisis and the children are gone. Some fathers suddenly mobilize themselves then to try at least to save their sons. At least they may yet have time to put their lives and their families in order. But these efforts are generally in vain. The sons are too busy and too young to understand. They are usually still eager to please, hoping to be loved and mothered in return for romantic devotion to their wives. Sons are generally unable to listen to their fathers then. Or they refuse to do so.

The tragic pattern repeats itself therefore generation after generation. Broken hearts and dashed dreams are the rule. Fathers commonly try to hide this pain from others and from themselves, too. But even so, many of them know. And their wives, the mothers, also know. When they are no longer envious or angry at their husbands' greater freedom to move about, they know their loneliness and the depth of their despair. After the battles for the children's loyalties have been won and after they grow older, wives sometimes sadly realize that, like themselves, their lonely and hurt husbands also cry out to be mothered.

It is an unfair burden on women, but what choice do they have? Strong and mature men are scarce. Boys are by far more common than men. Beyond all the struggles and beyond all the wars, wives often see their husbands as well-meaning bumblers. Tragic figures almost grovelling to be accepted. Tigers in the office and little lambs at home. Almost lovable.

15

The Sad Tale of Daughters who Lose their Daddies at Adolescence. And more about Marie

Many fathers become anxious when their little girls grow up. Suddenly they are rounding out and some fathers actually get disoriented by the presence of a sexy teenager living in the same house with them p. 116

Many...young girls simply fail to thrive as adult women. In the past such women often continued living at home with their parents. Now they are more likely to live alone with a pet or with a girlfriend in a similar situation p. 121

Daughters are more fun than sons. They show their love more openly. They are like dolls, at least when they are small. They're sweet and cute and cuddly. They adore their daddies. They idealize them so much that they talk of wanting to marry them when they grow up.

Daughters are also easier to father. They rebel less. They help around the house more. They don't usually ride motorcycles. They are less likely to end up in gangs, or to use a gun.

Even though such clichés are less true now than they used to be, little girls often still have a special bond with their daddies. Daughters are not competitive with their fathers, as sons tend to be. But this romance between fathers and their daughters usually lasts only until the girl becomes a woman.

Maryanne was George's favorite child. She was the family's first-born and from the start the apple of her dad's eye. Mother was a happy-go-lucky woman, temperamental and childish. Often busy with girlfriends and shopping, Julie was not very involved with her daughter. She did what mothers are expected to do, but she also was jealous of Maryanne's special charm. The daughter obviously was dad's greatest joy and he was her hero. This picture of him was supported by reality. He was in fact tall and handsome, a decorated colonel in the U.S. army.

As a soldier George was often forced to be away from home. But he also did not mind it. He found only little solace with his wife. She turned out to be more child than woman, but until after the honey-moon he was blinded by her good looks. When he was in their house with her he did not have a sense of being at home. Until Maryanne was born. From then on he always rushed back whenever he could.

Not only was she the reason he came home more often but because of her he also stayed longer. Julie obviously noticed the change, and it brought up a previously hidden deep sense of insecu-rity, and more jealousy. She would explode angrily more often now, and accuse George of being involved with other women. This is why he was away so much. They would have loud verbal fights, often in front of the child. Silently Maryanne sided with father. He was a good and decent man, she thought, and she loved him even more when mother screamed at him.

Julie was unusually attractive and men had always pursued her. To be accepted, they were always eager to please her and she had her pick among many suitors. In marrying a decorated officer she expected to find a strong shoulder to lean on. Someone very reliable to care for her. She expected to make up for the losses of her unhappy childhood. Many people do not know that even in very good marriages it's impossible to be only on the receiving end. And although she tried, Julie could not provide the warmth that she herself lacked. Conscientious as a homemaker and pretty, she expected this to be enough. George enjoyed the envious glances of other men whenever they were out in public, but when alone with her he was lonely. Nobody to talk to, he thought to himself. Julie rarely laughed, she was typically tight-lipped, dissatisfied and jealous.

George wanted a wife. Julie wanted him to be her "mother." It didn't work. She resented him and her own life. After a while she refused to have sex. Two hostile strangers were now living together in the same house. But neither sought a divorce. He was a rigid army man who followed the rules, she a scared child who did not know what else to do. Or that a better life was possible.

Maryanne had grossly distorted herself to please her dad. He loved his daughter, but it did not stop this soldier from yearning to also have a son. He also did not hide this wish, and Maryanne even tried to please him by becoming his son. So she excelled in sports. And in school. Like dad, she became interested in world affairs. She studied the countries where her father had served and conversed with him about topics that interested him. They were good friends. Buddies. And then came puberty.

Suddenly dad withdrew. He was starved for physical closeness and for being loved and feared being near the attractive young woman who unexpectedly bloomed before his eyes. He stopped hugging her when he came home. Even the occasional kiss on the check was perfunctory and short. They hardly talked anymore. George was angry at women and suddenly his sweet little girl had become a woman too.

Maryanne was deeply hurt but went on trying to please him even more than before. She didn't understand why he had suddenly rejected her. What did she do wrong? So she tried harder. And besides, what else was she to do? She was much more scared of losing her daddy than she was angry at his sudden withdrawal. Then it slowly began to dawn on her that her father was confused by her growing femininity. So she tried to hide and undo it. By the time she was 15 she had gained lots of weight. Perhaps this would help.

Maryanne's appearance became formidable, somewhat regal, but no longer soft or feminine. Her demeanor was glacial. She would never reveal any disappointment or express any hurt. But inside she was choking with rage. With frustration. She finally realized that she would never make it as her father's son. In that role she could not excel. And as a woman she did not like herself. Surely she did not want to be anything like her mother. She had nowhere to turn.

Many fathers become anxious when their little girls grow up. Suddenly they are rounding out and some fathers actually get disoriented by the presence of a sexy teenager living in the same house with them. Father may have enjoyed playing with her or rubbing her back to help her fall asleep when she was little, but all this is impossible now. No more brushing her hair, hugging her or holding the soft little hands in his. Pretty little girls, like kittens, are so enjoyable. But neither stay that way. Father enjoyed her dancing or her joyous carefree laughter and then, suddenly, she begins to grow breasts and to have periods. Now what?

It is not uncommon for fathers to feel cheated, angry and lost at such a time. As if suddenly someone had whisked their cute little girl away from them. Instead, they have a young, attractive and desirable woman around. Looking at her they may at times even become sexually aroused. This, they know, is wrong and forbidden. Besides they have always been uncomfortable around sexy women. And they still are. Such fathers distance themselves. No more hugging. No more back rubs.

From the daughter's point of view all of this could not have come at a worse time. The transition from child to woman is often very frightening. A time of profound self-doubt. Major changes suddenly occur in her body. New and mysterious yearnings begin to stir powerfully within her. She is suddenly thrust into an unknown place in an unknown role.

Suddenly she is no longer the cute little girl that everyone loves, everyone hugs and everyone welcomes. These all have totally different meanings now. She must suddenly curb herself, she somehow understands. Her openness could be mistaken for a sexual invitation. Up till now she was free, able to be herself. Friendly in an unrestrained way. Suddenly she has to be cautious. She can no longer smile spontaneously at people. These are confusing times. More than ever she needs her daddy to guide her. But he has disappeared. And he makes himself unavailable.

As in Maryanne's case, daddy often is the parent that the daughter was always closest to. Not, as Freud believed, because she secretly wished to be involved with him sexually. The reasons are much simpler and less fancy. And much more obvious. Emotionally, dad often is the mommy. The one the child trusts the most and feels safest with.

And besides, children are often more critical of the same gender parent. Kids often realize even while they are still rather little that when they grow up they will be like dad or like mom. So they scrutinize the same gender parent more carefully to see how to be. In so doing they often also discover what they don't like.

Children not only incorporate traits of both parents, but they also reject some. Character is determined only in small part by the genes. It is amazing how much children stand, walk, talk, eat, and assume bodily positions and habits of one or both parents. Much of this is slowly learned by imitation from birth on. Many careful "observations" are involved.

Children also tend to distance themselves from the parent of the same gender in order to form their own identity. (This task is considerably harder for sons than it is for daughters, as we shall see in chapter 22.) The parent of the opposite gender is often used by the child for support in this struggle. This is why opposite gender parents are normally idealized. Children of two-parent families clearly have it easier in this regard.

Little girls are therefore often closer to their daddies than they are to their mommies. And the opposite for boys. It helps them in defining themselves as separate people. Girls sometimes become extracritical of their mothers as they grow up. And fathers enjoy their daughters' extra adoration. Many men never had such an openly loving relationship with a female before. Fear of rejection may have prevented them from ever daring to be so close and to risk so much. This is one more reason why their enjoyment of daughters is so great when the girls are little.

Daughters often sense their daddy's carefree happiness around them. This stimulates them to make themselves even more lovable. Many daughters get their basic training in flirting this way. And mothers sometimes envy the loving bond that exists between the two. The love affair is nonsexual but it is a love affair nonetheless. And then suddenly father, the lover, jilts the girl "for no reason at all."

Not surprisingly many young women begin to hate their growing femininity and their sexuality. These "caused" their loss. They also learn that men are not reliable. Why would a stranger be less fickle than dad? They were safer in the world of childhood. The double messages of the adult world are confusing. They begin to hate it, and themselves.

Worse yet. Boys don't just want to be playmates anymore, but bedmates. Everything is different. Not only can she get pregnant now, but she can also get AIDS. And her rock and protector, her friend and guide, her daddy, is suddenly absent. There's no one to help her out of this confusion.

A young woman with such experiences cannot enjoy her entry into womanhood. Her new ability to create life is not experienced as a blessing. She understands why not so long ago women referred to their periods as "the curse." For her, the passage into adulthood is especially painful and unhappy.

For many girls this is the beginning of a lifelong disappointment in men. They are not dependable. Even the best of them are not likely to be big heroes. In a crunch, when they're needed the most, they're not likely to be there. Beyond their swagger and their boasting they are little boys. Irresponsible wimps. Pathetic jerks. Royal losers. Nobody to lean on. Nobody steady to count on during the storms of life. Even in decent marriages or in other good relationships, women often sense that they are psychologically stronger. They must depend only upon themselves. The hero of their childhood has let them down.

Marie, whom we first met in chapter 9, also resolved her life this way. At 33, she finally married a man 18 years her senior. He admired her body. Her looks. She admired nothing about him. But he was a successful businessman, well-to-do, rather handsome and physically fit. From the moment he laid eyes on her at the door of his hotel room, he was smitten by her. She came to see him as she did the others, but unlike them he tipped her $200. He did so that first time and every other time that they had similar encounters. And from their first date on he insisted that she quit this life. He proposed to her then and there.

He knew nothing about Marie except how she earned her living. But he obviously was in love. From that moment on she secretly despised him. She knew that he was a frightened child, if not a fool. As a human being she valued herself much more. The fact that others looked down upon her because of her work never bothered her.

One day she agreed to marry him anyway. What else was she to do with her life? She never met a man that she did not despise secretly. Including her pathetic father. And Marie knew very well that everyone had to be practical. She was a survivor.

They had two children, a son and a daughter. The children never knew anything about their mother's background. She was not ashamed but it would have confused the youngsters. It remained a hidden and locked secret. But she was comfortable with its existence. Not the least bit afraid that it might get out one day. It remained a secret for practical reasons only.

Her husband remained worshipful. Fifteen years later he died of a massive heart attack. The children were still in their early teens. She continued to father them as she had all along. Their father never even tried. In a sense all she ever had was three children and no husband. He left a large estate and she was well off. Very well off. But this did not protect her from always being lonely.

Marie was a good actress and excelled in manipulating people. Without malice. She knew what she had to do and did it. But she was not involved. Always playing a role. Emotionally she never had a home. Except as a very young girl and then again as an old grandmother. She enjoyed the grandchildren. And she never drank on the days when she would see them.

Fathers sometimes harm their daughters in other ways than by withdrawing from them at adolescence. For instance, some actually force themselves on their young daughters sexually and use them as if they were their property. Others don't like their daughters and reject them even as little girls. Many fathers are insensitive. Uninvolved. Harsh. Perhaps rigid. Cold. Even cruel.

And some daddies always overprotect their little girls and hardly ever push them to grow up. Their daughters often remain emotionally, intellectually and professionally below par. Sometimes also socially. For some such women life is but a game. They play at it as if they were dolls. They pretty themselves up all the time but are often remote even in bed. And as mothers they are busy and cute but not dependable.

The fact that Maryanne and others like her were dealt a bad hand by having a sick and needy mother is usually forgotten. But the anger at father and at men in general remains. Father was available at one point. Unlike mother, he held out the promise of loving closeness and he did not follow through. The expectations from father were high. This is why the disappointment in him is deep, the rage lasting, and the pain searing.

If such women marry, they often divorce. They don't really dare to love and they don't want to give. Why be involved in a serious and lasting relationship? They don't trust anyone enough for that.

And sometimes, when the disappointment of daughters in their dads is extreme, they grow up and stay away from all men. They want nothing to do with any of them. A few become lesbians. Many more young girls simply fail to thrive as adult women. In the past such women often continued living at home with their parents. Now they are more likely to live alone with a pet or with a girlfriend in a similar situation.

Millions of quietly hurt ex-daughters live their lonely lives this way or another, watching the days and nights pass by and fade away. At least we no longer shame them by calling them wallflowers, old maids or spinsters. They are true victims of poor mothering and of poor fathering.

Such women live mostly in big cities where loneliness can be hidden by anonymity. Here decent and sad human beings can at least try to find a little camaraderie in a cold and untrustworthy world. Such women often shrivel up and die inside while still very much alive. Years before they actually get old. Life slowly leaves them before they leave life. The only time they were really alive was as little girls.

16

Homosexual Men
and their Fathers and Mothers

*No one is quite sure yet why some boys...become
homosexual men, and others do not. Some believe that
the real reason for homosexuality is genetic or
hormonal, and not to be found in past events....But...
it cannot be that the all-important relationship between
a son and his father does not also play a role p. 125*

*It makes no sense to celebrate homosexuality
any more than it does to condemn it. But more correct
and better fathering and mothering may
lessen the confusion in the next generation p. 128*

Here is one possible scenario of a combination of events that sometimes leads to the creation of a male homosexual:

The parents are young and both mean well. Both are immature and unprepared for parenthood. Both are therefore very frightened by the arrival of their new baby. It happens to be a boy. The mother can hardly believe that she was the one who created this life. She is overwhelmed by joy and also by fear of her new responsibilities. She panics. Herself barely out of childhood, she now holds not a doll but a real baby in her arms.

From time to time mother almost freezes. Her arms are stiff as she handles the little creature. She feels guilty about her clumsiness when she notices it, which stiffens and tightens her even more. To make up for this sense of inadequacy, she is even more conscientious

122

than before. Now she tries even harder when she feeds and cares for the baby. But she herself still wants to be given and can't yet really give much to anyone. She herself still feels like a needy baby. Frightened. Overwhelmed. Confused. Even physically uncomfortable, tired and in pain.

Mother is also angry, at first mostly unknowingly. The baby is so demanding. So unreasonable. Not only has it stretched her young body out of shape but it also is depriving her of sleep. And of opportunities to have fun. She has become a prisoner and this young creature is her warden. She also resents the fact that the baby is often inconsolable. It does not always calm down even in her arms. Or on her bosom. The baby is rarely pleasant. Instead of smiling and cooing happily as she expected babies to do, this one whines a lot and complains without end. All this deepens her sense of being inadequate. She tries to hide her anger but sometimes it shows through.

Mother can't help it. She catches herself looking at her baby coldly. It is the cause of all this trouble. Hiding her resentment is an effort too, and she is already very tired of trying. She is even more guilty now. It's all a cursed mess. No joy.

Father is proud. He has a son. Happily he passes cigars all around. The new baby proves his potency. He too is scared but then, he has to take care of the baby only for brief periods of time. It helps him to remember that this is mother's job. But he really feels inner joy on the occasions when he holds the baby in his arms, and he is comfortable holding it. His big chest and muscular arms welcome the child's little body. It makes father feel even bigger and stronger.

For awhile all is well. The baby "knows" safety in father's solid embrace and craves to be there. Sometimes he smiles broadly when he "recognizes" his dad and is calmer when held by him. Mother is jealous and gets angrier. Sometimes she is a little rough and impatient when she handles the baby.

But the honeymoon with father does not last forever. The baby grows and becomes a toddler. He now has a will of his own and has learned to say "no." Father gets impatient with him at times. The boy is not quite so cuddly anymore, and he doesn't listen. He is stubborn. He cries a lot. And he sucks his thumb all the time.

Father is a he-man. He wants his son to be one also. But the child appears to be scared of everything. And he is so pale. And he whimpers. Father tries to correct the situation. The boy needs a strong hand. So father becomes not only firm but also harsh. He raises his voice too often and much too loudly. He punishes when a stern word would have been sufficient. He's impatient and disappointed. The boy is not the son he wanted.

Without even noticing it at first, father begins to reject the boy. Despite this and mother's impatience and lack of sympathy, somehow the child survives. We humans have a miraculous capacity to make do even under adverse conditions. But the boy's body "remembers" the good old days and pines for the comforting physical contact that he had with father long ago. He always wants more of it. But father is no sissy. He doesn't want his boy to be one either. He reacts with disgust to the child's attempts to climb into his lap. Instead he treats the young son roughly, toughly, and gruffly. John Wayne-like. The way "real men" are with each other. But the little boy still craves, wants and needs tender reassurance.

All this is something that neither father nor child understands or thinks about. But this is the way they feel and the way they react. The little child inside the growing boy has no one to turn to. In desperation he tries to cling to mother. He tries almost anything to please her. It does not work. Eventually he turns to run with and after other children. With other little boys like himself he sometimes finds a little peace. By chance he discovers that innocent occasional physical contact with another boy is enjoyable. The rest is obvious.

Other variations of this story exist. For instance, sometimes mother attaches herself to the infant for her own needs, and then begins to use the toddler and the growing boy as a controlled companion. As if he were a substitute husband. Or even an indentured servant, chattel. Father is shut out. He is hurt and angry.

Defeated. Crushed and resentful of both wife and child, he loses interest in his family. The son learns the "lessons" of his bitter experience: all women are dangerous. They use men. They are disloyal to their husbands. They are to be avoided.

No one is quite sure yet why some boys reach such incorrect conclusions and become homosexual men, and others do not. Some believe that the real reason for homosexuality is genetic or hormonal, and not to be found in past events. Most probably, the combination of two or more of these factors tips the scale. But leaving all this aside for the moment, it cannot be that the all-important relationship between a son and his father does not also play a role.

It appears that we are witnessing a dramatic increase in the number of male homosexuals. Perhaps it only seems so because we finally see in the open that which was previously hidden in the closet. But in any event, less shame is attached to homosexuality now since the stigma of "sin" is no longer such a potent threat. Old prohibitions carry little punch in a permissive age. But the increase in the number of male homosexuals may reflect more than merely a change in values. In many families fathers and fathering are in very short supply. Boys often continue to yearn for a dad to love and to be loved by, especially when mom was experienced as not nurturing enough. To grow up they really need someone sensitive and loving, present and patient, supportive and helpful.

This is how children experience daddies and this is why they love them so much: they accept unconditionally. This also is their weakness. They do not father.

The push behind the homosexual (and heterosexual) search for a partner is often so desperate and so determined that it cannot represent a sexual urge alone. The hurt that results from jilted relationships is also too deep to be explained this way. Lust and genital hunger have urgency. But the drive to find and to keep a safe haven is much more powerful than that. It comes from another source. These are not yearnings of the penis but of the heart.

What are these yearnings for? Their intensity and persistence suggest the answer. The yearnings are for a long-lost love relationship, like the little boy's relationship with his mothering dad. This explains why homosexual, and many heterosexual, relationships are so full of pathologic jealousy. The partner is much more important than a mere sexual lover. Any threat of loss is extremely frightening and feels as dangerous as the sudden death of mother would really be for a baby. It gives rise to the terrible fear of abandonment.

And why don't homosexual men try to satisfy their yearnings with women? Because no woman can be expected to provide solace when mother, the first and most important woman in their lives, was not experienced as doing it well enough. Every woman afterwards reactivates the old physiologic reactions of dread and distrust. Why would a stranger be less engulfing and more physically welcoming than one's own mother? Our bodies store impressions long before our brain remembers. Such impressions are historically not necessarily accurate. An infant's mother can thus be "remembered" as dangerous, hostile, cold, ungiving or even hateful, when in fact she was well-meaning and in her own way loving. What matters is that the tiny organism somehow experienced father as the welcoming one, and physical closeness with a woman as dangerous.

Homosexual men can have women as friends. They can be their companions and buddies. But even the idea of physical involvement with them generally raises anxiety which tenses the man's body. All living things react this way to perceived danger.

Normal sex requires trust. Relaxed togetherness. A willingness to be open and vulnerable. But homosexual men often experience the very opposite with women. They close up. They freeze and withdraw. Women cannot be the object of desire. They are the ones to avoid and to stay away from.

Not so men. Their company and closeness are yearned for since all warm-blooded creatures need and seek some physical contact for reassurance, and not only when they are young. Men who had a distant mother and some but not enough of a loving dad are literally starved for such contact. To survive, some become homosexuals.

Their bodies do not know any other option.

The tortured inner life of many homosexual men is centered around the recurring question: "Did my daddy love me?" Why is this so? Because their daddies were all-important. They nurtured. As in the scenario at the beginning of this chapter, daddy was the softer and the warmer parent. The more giving, the more loving and the more welcoming. And at least for awhile, the more available. Daddy was the "mother." And as we have repeatedly seen, children are normally most loyal and most attached to their mothers. This is true even when the "mother" is male.

Such confusion can be harmful for boys. And now that fathers are urged by the popular culture to mother much more, this may well get worse. Such boys may continue to seek mothering from men. Some may never have the option of being involved with women and will have to forego the chance to build a "normal" family.

We have already seen in chapter 2 why dads must become fathers in order to raise healthy children. It is now even more obvious why this is true for sons. But daughters too may be damaged by fathers who mostly mother and don't father enough. As grown women they often associate only with older men. Such arrangements have advantages but a price tag too.

As a result of the sexual revolution and feminism, being a mother is not quite so important as it once was. In the past, women and men both used to regard motherhood as a woman's most highly valued status, and girls still strive to walk down the aisle in white purity for this reason. But now women who are conflicted about their femininity and who reject motherhood do not have to see themselves as failures. Other honorable options exist nowadays. And mothers who are openly impatient with their endlessly demanding babies can more comfortably cite their professional duties and interests as being more important than the child. Now more than ever, many more little baby boys and girls depend on their daddies for mothering.

This need is being met partially by the increasing number of men who were led to believe that it indeed is their job to mother. Daddies are now present in the birthing room. Many have kitchen duty 50% of the time. They are proud of being childlike buddies to their children and participate eagerly in their daily care. But since nobody lets go of one's "mother" easily or without pressure, so much mothering by daddies may be dangerous, especially for sons. Such boys may continue to find men more understanding, more sensitive, and emotionally more present than women. Some of the increase in male homosexuality may thus be an unintentional side effect of feminism.

Condemnation of homosexuality has never deterred those who for reasons of nature or nurture had no other choice. It only drove them underground. But sexual orientation, like everything else, runs on a continuum. Many men have some freedom to go either way, and in the past, when homosexuality was defined as bad, they often preferred the socially acceptable alternative.

But now that the old prohibitions are gone, more men drift towards it. With shame playing a lesser role, almost any lifestyle is regarded as having equal merit. But only those who are not totally repelled by physical closeness with women actually have a choice.

Beyond all the political battles, homosexuality is in fact for many men neither a chosen nor a preferred lifestyle at all. Instead, it is a fixed position that those involved are unable to leave, whether for genetic, hormonal or historical reasons. The words "choice" and "preference" both suggest the presence of freedom to pick whatever the will dictates. We are free to choose chocolate, vanilla or strawberry ice cream as we prefer. Choices can also be changed at will. Such freedom to choose exists only for true bisexuals, men and women near the middle of the continuum. They can even find competent help now to lessen the physiologic confusion. But the others are caught wherever they happen to find themselves. It makes no sense to celebrate homosexuality any more than it does to condemn it. But more correct and better fathering and mothering may lessen the confusion in the next generation.

A recent photograph in a newspaper showed a mass demonstration of homosexuals in New York. Thousands of young and older men and women filled the street. Mostly men. Twenty or thirty abreast made up the front line of the long march on Fifth Avenue.

They were holding up signs with various slogans. Some were holding hands. Some were hugging. This was a peaceful demonstration. No violence. Only pain and anger. And an attempt to no longer live in hiding and in shame. One slogan was missing, the one that should perhaps have been at the head of the march: "Where Have All Our Fathers Gone?"

17

A Story of Four Generations

The children had no room to breathe....
Tom never noticed that they were too
young for all that pressure p. 132

Tom grew up in Belgium during World War II. His middle-class family lost everything they owned. The Germans confiscated and killed, the Allies bombed and destroyed. The family was reasonably well off before, but now everything was gone. They all crowded into a very small apartment. To get a little fresh air they would go to spend the day in "the country," a tiny plot of land with a toolshed where they grew a few vegetables. This kept them from starving. Tom remembers his father walking with a broom and a pail in the streets of their city to collect horse manure for fertilizer. He was disgusted but understood the need. He too wanted to survive.

The whole neighborhood caught fire one night after a massive bombing. Grandfather and Tom's dad ran frantically into the burning attic to save some hidden family treasures. Grandpa was overcome by smoke and died. Father fared better. Only his spirit broke. Afterwards he always walked stumblingly, like a dazed man. He would hardly see the radishes that he pulled out of the ground. Memories about the women in the family were all vague, but Tom knew somehow that they were all very straight-laced and strict. He remembers no tender moments.

So he escaped. All alone. While still a teenager. First he hitch-hiked to Switzerland, eventually arriving in the United States. To survive, he lied. He manipulated. Once he even stole. A kid on his own. Smart, socially clumsy and desperate. He was determined not to live like his father and he never overlooked a helpful angle to get ahead. Eventually he became a successful businessman. The father of three children. An owner of horses and of a big house. A community leader.

And he became a collector. First and foremost he collected money and gold coins. He never had enough. And he collected stamps. And all the letters he ever wrote and received. And interesting scraps of newspapers. And old cars. But still and all, he never had enough. He never felt safe. He was always afraid that he would lose everything.

Even as a youngster he knew that when the day came he would be very different as a father. He would be more present. More involved. He would guide his children more and set the tone in the family. This he did. From his "command post" in the living room he directed everyone's affairs. Autocratically. He admired Patton. His wife, a quiet and obedient woman, was glad to have an active and assertive leader around. She did not always agree with his tastes, or even with his decisions. But she was glad someone was making them. With his wife but a shadowy figure in the background, the children depended on him to also mother them.

Tom was especially concerned with bringing the children up the right way. He made sure that they went to the best schools, after researching the subject thoroughly. Some of these schools were far away. But no distance was too great to get away from the possibility of having to collect horse manure in the streets. He exposed the children to books, to ideas and to good teachers. They hiked together in the mountains. He taught them survival skills and insisted that they become independent and able to fend for themselves. His standards were unrealistically high but he did not know it. He expected the children to adhere to them even when they were still quite small. In spite of his busy schedule he took time with each child. He was the very opposite of an absent father.

But the children had no room to breathe. They got good grades in school to meet his expectations but internally they always failed to measure up to his demands. Tom never noticed that they were too young for all that pressure. All three kids blamed themselves for not trying hard enough, though they always did.

Tom Jr. almost died in a serious suicide attempt. He was barely saved. Not only was he fathered harshly but he also was not mothered well enough. The other son is socially still a child, still catching up. The third is a quiet, withdrawn scientist attending to computers. With little human contact.

The children knew that Tom meant well. But he was so intrusive, so insensitive, so authoritarian. Such a poor model for human relationships! This is where they all have serious difficulties. And where was mother? Hidden in the background. They could never be openly angry at such a nice lady, but it was easy to be furious at father.

Tom had worked extremely hard to build a close family, but it did not jell. He gave the children much more than he ever received from his own father, but not having had a good model, he improvised. He was harsh. Arbitrary. Anything meaningful in life had to be difficult. Success was measured by overcoming hardships. Competition was all. Relaxation was a waste. Because he was so obviously well-meaning it only bred resentment and hopelessness, not open rebellion. The suicide attempt came as a shock to everyone. But it might have been predicted.

Hard work and the cultivation of the mind is what Tom believed in. This is how he attempted to prepare his children for life. How was he to know about emotional needs? Nobody ever recognized his. He ended up being grossly insensitive since no one was sensitive to him. We can only know that which we were exposed to. Tom remained perplexed and could not understand: why would a child of his try to kill himself? What had happened? For him it remained a troubling enigma that made no sense.

When the kids were small Tom also micromanaged their mothering. And he often tried to mother them himself, "correcting" his wife. Thus he remained the central figure in their inner lives. More so than the real mother. She was reliable and loyal but much too passive and emotionally distant. The children liked her, but they remembered and especially appreciated Tom's unusual dedication to them. Even so, they were uncomfortable around him. He knew that they often stayed away to avoid him.

Now that Tom Jr. also has a son he wants to father him better. He's allergic to anything authoritarian. He's even suspicious of reasonable authority. He makes sure to never be intrusive. He gives the kid lots of freedom, lots of breathing room. He is exceedingly sensitive to the child's emotional needs and does not want him to be afraid. Or hurt. He knows that children must find themselves and express themselves. It's good for children to experiment. Not to be choked in the yoke of too much discipline.

But he is not strict or firm enough. The other day the son came home from school with a bad report card. And his friends sometimes do drugs.

• • •

And so the cycles of pain and despair repeat themselves. Until someone, somehow, begins to father the next generation more competently.

18

Growing Up is Hard to Do

He was my hero. I do recall the stories
I used to tell the other kids about an
important and powerful man. He used to
fly in on a moment's notice. I'd see
him for a few precious hours p. 135

Probably there are many kids who
don't see too much of dad...dads
who don't visit as they should p. 136

Here's a touching story written by a sensitive son about his relatively absent father. The pain and hurt are obvious. So is the damage. Written by Travis Simpkins, it was published in the June 21, 1993 issue of *Newsweek*:

I'd like to think I'll be a better father, that I have learned from Dad's mistakes. On most days I can buy that. But there are times when I look in the mirror and see who I've become, and think of who he's always been, and I'm not so sure. You can't pick up a newspaper without reading of the nightmare that is child abuse, or how alcohol is ripping families apart. I see these articles and feel a little foolish for my anger. My father was neither abusive nor alcoholic. He was simply absent.

Dad did always love me. He still does—or so he says on the rare occasions when we catch one another on the phone. He had his priorities when I was young, and now I have mine. I'm in jail, and my primary concern is my trial. I'm sure he understands. I always did.

My parents married when they were young and idealistic. I

was only 2 when they gave up on their marriage and went their separate ways. I stayed with Mom. Dad probably wanted it that way, as he needed to "stretch his wings" (his words, not mine).

I don't remember much of him in the early days except that he was my hero. I do recall the stories I used to tell the other kids about an important and powerful man. He used to fly in on a moment's notice. I'd see him for a few precious hours. He drove flashy rental cars, wore expensive suits and took me to top-dollar restaurants. It enthralled me. This man was so big, so much larger than life. He was my dad and, in my eyes, the king of the world. I recently asked Mom how many monthly child-support payments he made in those years of absence. Her face drew into a tight smile, the kind that only painful memories can bring. She said she wasn't sure, but she could probably count the number on one hand. I guess he had other things to spend his money on.

As I grew older, the visits became more and more infrequent, sometimes a year apart. Nonetheless, what they lacked in quantity, Dad made up for in quality, or some cruel parody of it. He flew in from Los Angeles, New York or San Francisco. He dropped names left and right, always on the brink of really big success. He remained my hero.

Such is the innocence of youth that when he called, always a few weeks after Christmas or my birthday, and told me the package I never received "must have gotten lost in the mail," I believed him wholeheartedly. Until I was 13 or 14 years old, I was afraid to mail a letter for fear the same fate would befall it. But as the years rolled on, the truth about the letters and packages, the truth about everything, became painfully obvious. I tried for a while to stick my head in the sand. This wasn't the same as learning about Santa Claus or the Easter Bunny.

The road from realization to acceptance is a lot longer than it looks. I've been on it for the past five years, and I'm not all that far from where I started. "The past is the past" is a nice catch phrase, and one I've tried in vain to make myself believe....My father and I have a hard journey ahead of us, provided we can find the time. There is sorrow in his voice when we discuss the past, and I know that if he had it to do over, he'd do his best to do it right. Second chances are few, and it's much easier to do it right the first time. That's become painfully obvious to me as I live with the consequences of my own mistakes every day.

My dad loved me as only a father can love a son. I don't question that. But he was also a self-centered, egocentric s.o.b. who let me down when I needed him most. A part of me will always be that kid at the window waiting and waiting with his nose pressed against the glass. Knowing that if Dad said he was coming, he was coming; but waking up curled beneath the window, alone. I don't want to sit and cry about the scars his actions may have left....But I have a very hard time letting people in. Trust is not an easy word for me to say, and it's almost impossible for me to feel it. I learned a hard lesson a long time ago. It's not one I'll risk learning again.

Now that I'm older, ironically, the tables have turned. It's Dad who seeks out his son, and it's he who is let down. Not so long ago, we took a trip, my dad and I. I was in trouble with the law, and Dad flew in from New York to help me....It was a gallant gesture, but neither of us could find our way around the wall that we'd built. We talked of business things, politics, a weakening dollar, you know, the important things. Eventually the conversation turned to the past, and at one point this baldish but still distinguished 43-year-old man looked at his 19-year-old son, who outweighs him by 30 pounds, and asked with tears in his eyes, "How did you grow up so fast? What happened to my little boy?" I suppose I could have said something witty....But I looked at this man who was once my hero, and I saw the gray in what's left of his hair and the wrinkles around his eyes. I understood his frustration at being unable to solve my problems. It was then I began to replace anger with compassion as I realized he was just as human, as vulnerable, as I. I love my father, but looking in the mirror sometimes I get a little scared. We are just so damned much alike....Probably there are many kids who don't see too much of dad...dads who don't visit as they should. If I'm lucky, a handful of those fathers are reading this...maybe you should take time to consider how important whatever else you've got planned is. We do grow up fast. Just ask my dad, or better yet, ask yours.

Simpkins was 20 years old when this was published. At the time he was in an Atlanta jail, awaiting trial for armed robbery.

The fact that he's young is the only silver lining in this sad and touching tale. Unlike his dad, he still has time and a chance to turn his life around. Sensitive and wise from having suffered, his children are likely to have a father who will be more present. He too will make mistakes, but he'll be there.

19

A Page from a Father's Diary

*The pain and suffering of a living
creature did not bother you at all p. 138*

Your cute little face, Ronnie, wet with tears, keeps flashing in front of my eyes. I cannot fall asleep. I see you again and again, so very hurt at first. Then angry. And finally stubbornly refusing to let me console you. I'm troubled by what happened between us earlier. So here I am with my diary again. Perhaps writing will bring me a little peace.

I was eager to spend a relaxed few minutes with you when I came home. It was a very long day at work. I missed you. So I thought of you lovingly and looked for you when I parked the Chevy. But though I heard your chattering happy voice, I did not see you at first. Then I heard you laughing loudly. You were probably having a lot of fun, I thought. Playing with your friend Sammy. It was at that point that I began to also hear the long wailing, whining cries of the cat.

The two of you, happy and carefree little boys, were across the street. You were standing beside the covered garbage can and Sammy was sitting on its top. The end of the cat's tail was squeezed between the garbage can and its cover. How much you both relished your power to cause pain. The cat's screaming did not bother either of you. It was all innocent but very cruel play.

I pulled Sammy off and released the cat. You both protested. Why was I interrupting your fun? Sammy became belligerent. It was his house, he said. I should leave and let him be. You were just quiet. Stood there silently, looking. At him and at me. Not knowing what to do.

Even before this happened I thought that Sammy was a troubled little boy. He wasn't supervised enough. For a 4 1/2-year-old he was allowed to play outside the house much too late. He was often ill-mannered. You told me that sometimes he beat up on kids smaller than himself. And he was a little rough even with you. But I figured that you'd work things out somehow. Aren't you best friends? Besides, there are not too many little boys your age on the block.

I tried to explain. To reason. But this never works in the midst of anger and disappointment. And then you also began to talk nastily. This was too much. I simply took you by the hand and walked you back home. Now you protested more loudly. You didn't want to go home. You were just playing, you shouted. I knew neither of you did it out of malice. But the pain and suffering of a living creature did not bother you at all. You even enjoyed it. I had to do something. This could not be allowed to pass.

Your mother tried to help by taking your side. "He's only a little boy," she said. "And a good boy." You are. And I love you so much. Her words made it harder for me to remain firm. And it did not make it easier for you. You cried. "There will be time to teach him later, when he's older," she said.

But I did not let you go out to play that evening. Such lessons, I still believe, must be learned early. Whenever the opportunity presents itself. Compassion cannot be taught in a formal way. It is never learned in a classroom unless the child already half-knows it.

You were pouting. Angry. Embarrassed. I held you firmly in a loving embrace till you calmed down. Then we talked.

I have tears in my eyes as I write this. I was pained by your pain. Disappointed and hurt by your anger at me. I love you very much but you really don't know it at times. You complained that I was not fair. You wanted me to leave you alone. You wanted to be with your mother. Unlike me, she understands you, you said. She is nice.

I knew I was right to do what I did. I also knew that your words merely expressed your hurt and your anger. Even so, they hurt me. Not so long ago I was also a little boy, sometimes angry at my father. I too often wanted only whatever I wanted at that moment. It's ironic. I did not see his pain then, as you didn't see mine. But my father, unlike me, was often too busy. Preoccupied with his own life. He was not as involved with me as I am with you. So I often had to learn things the hard way. I bumped into people. I paid a price. So I want to make things easier for you. But you don't see it. You're just furious. Even your mother disagrees with me.

What happened today will soon be forgotten. But will a residue of your anger remain? And I know that I will have to repeat such confrontations. Again and again. Sammy screamed that I was unjust, a dictator. I worry. Will you ever know that what I did was right? Will you understand that all this had to happen because I love you?

It pains me. You are already losing your carefree innocence. I noticed it first when you were two. Your sister was born. You became more solemn and more quiet. Sometimes angry. Your clear eyes were beginning to dim. Clouded by a frown. Your body used to fold itself so completely into mine before that. Especially when I rocked you to sleep. Now there is something, a little something, that separates us. Even when we are together. I miss my sweet little boy.

You are my first-born, my only son. I so much want to see you grow up to become a good man. Self-sufficient, proud of your life and content. But from time to time I already sense in you a hidden resentment. As if you have been done wrong. And now this incident. One more item for you to add to your growing list of injustices, supposedly inflicted by me. God, how much I wish you to see that I'm only doing what I must. I'm your father! I have no choice. But I also know that you cannot understand. You have not even reached your fifth birthday.

But much of what you must learn cannot wait for another day. So

I will continue to do my job. And console myself by writing in this diary. Perhaps you'll read it one day. Perhaps you'll understand then.

20

Fathers Running Away in Panic after their Child is Born

*People generally tend to believe that the
one who shouts the loudest is the boss p. 142*

*New fathers are [sometimes] overcome by a huge
and "unexplainable" wave of inner turmoil, as
if they were about to be washed away p. 143*

Fathers sometimes panic when their first child is born, and a few suddenly disappear at that time. They feel abandoned. It makes no rational sense, but then we humans are often irrational. Such running away is a thinly disguised form of a nervous breakdown but it is hardly ever understood as such. After a while some such fathers return home. And others are never heard from again.

Men often attach themselves to their wives in a bond that resembles the one they had with their mother as infants. The wife is the source of their emotional security. Although grown up and perhaps competent otherwise, many still feel like dependent and anxious little children at home. This is embarrassing, which is why such men always hide it, often even from themselves. And why most people deny even the existence of such a dependency.

The attempts to deny this hidden emotional dependency take strange forms. Husbands are sometimes eager to show others that they can ride roughshod over their wives, to disguise their real vulnerability and weakness. Such behavior is not necessarily conscious. All living organisms try to look powerful to discourage those they fear might harm them.

The children and strangers who don't know the family usually get confused and think that they see a gruff-sounding and bossy husband. People generally tend to believe that the one who shouts the loudest is the boss. Even the wife is sometimes unaware for a long time of the real power in the relationship. But in fact screaming often hides a sense of weakness and smallness. A coin in an empty vessel makes the most noise.

The wish to appear big and strong commonly shows itself quite early. Little boys brag about their daddies, teenagers want to demonstrate their physical power, and grown men often tell exaggerated stories about their sexual conquests and exploits. This also is one reason why some boys deliberately act as if they were insensitive and why they are disrespectful, and at times even abusive, of their girl friends. It "proves" their total independence. Such behavior often continues when they become fully grown men. The facade that was stuck on for so long eventually becomes an inseparable part of the character. Then they marry.

One day such husbands are in for a shock. They panic when their wife threatens to leave or when she files for a divorce. Then the chips are down. They are not such big heroes after all. They feel abandoned and scared like little kids lost in a crowd.

Strangely, many men have the same kind of reaction soon after their wife gives birth. Sometimes it happens even before the baby arrives. Some studies show that 25% of battered women may be beaten when pregnant. Some husbands get panicky as if they were being left behind, all alone in the universe. This also is what men and women often experience when they suddenly discover that their spouse is having a love affair with someone else.

And in a way every new mother is really having an affair, one of the heart. She has a new love. Most of her time and energy are now given over to someone else: the baby. She is not only wife now but also mother. No longer is she attentive to her husband alone. Some men flip out under the pressure of this confusing new situation.

Such new fathers are overcome by a huge and "unexplainable" wave of inner turmoil, as if they were about to be washed away. They feel suddenly displaced. Deserted. Altogether unseen. Altogether unattended to. In fact they have not been abandoned at all, but they can't shake the feeling. Sometimes they get angry to hide their panic. This is a popular tactic which many people use to hide their sense of helplessness. Some husbands even experience the wife as disloyal at such times. They usually know that this is crazy, but knowing does not change how they feel. Many men drink more now, they become interested in other women or they withdraw into themselves.

And some men suddenly disappear at this juncture. They become homeless wanderers. Here and there they stop, but they never find rest. Or peace. They are stuck with lots of guilt and with shame. Deeply hurt, they also experience seething anger at no one in particular. From then on this is their daily bread. Some such men become homeless alcoholics. They just work and drink or drug themselves to make the pain bearable, at least for awhile. Soon they must numb themselves again. The sharp teeth of irrational fear do not let up for long. One day they die. Often all alone.

Other people who don't know the whole story of such men usually judge them harshly. They are cowards. Irresponsible deserters who don't want to support their wives and children. And they often think of themselves in the same terms. This is the source of their current shame. So they live in hiding. Nobody knows their whole tragic story, and they don't understand it enough to tell it correctly. They barely survive in their lonely despair. Misunderstood. Friendless. Anonymous.

For Joel it was a little easier. But not much. He was a bright and promising 25-year-old college graduate when he married. As a teenager in the 60's he experimented with drugs, like everyone else. It was fashionable. In school it was so common that those who did not do it stood out. His family was wealthy and he always had enough money to get a fix. They didn't give him much else. The rest of the story resembles many others: his mother spent her days playing tennis and bridge. His father was a successful builder. Joel was a lost kid. His childhood was difficult. But then, is this not true for almost everyone?

The young couple did not plan to have children. That was for squares. They also knew that they were not ready for parenthood. Sandy had also done plenty of drugs, even before she met Joel. And she drank daily. Both her parents were alcoholics and she grew up smelling liquor all the time. When she and Joel got together they clung to each other like two frightened orphans lost in the forest on a cold and dark night. They themselves describe it this way. At long last, each of them had found a true companion.

But they were both very fertile and Sandy soon got pregnant. It proved again that birth control was not 100% safe. Quickly they agreed that she would seek an abortion. To them it was self-evident. The best solution also for the unborn fetus, they convinced themselves.

But three years later she became pregnant again. This time they were nearing 30. The biologic clock was ticking. Sandy did not suggest an abortion this time and Joel did not dare to bring the subject up. So they never discussed it. And before they had really considered what to do, Sandy was in labor. She delivered a healthy, seven-pound baby boy. Everyone congratulated them.

Johnny was cute. But he did not bring much joy to either parent. Mother just did not know what to do with him. She always worried that he would fall out of her arms and get hurt. So she held him too tightly. The baby was colicky and very demanding. She would get angry at his endless boohooing and whining. This embarrassed her. So she tried to hide it, but her body rigidified from the tension. For relief she drank more now, and more often. Her mother would come over to see that the baby got fed and changed. Sandy had so many hangovers that they began to hang together. Often she was out of it.

This frightened her more. Most of the time she sounded impatient and angry.

Joel was cool. Nothing fazes a man like him! He tried to hide how scared he was even from himself. Panicky in fact. This was silly, he understood. There was no cause for alarm. But he was alarmed anyway. And wired all the time. Nothing was taken away from him, he reassured himself silently. But even so, he felt jumpy inside, completely unable to concentrate. He couldn't go to work, so he hung around the house doing nothing. Even this did not help much.

Only when he and Sandy were physically close did he become somewhat comfortable. They were therefore in bed having sex practically all day long, but he resented her leaving whenever she took a short break to care for the baby. And what was he to do before or after sex? Even marijuana and heroin did not help enough. So he began to use cocaine. So much in fact that money became a problem. But he had good credit cards. Soon he built up a huge debt.

One day he simply informed Sandy that he was leaving. With a couple of friends he would climb mountains in Tibet. Maybe he'd spend some time in India too. He planned to stay away for a month but returned over two years later.

Three-year-old Johnny did not know the strange man who came to live with his mother. Now he resented being displaced. And Joel was like a stranger even to Sandy. Alcohol and drugs had become her closest buddies while he was gone, and she would not give them up now. Besides her parents, Johnny had been the only human she had any contact with. The reconciliation of husband and wife was slow and very tentative. Something was destroyed between them and it could not be repaired. She no longer trusted him fully. He did not protest. She was right. Their relationship was never again what it used to be.

Stories like this do not get much media coverage. What's the point? People don't like tragedies. They want to blame someone. And here everyone is a victim. No one is a villain. Joel's mother and father were also not mothered properly, nor were they fathered well.

They did the best they could with their son. The story of Sandy's parents is practically the same. Such parents cannot but raise troubled kids. And when such kids grow up, they also don't know how to parent their children well.

Johnny really did not have it so bad. Many fare much worse. At least after the age of three he had two parents living with him. And both meant well. They really tried and did all they could to help him. Many families are much more disorganized, and they are becoming the majority rather than the exception. Such stories are not news anymore. They don't even have much human interest value.

Young mothers are generally a little better off than new fathers. Even if mother is immature and like a little girl, her body nevertheless is competent. She is an adult at least in one area: she's capable of producing new life. She may be emotionally and intellectually way behind, but biologically she is ready. This helps her self-image a lot.

Young fathers do not have this advantage. Emotionally they are often more needy and more immature than their wives. Many are also underdeveloped intellectually and professionally. Often they're school dropouts who can hardly read. Without elementary math skills. This condemns them to have only marginal and low-paying jobs or to be chronically unemployed. With little hope of ever having a better life. It is not a great human achievement to make a young woman pregnant, but this is often all such young fathers have to boost their self-esteem. They may have tried everything else to support their manhood. Joining a gang. Being tough. Driving fast cars recklessly. Carrying and using guns. Or switchblades. Nothing fills the inner emptiness.

But when such a young man finds a woman it sometimes helps anchor him. Her loyalty is life-sustaining. Gang members and ordinary people therefore sometimes kill for a woman. It's an old story whose details fill all of literature. This is why such a man may lose his balance when he becomes a father. Suddenly he is being shoved aside if not replaced altogether. No longer is he number one with his wife. Her attention and love must now be divided. He panics.

And some young fathers are really rejected and excluded. On purpose. The wife really prefers the baby over the husband. Immature mothers often feel safer with a baby. They can have total control over it. Mother not only produced it but the baby can't survive without her. Next to her baby she is and feels powerful and needed. Often for the first time in her entire life. This is intoxicating stuff.

In such a drunken-like state mother may really reject her husband and form a pathological bond with the baby. It gets all of her love. All her attention. She may still cook and have sex with her husband, but she has no emotional supplies left for him. He may be the breadwinner but even so he is an outsider. Barely tolerated. But only if he does not interfere too much in the ongoing love affair between mother and baby. He is a stranger in his own home.

To compete on a level playing field, some such fathers then regress. They want what the baby has. To be held. To be loved. To be fussed over. To be warmly welcomed. They want their wife to be exquisitely sensitive to them also. Perhaps if father is needy enough she will notice him and divide her favors. But such regression usually alienates the wife even more. The husband gets even less.

This is when some fathers feel that they can take it no longer. They disappear. Better and saner solutions do exist, but such young dads don't know what they are. Or how they could change things. They're starved for acceptance and welcome. By leaving they at least don't have to witness their wife showering her love on someone else.

THIRD SECTION

...

THE MANY TASKS
OF GOOD FATHERING:
A MANUAL

21

A Simplified Formula for Raising Healthy Children

Everything conflictual belongs in the
open. Insist that every disagreement
be put "on the table." Nothing should
be hidden under it p. 152

Relationships stand on mutual respect
and they collapse sooner or
later without it. Remember that
children too deserve respect p. 153

To raise healthier children we must...change course.
We must make room for the expression
of feelings but hold everyone responsible for
every single act. Always p. 156

Here is a simplified formula for raising healthy children:

1. Make room for your child to feel anything openly and to express it powerfully as a feeling. Anything. Even objectively unjustified anger at you. Chapter 23 explains why. Help the child to distinguish thoughts from feelings and always insist that any and all decisions and acts be based on reason and on thoughtfulness. At all times. It is never safe to make an exception to this rule.

2. Similarly, encourage your child to discuss with you any and all thoughts, even if you believe them to be silly or bizarre. Explain why you think that some things make no sense, but listen first. No subject is taboo. Listen respectfully and explain your position patiently. Don't discourage a child even by frowning your disapproval. Children notice such things. Explain on the level that suits the child's age and understanding.

3. Agree and approve quickly when you do. When you disagree, do so as matter-of-factly as possible. Not angrily. Children don't know what they have not yet learned, and learning often requires repeated teaching. Don't hold back your critical comments, but don't "bite" the child when you are critical or when you disagree. Sometimes you will be provoked into anger. No need to hide it. You too have feelings but make every attempt to express them without excess. Children attach an extra importance to your reactions because of your special position as a parent. Never act out of control. A loud voice or angry words are not wrong when they are justified and needed. But don't insult, never humiliate and never induce guilt in order to prevail.

4. Everything conflictual belongs in the open. Insist that every disagreement be put "on the table." Nothing should be hidden under it. Nothing a child thinks or feels is bad. Even objectively shameful and wrong acts are best looked at and examined in the light of day. Everything can and should be discussed. And resolved rationally.

5. You and everyone else in the household must also be totally committed to living by what makes sense. Always. No exceptions. What makes the most sense must always prevail. Don't ever yield on the basis of strong feelings alone. But be sympathetic and wait a little when your child (or anyone else) is gripped by a storm of strong emotions. Especially then remain firm. Reality must always come first.

6. All your relationships should also be rooted in reality. Do not ever base a relationship on feelings alone. Relationships stand on mutual respect and they collapse sooner or later without it. Remember that children too deserve respect. Always insist that they treat you, themselves and everyone else this way.

Sane relationships are based on a solid commitment to maintain the relationship provided that it does not become abusive to either party. In such relationships there is room for the expression of any and all feelings and all thoughts. But there is never room in them for disdain, for reasons explained in chapter 24. Insulting or dismissing the other person is not acceptable. And neither is physical or even emotional withdrawal.

• • •

All this is easier said than done. But it can be achieved. It requires that thinking and acting be completely separated from feelings. They must always be kept apart. This is possible. Several of the following chapters have specific suggestions, especially chapter 29. With time and hard work such a way of living can become second nature and no extra effort is then required to achieve it. Actions and decision making are then usually free from the distorting power of emotions. Many tragedies are thus avoided.

All living creatures survive longer when they are on the alert. Even the biggest and fastest animals do not always prevail in the jungle. They catch and kill only those who get close enough to their path. These are the ones who usually were a little less careful, too young or too old. We humans have double protection. In addition to all the alerting mechanisms of animals we can also think and plan ahead.

With the help of our thinking brain we learned to protect ourselves not only from bears but also from bacteria. And we became the best hunters and the best fishermen. We observed and saw that the behavior of animals was predictable. They follow their instincts which, like feelings, are independent of thought. Animals don't think much. We who can see distant consequences can trick them. But when we don't think we too get tricked.

Feelings are instantaneous. This is their advantage. But they do not normally integrate new information, which is their disadvantage. This is why they often mislead us. We've already noted that feeling patterns get fixed very early in life. Later on they frequently don't fit the reality of adulthood.

It is easy to understand why parents and religions throughout history have always demanded that children and adults suppress their feelings. They knew that not only physical survival but also civilized existence itself depended on people acting thoughtfully. Law and order cannot be maintained otherwise. Feelings can be dangerous. In anger and fear people sometimes hurt others, destroy and even rape or kill. Or they rob and steal for greed. Unrestrained, feelings destroy communities, nations, property and freedom itself.

Rigid self-discipline was therefore highly valued. And it was often enforced too strictly. Feelings were suppressed to help achieve such discipline. Most religions consider it a sin to yield to these powerful forces and the legal system defines many impulsive acts against others as crimes. Rationalists regard feelings as inferior because they lead to irrationality. But all this downgrading and bad-mouthing of feelings has never worked to weaken their power. Neither has hiding them. Or denying their existence.

The opposite is true. Residues of suppressed feelings accumulate in the body. They create internal pressure. Like the steam in a boiler, this pressure always pushes for release. Sometimes the pressure causes symptoms to develop. Sexual impotence, psychogenic infertility or difficulties in thinking and in concentration, as well as obesity, anorexia and many other harmful disabilities are all costly ways used by the pressured body to preserve itself. They all serve as escape valves, lessening the chances of an explosion.

The internal pressure of hidden yearnings, wishes, fears, hurt and anger is often literally destructive. Drugs, alcohol and smoking all represent efforts to keep this inner pressure from breaking through. To maintain the suppression. In order to remain effective such poisonous substances must be used regularly in frequent intervals, since the pressure of suppressed feelings builds up rather quickly. It can be like an internal time bomb.

We now know that it is undesirable and dangerous to suppress feelings. The old system didn't work well. Modern psychology has shown that we are better off when feelings are expressed. *But we forgot to make sure that we must still act rationally, that we must first detach our actions from the feelings we experience.* Now we also do what we feel like doing. Now "decisions" are often made by emotions.

In the name of nonsuppression of feelings almost any kind of behavior became permissible. Almost any pathologic lifestyle is "in" now. Our new license to express our feelings has been used to discard many old standards, the ones that made a decent life possible. Here are two of several bumper stickers seen on a new and expensive car recently: "There are no fees in our intercourse club. No dues. Just come" and "Yes, I do fuck on the first date." The well-dressed driver was not a bit embarrassed to be seen in that car. What feels right is right. We've swung all the way over to the other end of the spectrum. We suppress nothing.

Freud was personally a rigid son of the 19th century. Super old-fashioned, proper, responsible, thoughtful and nonimpulsive. So too was his society. Living according to feelings was not even imaginable by such people. They pushed for less suppression without understanding that this can be dangerous too. They could not foresee the possibility of excessive looseness or too much freedom. It probably did not occur to any of them that a civilized person would even seriously wish to live according to the dictates of emotions. All they knew was that the then-current Puritan ways caused a lot of harm. They were constricting and choking.

The psychologists and psychoanalysts who followed them have never slowed down long enough to notice that the situation has basically changed. They still concern themselves mostly with freeing people from a harsh and punitive superego. But nowadays there is not enough suppression. Anxiety is bubbling up because there is not enough structure in the lives of most people. Not enough containment. The boiler is broken. There is no head of steam left. The engine has stalled.

Now many youngsters are stuck. Not motivated to care even for themselves. Typically irritable, they are openly angry but often about nothing specific. And now they also have assault weapons in their hands. Unable to concentrate on studying anything, many are impulse-ridden and thoughtless. Dangerous to themselves and destructive to others.

We have gone too far. To raise healthier children we must again change course. We must make room for the expression of feelings but hold everyone responsible for every single act. Always. Under any circumstances. It is timely to question the justification for the insanity defense. Sick individuals can also destroy societies. The public must be protected from them too. They must be locked up even if not punished. In hospitals if not in prisons.

Children who are fathered well will generally be responsible for what they do. Well-fathered youngsters are also self-starters. They live with self-restraint and with self-discipline. Typically they support themselves financially. They are less likely to remain dependent on their elders or on welfare checks. Making sense really makes sense.

Specific suggestions to help your children reach this goal are to be found in the following chapters of this Manual.

22

Push Sons to Leave Mother's Apron Strings and Help them Stand Tall as Men

Fathers...must pull their children away
from holding on to mother when they
objectively no longer need to hold on.
This is how children begin to discover that
they can be self-sufficient p. 160

Boys rarely become men without a strong male
influence, but everyone needs persistent pushing
and pulling to find the courage to leave behind
the slavish desire to remain small p. 164

To succeed as a father you must be seen
as a strong pillar of stability. Sons always
look for weaknesses and inconsistencies in
the one who fathers. Anything to circumvent
his or her demands p. 166

Everyone has seen it on TV. A 250-pound-or-so 6'6" giant football player looking into the camera that happened to focus on him, sheepishly calling out "Hi, Mom." But hardly ever "Hi, Dad." This apparently is so natural that few people even wonder about it. But why in fact are these tough guys so eager to greet their moms? Why is this such a common and natural inclination?

Because mother is not only life-giving but also every baby's source of food, warmth and reassurance. This lasts for years. She often remains all-important even later on, when the kids have become adults. For life. This is how highly we value those who provide us with the basic sense of safety. We'll soon see why grown women may yearn for mothering a little less than men, but in general people often continue to seek some sort of mothering for as long as they live.

Little children reach for their mom in fear. This habit of reaching out for reassurance commonly returns quickly when grown men and women get anxious. They again seek solace in the same old way, though usually not with the same person. A wife, husband, friend or lover generally takes mother's place.

This partly explains why most men feel safer in the company of their women. Typically they get anxious when their wives or girlfriends leave them for any reason. And adolescent boys are driven to get into girls' pants not only for release of sexual pressure. They have a one-track mind also because they become more settled in the company of a girl. Likewise, the men who brag about their sexual exploits and conquests often do so more to reassure themselves than to impress others. Again and again they confirm their ability to always find a safe haven.

For many men, being acceptable to women is therefore of the greatest importance. Some become compulsive pleasers for this reason, and they distort and bend themselves out of shape in order not to alienate the opposite gender. Some "kiss up" without a sense of revulsion, sacrificing their dignity and self-respect for acceptance. This also explains the ongoing popularity of girlie magazines. Since the sexual revolution real sex is not so hard to find. But the fantasies of finding a perfectly safe, soft and wonderfully receptive female body that is always welcoming persist as ever. "Here comes the bride" was and still is the most stirring moment of marriage ceremonies.

It is not surprising therefore that many men are secretly also afraid of women. And angry at them. At least from their perspective, women have so much power. And this also is why some men enjoy disappointing or hurting females, or even abusing them. The revenge of the weak. But one way or another, the relationship with women is commonly a central concern of men. It surely is the most important worry of heterosexual singles. Women obviously also seek the company of the opposite gender, but generally they are not quite so intensely worried in this search. Males and females have the exact same yearnings and needs only while they are babies. Then they all want to be safe in the cuddling and serene arms and bosom of a loving mother. But alas, perfection is not even attainable then.

Every baby experiences at least occasional moments of panic. Everyone had to wait sometimes for solace and for reassurance in moments of fear. What we wanted, needed and expected did not always come soon enough. No one can remember such experiences because babies have no memory, but our bodies remember. Without conscious awareness, everyone tries very hard to avoid re-experiencing such "unknown" fears. They are so terrible because they were faceless, meaningless and endless when first experienced. This is why practically everyone continues to wish for a good "mother" as the best protection from such dread. At moments of panic it is especially important for people to be seen and to be held, to be reassured and to be touched. Solace is the immediate result of being loved, accepted and welcomed. Loneliness is the absence of these.

When they feel safe, toddlers are eager to walk away from mother for a little while. They even fight for their independence. But they also expect the mothering person to be nearby whenever they feel a need for her. They want mother to always remain in sight even when they stroll away. If they have a choice, young children never leave her protective presence for long. Or completely. And as grown-ups they usually still want someone like her to be close by. To be available when needed. This explains the strange behavior of the football players.

We humans normally hold on to our "mothers" for as long as we can and refuse to let go. Even little birds whose dependence is relatively brief must often be pushed out of the nest to force them to begin flying. Humans are totally dependent for much longer and they become habituated, if not addicted, to it. They don't usually assume responsibility for their own care without resistance and many fights. In some "primitive" cultures mothers paint their nipples with a black and bitter substance when their babies are old enough, to wean them and to force them off the breast. Psychologically this must be done with everyone.

It is the job of fathers to help do it. They must pull their children away from holding on to mother when they objectively no longer need to hold on. This is how children begin to discover that they can be self-sufficient.

Beyond the initial excitement of discovering their new abilities, youngsters must often be forced to do what they already know how to do. This often is the only way they realize how much they can do. Thus they gradually become competent and independent as individuals. It is a painful and fear-filled process, but no pain no gain. Youngsters slowly notice then that even when alone they can survive with hardly any anxiety. Raised this way they become well-contained within their skin. Well defined. Whole.

The main reason that girls are attached to their mothers somewhat less than boys is their anatomic good fortune. All children must have a counterforce to help them put some distance between themselves and the powerful magnetic pull of mother. Father is ideally situated for this purpose and daughters naturally use him to get a little breathing room. This enables girls to define themselves slowly as separate beings, and this is why girls are at the core a little less anxious than boys. Emotionally stronger. Females tend to individuate more fully than males, and they even mature earlier, not only physically.

Consequently, women often hold families together. Their feet are generally planted more solidly in the ground of reality. Hard as life often is for them, it nonetheless is emotionally and physiologically less wearing than the life of men. Now that mothers usually no longer die at childbirth, as a group they also live longer. Over time even biology is affected by the presence and absence of chronic stress.

A special "romance" commonly exists between little kids and the parent of the opposite gender. Mothers usually expect more from their daughters and they are at least somewhat less patient with them. And fathers are more demanding of their sons. The same gender parent is also a closely observed model whose real and imagined shortcomings often stand out for the child all too clearly. Children are therefore more critical of and much more competitive with the same gender parent. As a result, there is normally less conflict with the parent of the opposite gender. For girls all these factors combine to cement a very helpful relationship with their daddies, at least until puberty.

But boys are not so fortunate. They too have a "romance" with the parent of the opposite gender but this only gets them into deeper trouble. They get even more tightly bound to the all-powerful mother with whom the attachment is already much too strong. And the more tender and doting mother is, the more constricting the bond with her becomes. It sharply limits the space within which sons can become independent. Without the consistent presence of an active father who intrudes on this relationship with mother, sons have no one to push them to do what they don't want to do anyway. And not enough fathers are willing to take on this difficult task.

Girls also have it much easier for another reason: they can see that mother is the one who often sets the tone in the family. Even father may not dare to displease her except indirectly and passively, if at all. And it always is safer to side with the most powerful force around. So daughters can both separate from mother and still identify with her and become powerful as women. But when boys identify with mother their self-image as males often ends up being somewhat defective. Masculinity is associated with weakness.

Furthermore, the one who mothers typically gives, while the one who fathers is supposed to demand. It is normal for all of us to prefer ideas, situations and people that make our life easier, not harder. No one is eager to become involved in things which require effort. Mother usually continues therefore to exert an extremely powerful pull, even if some of her ways are resented. No one leaves the source of their security voluntarily.

Many sons thus remain attached to mother and they put off defining themselves as separate and independent beings. They never even notice that to feel safe they have in effect accepted a lifelong emotional position of houseboys and dutiful servants. In slavery one can at least count on being protected by the master.

Without sufficient good fathering sons tend to remain mommy's little helpers. They usually side with her and in return she shields them from the demands of reality. From father.

Jonathan's dad was an alcoholic. During the day he worked in the factory. The evenings he spent in the neighborhood bar. A police car would bring him home from time to time, after he was involved in a fight while drinking with his buddies. The fights were never serious and the policemen all knew him well and liked him. They grew up together. Everyone knew that he was really a frightened little man trying to look big.

Father occasionally also fought at home. These fights with his wife were always very loud and quite ugly. The kids would cower and hide under the table or behind a cupboard, to avoid being hit by a flying pot that one of the parents would hurl at the other.

One of the five children suicided at 22. Another died of chronic liver disease in his forties. Like his father he also drank. Of the three others, the girl attached herself to her grandfather who was a good, solid man. This saved her. The youngest boy had no one in his corner and remained confused and ineffective. Never earned a living. Always looked for someone to take care of him. He married and divorced several times. But Jonathan did well. He was mom's favorite.

She doted on him. He looked after her. He always defended her against father's loud accusations. She pushed him ahead, gave him what she denied to the others and supported him both emotionally and financially. This gave him the strength and the courage to despise his father openly. He even told him so on one occasion. Father and son would sometimes actually get into fist fights. It was not only ugly but also dangerous.

But Jonathan prospered. As a businessman he was innovative and built a flourishing company. Having made lots of money, he married and fathered three children. But as a grown man he was no less confused, and as lonely, as he was as a boy. In a real sense he was fatherless, without a male model to learn from and to emulate. And he also remained unsatisfiable and disappointed in his marriage. No wife could be as solicitous as mother was. And in addition, Jonathan's wife, Evelyn, was very insecure. And jealous. She always tried to come between Jonathan and his sister. She wanted her husband all to herself and interfered with any relationship he ever had with a friend.

At home Evelyn made every decision, down to the smallest one. He did not object. After all, he was used to this system from his days with mother. But secretly he also resented it. Jonathan retaliated by being aloof and unreachable. He was always at work or out on the golf course. The raising of the children was left to mother.

The two sons resembled Jonathan when they grew up. Below the bravado they too became nonassertive wimps, like their father. He was a giant only at work. They too became successful professionally. But with the women they dated they were like helpless little children.

The older son got involved with a pretty and competent classmate in college. She eventually rejected him. With him around, she was always alone. She wanted to marry a man, not adopt a boy. He was heartbroken and perplexed. Why would she let go of such a "successful specimen," one who was handsome and lettered in football?

A year later he married a much less accomplished woman. She admired him greatly since emotionally she too was a child. Each of them expected to be mothered by the other and both were disappointed. And very angry at each other. For solace and to get even they both became involved in many sexual affairs. These too turned out to be disappointing and painful. So the wife clung even more tightly to their one son. Jonathan's grandson so feared the choking hold of clutching women that eventually he turned to homosexuality. The story is similar to that told in chapter 16.

One of the most important and most difficult jobs of father is to help his sons find enough room to become men. Fathers must stop sons from remaining clingers to their mothers so that they develop their independence as individuals. Daughters must also have such help to let go of mother's apron strings, but they will usually reach for father naturally. Not so sons. They must be pulled and often even forced to take father's hand. Otherwise they are likely to fail to become self-sufficient.

Father can perform this task well only if he himself is emotionally no longer a child. But with guidance every father can somehow force himself to stand at least a little taller. This is absolutely necessary if he is to help his sons and daughters to stand tall. See chapter 6 for suggestions. Boys rarely become men without a strong male influence, but everyone needs persistent pushing and pulling to find the courage to leave behind the slavish desire to remain small.

Here are a few more specific suggestions for fathers who need assistance in helping their sons grow up into healthy manhood:

1. Spend enough time with your son. Boys must know their father as a strong ally and as a reliable friend. Not only as the one who restricts and punishes. Like mother, you too have to become very important in your son's life. Actively make efforts to do so from early on.

2. Remain reasonable even when provoked. Toddlers and older children are often grossly unreasonable and demanding. Even then don't lose your cool too often and never lose control of your actions and behavior. Model reasonableness. Remain patient for as long as it makes sense.

3. Do useful chores with your son and challenge his growing abilities. Clean up the garage together. Teach him to cut the lawn. To figure out the correct change. To construct a few shelves. Discuss ideas on his level, and obviously do this with your daughter too. Help all your children with their homework and school projects, but don't do it for them. Do not allow children to give up when the going gets a little hard. Scolding doesn't help much but being firm does. Even little kids can do little tasks competently. They should be helped at first and pushed later on to do so. Do not settle for less than what your son and daughter are capable of.

Mother will hopefully support your efforts, but sometimes mothers also reject fathering. This is not necessarily prompted by a wish to have you fail. It may only reflect some old confusion remaining from the time she was a child. Help her. Insist and remain firm. Even fight (verbally) to maintain reasonable demands of your children. Remember Jefferson's words: "In matters of style swim with the current. In matters of principle stand like a rock." Do not yield unless you have been unreasonable in your demands. Always double-check yourself. Both mother and son will eventually be grateful for your firm insistence.

4. Help foster your son's male identity. Pitching baseballs or encouraging your son to play hockey or football is good but not enough. Such activities should also not occupy most of his time. Masculinity is much more than physical prowess or excellence in sports. Making disrespectful remarks about girls or women is not a sign of healthy masculinity. Nor is telling stories of sexual or other conquests. Any bully with a gun can act tough. And even wimpy boys can put out a campfire by urinating on it.

The best way to build up your son's male identity is to live self-respectfully as a man. Be a good model of vigor, integrity and rectitude. It requires courage to buck a popular but wrong trend. Dare to be right even if it is politically incorrect to do so. Honor your word. Stand on principle. Demonstrate loyalty. Truthfulness. Self-discipline. Responsibility. Compassion.

Your daughter should also be pushed to develop these same qualities, but your son must see his father (or another fathering man) live this way to develop a self-respecting male identity. Girls can become good women by incorporating desirable qualities of their mothers, but not boys. They usually get confused by identifying with mother. They also need to look up to a man.

Remember that stubbornness is not the same as strength. Yield gracefully and quickly when you are wrong. This does not compromise your masculinity. The current fad of making peace with one's internal father in enclaves of men is not enough. The beating of drums is also not important for learning to be properly assertive as a man.

5. Live in a way that commands respect. To succeed as a father you must be seen as a strong pillar of stability. Sons always look for weaknesses and inconsistencies in the one who fathers. Anything to circumvent his or her demands. Do not make it easy for your children to disqualify you as a legitimate and just authority.

6. Interfere with your child's excessive pursuit of comforting. Little kids often run to mommy to get a hug when they are a little anxious. This has a calming effect and is good for them. Children need it. Their bond with mother is essential for healthy emotional development. But such behavior must lessen with time.

It is best for children to learn early that a little discomfort is tolerable. Many never learn enough of this. The achievements of such people are limited because minor difficulties bring them to a complete stop. Their pain tolerance remains too low. Do not let your children comfort themselves too much, too often or at the wrong times. But also remember that they need more comforting when very young and when they are not well.

7. Don't allow overpampering. Mothers naturally tend to be protective of their young. This is true among us humans as it generally is in the animal kingdom. It makes sense. Children are blood of the mother's blood and flesh of her flesh. But when mothers overidentify they tend to overprotect and overpamper. This infantalizes the child.

Even infants should not be infantalized. Baby talk is almost always wrong. Some competence exists at any age. Help children discover it and teach them to enjoy it by praising their realistic achievements. Even very small kids respond well to respectful recognition.

8. Prevent mother and others from projecting their fears on the children. Some mothers worry too much. Their children tend to become complainers. They discover that this is a good way to get attention. Every little booboo becomes a major calamity. Such children want their temperature taken every time they don't feel so good. And they often insist on staying home from school.

Matter-of-factly but firmly resist such requests. But remain patient and reasonable. Remember that if your child behaves this way it probably is because it worked earlier. Stop it now. And also help your wife see the bad effects of her excessive worrying. But don't do so in front of the child.

Too much of anything is by definition wrong. Even too much loving concern for the child. Even too much love.

9. No Regression. Prevent your son from taking needless refuge in mother's lap. Parents often so enjoy holding and touching their youngsters that they do it too much. Little boys are thus often able to use mother's lap as a comfortable refuge when they can do very well without one. Stop it when it's excessive. Instead, you hold your child sometimes. But not too often, not merely for your own pleasure and not for too long. A father's lap is also reassuring, but in a different way. It is firmer. Less cuddly. But it provides warmth and a sense of strength and safety nevertheless.

Growing boys often make themselves look needy and they sound whiny to justify remaining in mother's arms. And they falsely claim helplessness. If nobody challenges them they will soon believe such claims. As adults they will also degrade themselves for a woman's embrace. It is best to interfere with this tendency while a boy is still very young. Three years old is not too early. Perhaps even earlier. But make sure to base your actions on careful and repeated observations of the child's real needs. Do not interfere with the normal, natural and desirable contacts with mother.

10. Do not allow for an unholy alliance to develop. Mother sometimes makes father look like an ogre. This can be entirely innocent: "Wait till dad comes home. You'll get your punishment then." Do not allow yourself to be cast in this light. It's especially damaging to a son if father is known essentially as the "bad one." Your children should know you as firm but fair. The enforcer of reasonable standards, even if such standards cannot be met easily. But not as capricious or bad.

Even mature and well-meaning parents "bribe" their children at times. Both fathers and mothers want to be loved, so they sometimes give too much. Or permit what should be forbidden. Mother sometimes contradicts father's demands for the same reason. Make sure that neither mother nor anyone else sabotages your fathering efforts, and by the same token never sabotage your wife's fathering. If your wife or you must correct each other with more than a gesture or a word, do so when young children are not around to hear and see it.

Remember that mother is not necessarily an enemy even when she interferes when she ought not to. Do not wage an all-out war immediately. Help her see that she is damaging the child. Most mothers do not want to do such a thing and will stop.

Above all else, never allow your son and his mother to exclude you intentionally. Mother should never use her son as an ally against father unless he poses a real danger. She should not make the son her confidant. This position is reserved for you alone. You are her husband. The consequences of pathologic relationships between mothers and sons are usually most damaging. The stakes are very high. Suicides are common.

11. Insist that your children learn to mother themselves. Help both your sons and daughters learn to mother themselves while they're still very young. Girls usually learn it faster and better. Boys are often much more stubborn in refusing to take care of themselves. They don't want to give up being mothered by mother, and this is why they often refuse to learn how to treat themselves more competently. Insist especially with sons. Be firmer with them on this score. You must win and they must lose. In losing they win. Also see chapter 31.

Mothers sometimes love their role as a mother too much. For this reason they may pamper excessively. "But he (or she) is still so young," she may innocently say. Such pampering is damaging to the children. Stand firm but remain reasonable. It will help you to remember that it is natural for most mothers to err this way.

12. Do not divorce your children even if the marriage breaks. Remember that a divorce applies only to a spouse. Not to the children. Your responsibility for fathering becomes even greater after a divorce. This is true for children of both genders but it is crucially important for sons.

Daughters can become reasonably competent women even when fathered by mother alone. Not so sons. When they live with their mother they need your consistent and committed involvement nonetheless. And they need a lot of your time and wisdom when they live with you.

Insist that your teenage sons live with you even if this is very inconvenient for you. Even if it crimps your lifestyle. They need an ongoing male model to grow up properly. This obligation saddles you with a double responsibility. To father and to mother too. Do not shirk either task.

23

Make Room for Expressions of Anger Yet Control Impulsive Acts

*Open and powerful protest...clarifies the
air and is thus useful in repairing
damaged relationships p. 172*

*Anger, like all other feelings, does
not follow the rules of reason and it
sometimes arises with great intensity
even when it makes no sense p. 173*

*Hate causes real harm. It also is contagious
and not always controllable. Hate commonly
leads to destructive acts of violence p. 175*

Anger is unavoidable in life, but as long as it only is a feeling, it is completely safe. Anger usually follows quickly on the heels of hurt, which also is unavoidable in any relationship. We get hurt when things don't go our way, when the wishes and plans of others interfere with our own, or when we feel slighted and unloved by those who are important to us. The pain of hurt is diminished and its life span is shortened when we have the freedom to express our anger about such situations. Anger is thus a self-helpful form of protest.

But even so, parents often disallow open expressions of anger for fear that it might lead to violence. They do not realize that children can be taught that any and all acts can and must remain totally and always under rational control. This is made easier when the power of feelings is lessened by allowing them to sometimes be vented verbally.

This fear of violence has caused many well-meaning and loving parents to inadvertently damage their children. In many cultures even angry words or thoughts are disallowed. The unspoken expectation is that suppressed anger will lessen the likelihood of dangerous and potentially harmful eruptions. But now we know that the opposite is true. Justified and even unjustified angry protest that is repeatedly being pushed underground commonly turns into seething hate, which is very dangerous. Nothing is lost in the universe, and anger too does not just evaporate when we put it out of sight.

Storms of feelings that we try to hide leave a residue within us because it is against our nature to close the books quickly on unfinished business. Such anger smolders. And its residue often causes much harm, unlike open and powerful protest which clarifies the air and is thus useful in repairing damaged relationships.

Because expressions of anger are widely forbidden, millions of people exist with dangerously high levels of such an accumulated residue, the result of suppressed protest. Cauldrons of fury quietly boil beneath the tranquil surface of many very nice and very mild-appearing people. Many of them are always afraid of losing control. To protect themselves, although they may not be aware of it consciously, some become pacifists who compulsively avoid any and all confrontations and conflicts. They fear any situation that might detonate an inner explosion. That's why they take wide detours around anything that might overpower their defensive dikes. Almost everyone has heard of someone known to be peace loving and kind suddenly going on a wild rampage of shooting and killing innocent people. This intensifies and confirms the validity of the ever-present fears of losing control.

But in fact even the most intense verbal and vocal expressions of anger are completely safe as long as acting remains strictly separate from the expressions of the feeling. Children and adults can learn to live this way with relative ease. Once learned, the commitment to never act thoughtlessly should always be enforced. No degree of provocation ever justifies breaking this rule. To maintain the social order and public safety, the insanity defense can never be acceptable and should never be used.

Under such conditions it is completely safe for parents to allow and even to encourage their children to verbally express anger when they feel it. Even when objectively the anger is not justified. But violent acts, damaging property or even withdrawing into oneself are always out, no matter what precipitated the angry reaction.

Anger, like all other feelings, does not follow the rules of reason and it sometimes arises with great intensity even when it makes no sense. Our typical ways of reacting become fixed in early infancy, and feelings are therefore irrational much of the time unless they have been calibrated. But rational or not, they are powerful forces that determine most human reactions both to internal and to external stimuli. As grounding does to electricity so the open vocal or verbal expression of feelings causes them to pass through us more quickly and to do less damage. Unexpressed anger, on the other hand, like unrequited yearnings, burrows deep into the person and often interferes with the ability to remain logical and thoughtful.

This is not the only reason why anger is best expressed openly with the appropriate intensity, even if extreme. Another is that the freedom to have such expressions repeatedly confirms that the system is fair and just. Only here does protest find an open channel. Only in such a system can wrongs, and even what is merely perceived as wrong, be protested without fear of retaliation or punishment. Less bitterness and hardly any hate arise when fairness and justice can be expected.

But as soon as a storm of anger has passed it is always necessary to examine whether it made rational sense in the first place. Kids and even sensible adults whose expectations have not been met often perceive slights that did not really occur. Anger is quite often unjustified in reality. And the intensity of rage is therefore never an indication of the rightness of any cause.

It is obvious then why no amount of protest should ever alter an original decision that was right. Protest and anger often spring entirely from baseless disappointment, especially among the young. Anger is often directed at completely innocent people. The real causes often hide in long-past happenings, many even beyond memory.

A cool and objective examination of the real circumstances of any angry protest reaffirms the basic commitment to justice, and this slowly diminishes the frequency and power of irrational outbursts. The habitual bodily reactions of anger slowly weaken. Eventually anger reflects present circumstances only. This is why open expressions of protest are necessary even when the anger is unjustified in reality. Wrong perceptions can be corrected more easily after the underlying sense of frustration has been relieved.

Since our understanding of these issues is relatively new, it is not surprising that even experts are sometimes wrong on these matters. Psychoanalysts, for instance, confuse the issue by using the word "aggression" which is an act, to describe "anger" which is a feeling. The first is dangerous and hostile and therefore unacceptable, while the second is desirable, helpful and welcome. Like the analysts, so many parents are also confused. This is why many still squelch necessary and useful expressions of protest that are completely safe.

This lingering confusion persists because only relatively few people have actually seen that we humans have the capacity to control all our actions even under the pressure of extremely powerful feelings. Even white rage or red fury do not necessarily lead to violence. People lose control only rarely in societies and in families where everyone is always held responsible for each and every act. But not so when temporary insanity is a common plea. Everyone's safety is compromised when psychologic explanations have the power to excuse. We are damaging ourselves and our children by having too few standards that are absolute.

We humans are irrational by nature. But children slowly become rational when they are held responsible for everything they do. The open verbal expression of anger is the safety valve that enables people to discharge the pressure that might otherwise explode in thoughtless acts of violence and hate. Unlike verbal expressions, hate causes real harm. It also is contagious and not always controllable. Hate commonly leads to destructive acts of violence.

Parents whose feelings were unjustly suppressed in their own childhood sometimes tolerate and allow too much, including outbursts of rage that are contaminated by disdain. In the next chapter we'll see why disdain is dangerous. Such parents mean to save their children from accumulating residues of anger like those that they endure, but the result usually is far from what they wish for. Their children typically remain undisciplined, unruly and irresponsible. When the reasons for protest are not challenged often enough, children end up believing that they are always right when they're angry. This gives rise to narcissistic misfits who are insensitive even to their own real needs. Rather than become free-spirited and spontaneous citizens, such people often remain slaves to their own impulses. They also repeatedly get into difficulties for ignoring the rights and the dignity of others, as well as the law of the land.

Here are a few specific suggestions for parents to help their children express their anger usefully and safely:

1. Allow verbal expressions of anger in any intensity. In themselves such expressions are not disrespectful. It is not wrong for a young child to be very angry even at mother or father. But such anger must always be voiced in a basically respectful framework.

Healthy boys and girls are not always nice and clean. The rough and tumble of playing with other children often requires a shower at the end of the day. They sometimes even get a few scratches. This is how kids grow up. The same also with expressions of anger.

2. Never allow anger to damage relationships. Dismissal and disdain are therefore never permissible. Details in the next chapter.

3. Remember that loudness of protest in itself is not an indication of danger, only of the strength of the child's feelings. Never allow your child to throw or to break things. If circumstances permit, children may shout, scream or cry powerfully. But not in public places to embarrass you, and not to elicit the support of family members or bystanders. Even when your child pouts, do not allow withdrawal from the relationship with you.

4. Allow storms of anger to pass naturally. It may take a few minutes and it's best not to cut off angry outbursts in the middle. On the other hand, enough is enough. Do not allow the child to "milk" the hurt and anger endlessly in self-pity. Insist that the two of you discuss the real facts of the situation as soon as possible.

5. In the midst of angry outbursts people say things they don't necessarily mean. While no name calling or threats should be allowed, do not otherwise become confused by angry words. Only the overall music matters. But insist afterwards that proper apologies be made for inappropriate and unacceptable expressions.

One angry young woman cursed her abandoning father and with it all men as she was furiously raving against her fate. They were such irresponsible wimps, she screamed, pathetic creatures, little boys out to play, miserable shrimps masquerading as human. She wanted nothing to do with the best of them. As a religious woman she couldn't understand why God had created such defective beings. But a few short minutes later she could easily reflect upon the fact that such judgments were obviously wrong. Not all men were evil and not all were losers. Her husband, for instance, was a good man whom she loved.

Make room even for such exaggerated and generalized verbal expressions so that intense fury and frustration can find an open channel. But personal insults should not be tolerated. It is best when the protest can be expressed directly at the one who gave rise to the anger, though this is not always practical or possible.

6. Many parents overlook the dangerous signs of anger hidden under a surface docility. This can be deadly as described in chapter 4. Children who are scared also tend to hide and to deny their anger, since they too may be afraid of losing control. Actively encourage your child therefore to directly express his or her anger at you openly. Safety valves lessen pressure and the risk of explosions.

Lack of interaction with other children and preoccupation with violence or with survivalist themes are hidden signs of menacing inner rage. Fire-setting and cruelty to animals are other indicators of a gathering storm. Children who are too quiet, too obedient and too nice, and who are never angry, may be on the way to snapping or to breaking down. Mounting internal stress often shows in visible tensing of the body. It is always a dangerous sign that needs your attention immediately. Be gentle but firm.

7. Self-pity or self-righteous indignation are neither healthy nor effective ways of expressing anger. They do not give voice to powerful protest which is directed at others. Instead, the sense of having been victimized is used as justification to withdraw or to "get even." Therefore, allow no silent long looks of hate, no disrespectful expressions and no wallowing in victimhood. Everything belongs in the open, on the table, in the relationship with you.

• • •

The ugliness that is sometimes part of angry confrontations can easily be cleaned up afterwards, but the damage done when everything is kept inside is frequently irreversible. Constant pressure exacts a toll on machines and on people, and violence against others is not the only danger. The thrust that injures is often directed inwardly.

Children who chronically internalize their rage tend to become adults who suffer from various chronic illnesses and their life span is often shortened. No one is safe under the pressure of unexpressed anger.

24

No Disdain in the Fight
Against Authority

Disdain is destructive to all relationships.
It contains not only disrespect but also dismissal
of others, which is why it is ruinous p. 180

Explain that the strength of the anger
is not an indication of the rightness
of the child's cause. That needs to be
examined separately p. 182

Children can learn many hard lessons better and faster when they are rather young. For instance, that they cannot always have their way. When they are older they put up a bigger fight. It is easiest to teach such lessons in nursery or in grade school, but since little kids are so sweet we often indulge them. They get hurt so easily. Parents and grandparents want to avoid disappointing them, so they postpone doing what cannot really be avoided: facing life as it really is.

Children and adults who have not been forced to accept realistic limits on their behavior maintain their unrealistic expectations. When these are denied some become withdrawn and quiet, others tend to quickly be angry and self-righteous. As adults such people are often unfriendly and even haughty. They look down their nose at those who expect them to carry their fair share of any burden. They are deeply disrespectful. If other people count at all, they count less.

Our society now has many more narcissistic people like these because of years of insufficient fathering. Such people are smug. Holier than thou. Obnoxious. A pain to others, and themselves usually also bitter and unhappy. Never satisfied.

Such people react as if they had been personally wronged every time they are delayed or stopped. They usually claim to be unjustly and unfairly treated by everyone, a mind-set which justifies being careless with the rights and property of others. It follows, for instance, that they would drive aggressively and without regard for speed limits or other traffic regulations. Many car accidents happen as a result of such an attitude. Narcissistic people always expect to have the right of way and see others as merely being in their way. They explode angrily without any attempt to restrain themselves and become sullen when this avenue is blocked. Pouty. Passive-aggressive with a big chip on their shoulder. They are full of scorn and disdain. Such disdain must never be tolerated in children if they are not to behave this way as adults.

Disdain is destructive to all relationships. It contains not only disrespect but also dismissal of others, which is why it is ruinous. Disdain ends dialogue and breaks down the possibility of future communications. In the presence of disdain no sensible resolution of conflict is possible. This requires that a genuine correction be made.

We have already seen that anger and disappointment cannot be avoided in relationships. But they must always be expressed from a bedrock of respect. Fixed hate can develop without it, and this often is beyond repair. Disdain, disrespect, dismissal and an open attitude of distaste poison relationships. This is why they must be uprooted from the start.

Even so, such expressions should not be hidden if they exist. It is impossible to eliminate an unseen obstacle. It is best therefore for the disdain to come into the open, but then it must be met head on. Firmly, and without ever allowing it to prevail or to go on.

At any age a person must repair a relationship contaminated by scorn. Such a repair must be made in good faith and as soon as possible. The one who scorned must also pay some penalty or price, appropriate for the age and the circumstances. Disdain is like spitting on someone. Merely saying "I'm sorry" is not enough.

Children do not disdain when they are little. They get hurt. They get angry. But they do not see themselves yet as necessarily right, which is why they don't become self-righteous. It is best therefore to begin fathering the child when it still is soft and easily malleable. Narcissism should be squelched from the time it makes its first appearance, even under the age of three. Young children do not yet question the legitimacy of a fair authority. The task is least painful at that time for everyone.

But five- or six-year-olds can already be headstrong and rebellious. By then they ought to have developed some capacity for self-reflection, but many have none. They often can't see that other people may also have a valid point of view. Many kids can't even imagine it. They already show the beginnings of being nasty and contemptuous, which always indicates that disrespect and dismissal were not nipped in the bud earlier. Years later marriages and careers will end in pain because of it. Disdain and self-righteous arrogance are also at the root of many school failures. They sometimes even lead to crime.

Disdaining people don't get along well with anyone. They typically try to push themselves ahead at the expense of others since they see hardly anyone but themselves. As kids they were not forced to acknowledge the existence of other people or that others have rights too. They really don't know that everyone deserves to be treated respectfully. And they really cannot see that they themselves stimulate the many rejections that come their way. Typically they are cantankerous. Even wars have occasionally been started when such an attitude contaminated entire nations. Hitler whipped the Germans into a murderous genocide machine by convincing them that they were merely getting even: a historical wrong had to be corrected. Non-Germans were simply declared as less than human. The fear and hate at the root of disdain can be easily exploited.

Here are a few specific suggestions to help mothers and fathers who realize the need to combat this dangerous tendency:

1. Be very firm. State simply that you will not tolerate being dismissed and don't accept it in practice. Demand that your children stay with you physically and maintain eye contact even when very angry. Acknowledge their right to be openly angry and hurt but not disrespectful.

2. Give hurt and angry youngsters enough time to get hold of themselves. Don't rush things that are not rushable. Tell your child to take a deep breath through an open mouth and to exhale fully, after a little time has passed. This often helps to restore thoughtfulness more quickly. Angry children will refuse at first to follow your suggestions, so insist. But don't start a new fight at that time.

Tears sometimes well up after a few good breaths and this always is an important turning point. Welcome it respectfully by waiting for the child to cry for awhile. Let the storm of feelings blow over before you continue. But continue you must. A disrespectful outburst can never go unchallenged.

3. Explain that the strength of the anger is not an indication of the rightness of the child's cause. That needs to be examined separately. Admit that you may even have been wrong and that the child may be right. But even then disdain is not tolerable and not acceptable.

4. Engage the child with reason as soon as the storm has passed. Try to win the youngster over to seeing your position by being consistent, reasonable and fair. Be careful not to excuse the inexcusable and never beg. Even when you meet extreme stubbornness in your child. Your ideas may have to percolate, but at the end your position must prevail if it is right. This may take time. Let children struggle with the issues you raised at their own pace, but remember that all confrontations and conflicts must be resolved thoughtfully as soon as possible, ideally the same day. Withhold all privileges that are precious to the youngster until the conflict is resolved rationally. This maintains the pressure.

5. Never let an episode of disdain go by unattended. Indicate your disapproval with a stern look if the child provokes you this way in a place or at a time that does not allow for an immediate confrontation. As soon as it makes good sense raise the issue and insist on a correction.

6. Demand a proper apology in good faith. A statement made by the child to get you out of their hair is not enough and not acceptable. Such is not a proper apology. Punish a refusal to make a correction. Immediately stop every normal activity liked and valued by the child. Do not restore these privileges until the issue has been resolved properly.

7. You must remain in control of yourself at all times. The whole point and purpose of these interventions is for you to remain a respected model of authority for the youngster. Someone your child will continue to look up to after the hurt and anger are gone. Be most careful not to act in a way that will give anyone real reasons to disrespect you. It's OK to outshout a shouting child, but only if you're in full control of yourself. Never use physical force at times like these. It only hardens the resistance.

8. Sons and daughters need and want to have worthy fathers to confirm their own worth and to approve of them as human beings. They need and want a respected father to be proud of them. This is one reason why you must protect your self-respect at all times and why their dismissal of you should never be permitted.

A child may fight you ferociously but even so, children will quietly respect a father who can stand up in the heat of such battles without flinching and without folding. Secretly and beyond the confrontational storm, even rebellious children generally wish father to win. Always remember that your child is not the enemy, even when the youngster acts like a beast.

• • •

Remember at all times that these are not contests of power to prove your own greater strength. On the contrary, you sometimes ought to let children try to save face by pretending that they won. What really counts is what they do and how they behave from then on. By disallowing disdain and dismissal you are helping your child live respectfully with others, even during disputes. You are in fact providing the child with an important tool for success in life.

25

Set Limits and Instill Self-Restraint

*Many children never get rid of the strange notion
that they are entitled to have whatever they fancy,
even if it's only a passing wish...it is father's
job to correct the crazy notion that one should
have, or do, whatever one wishes p. 189*

*Without sufficient fathering youngsters
often have a frustration tolerance
that is much too low p. 190*

*Families and societies fail in the absence of
self-restraint. Fathers who instill it are in a
very real sense the trustees of civilization,
and they hold its future in their hands p. 193*

S aying "no" to a loved, innocent little child who barely understands anything is one of the most difficult tasks of fathering.
Remaining firm in spite of protests is more difficult yet. And
not yielding to any amount of charm, tears or temper tantrums is the
hardest thing of all. But it really is the kindest and the least painful
way to teach a child the unpleasant truth that limits exist, and that
they cannot always be avoided.

Setting limits, like everything else, must be age-appropriate.
First and foremost babies need to feel as safe as possible, since even

with perfect mothering they experience unexplainable and therefore terrible fear at times. Most of life is still unknowable then. This is why young children need lots of physical holding, calm reassurance and love. Most parents know this intuitively, and therefore they always want to comfort their little kids and lessen their hardships, disappointment and pain. But even so, it is much easier to teach two-year-olds than three-year-olds that they can't always have what they want. Even the best efforts of parents may fail if this struggle is not started until much later. It obviously is too late to start setting limits when kids become rebellious teenagers.

Every child wants, and at first even expects, to be loved uncon-ditionally. But such an impossible dream cannot really come true, although self-sacrificing mothers often confuse their children on this point. In fact, love too has limits, even the love of mothers. Yet many otherwise sane adults have never learned this simple lesson. They may never think of it, but even so they expect to be accepted and loved unconditionally. The false promises of the usual marriage vows add to this confusion.

As a result, many people everywhere experience deep distress because their unrealizable expectations have not come true. They become repeatedly angry before they give up in despair, and each time they are surprised and hurt anew when they are disappointed. Slowly they become bitter. Not having been taught early that self-love is necessary, they are really victims of poor mothering and of inadequate fathering. Since hope springs eternal it often takes a very long time before people get really disillusioned. Many continue to wait to be mothered by others till they die. Therefore, such people do not provide well for themselves financially, socially and emotion-ally. Many, many lives are wasted.

As children such people were not forced to accept the unpleasant fact that dreaming, wishing and yearning are all a poor substitute for acting according to the demands of reality. It always prevails. Their bitterness often causes them to reject attempts to help them learn to care for themselves. Without self-restraint they wallow in their hurt.

Without enough self-restraint youngsters also drive too fast, engage in sex and drink beer too early and take drugs for "fun." Many fail in school. They rarely read or consider things, and they reason too little and very poorly. Many youngsters never learn to really think. Impulsive and brash, such people hardly ever engage in self-observation and in self-examination.

This explains why many people nowadays no longer even believe that it is obviously wrong to push or to sell drugs, or to get involved in other illegal and immoral activities. Even good kids from decent and reasonably stable families are now often involved in criminal schemes, in rape and even in murder, sometimes without remorse. It is not poverty that breeds criminality, just as wealth is no protection from it. The absence of self-restraint is. Dangerous adolescents kill in cold blood even in suburbia. But fatherlessness mixed with the hopelessness of poverty frequently produce extreme brutality and a total disregard for life and for property. This is why violence is so common in ghettos. Despair in the absence of self-restraint is a deadly combination.

Children will always be angry when they are prevented from doing what they want, but anger is only a feeling and not dangerous as such. Aggression or violence do not necessarily follow, as noted in chapter 23. But for angry expressions to remain safe, out-of-control outbursts must be stopped while the child is still a toddler. No father can restrain a six-foot "child." By then all restraining must be done by the self.

But now fathers in general inject themselves too late into the lives of their young, if they do so at all. The values of TV and of peer groups are not challenged often enough, or firmly enough. Cars are sold in the U.S. with the words "TOTALLY RUDE" displayed on them in large letters, and some youngsters are eager to drive them and consider it a mark of distinction. It shows that the driver is not afraid to be rude. The 1994 movie "Natural Born Killers" makes light even of multiple murders. Our mores allow for such things. No one objects publicly and few people even notice. Similarly, many little kids are allowed to play video games in which they win points for killing and mutilating people and for destroying their belongings. They laugh with pleasure as cartoon characters torture less powerful creatures. They watch movies like "I Spit on Your Grave" and listen to songs such as "Be My Slave." Nobody prohibits such activities, though a fathering parent obviously should.

The most aggressive and pathological teenagers usually become models for kids without enough fathering. Gangs become their family and the street defines their values and their standards. It is common now to blame television for our lawlessness, but even watching a lot of trash does not in itself distort the character of children raised with the steadying presence and influence of a sensible fathering parent.

But without it young kids often become like packs of wild dogs. Allowed to roam the streets at all hours, they out-dare each other to appear fearless. Gangs in Los Angeles have actually killed, and they continue to kill, innocent passers-by who by chance wore a piece of clothing with the colors of the competing gang, the "enemy."

The combined efforts of local police and Federal law enforcement agencies have all failed to uproot the widespread criminality, and the recently enacted crime bill will also not solve the problem. Even 50,000 or 100,000 more policemen cannot do the job of millions of absent fathers. Fatherless homes are at the root of criminality. Without a competent father to set limits, restrain and support his children they do not become strong enough to resist the pressures of the street culture. The only escape many have is into prisons or morgues. The situation is often not much better in "good" schools and "good" neighborhoods.

Because of love or guilt, many fathers and mothers try to never deny anything to their youngsters, as if it were best to always satisfy every one of a child's whims. Many psychologists and self-help books have added to this confusion. Dr. Spock has never really been defrocked. Self-restraint develops only if the child is first consistently and reasonably restrained and limited from the outside. Bruno

Bettelheim was right: Love is not enough.

In rich societies such as ours we could afford to ignore such facts for a long time, which is why they have been overlooked. Most young kids have too many stuffed animals and toys, and they are rarely refused when they want more. No wonder that many become self-indulgent and sloppy adults, insensitive, irresponsible, disrespectful and lacking in initiative, good judgment and self-restraint. Even kids from intact families often look slovenly, dirty and loose, and their behavior matches their looks. Nowadays the habits of our throwaway society often also apply to personal relationships.

Many children never get rid of the strange notion that they are entitled to have whatever they fancy, even if it's only a passing wish. Parents who were poor as children are usually an especially soft touch, and so are those who see themselves as inadequate in the role of parents. They often give and give in without end, in order for the children to have what they themselves always wanted but could not afford. And also to make up for their other deficiencies.

Such eagerness to give is not limited to material things alone. Many parents feel guilty and condemn themselves when they disappoint the child in other areas too. As if disappointing and displeasing necessarily damage a child.

But in reality it is father's job to correct the crazy notion that one should have, or do, whatever one wishes. Not enough fathers understand this. Fewer yet say "no" firmly enough when this is called for. Their children therefore grow up always expecting and wanting more. They not only get hurt and angry when they can't have something, but they also become anxious. Since they live with a sense of deprivation, as if they have been wronged, they usually take from others but don't give much to anyone. Generosity and a genuine concern for all living and nonliving things are best taught at home while the children are still in nursery school, not in university seminars or from the pulpit.

Without self-restraint teenagers brazenly demand outrageous things, and getting them only confirms the correctness of their crazy expectations. It thus hardens them in their position. Many parents give money freely and without accounting, and too much freedom to decide how to live and what to do. The results are often tragic. Even the children of parents with moderate means generally have too many clothes, games, computers and cars. Even they are not expected often enough to become thoughtful or considerate. Many never learn to budget their time, their money or any other resource. They frequently act as if nothing in the world is scarce or precious.

Without sufficient fathering youngsters often have a frustration tolerance that is much too low. High schools all over the country are full of flashy kids driving expensive cars, the fruits of parental "generosity" or illegal activities such as drug dealing. Owning expensive things has in fact become for many kids the required ticket for being "in," as it is for many of the parents. This is how boys impress girls now and how they become popular. And the more freedom one has to be disrespectful and undisciplined the better. Even youngsters who know better are often eager to demonstrate to others that they too are "free" to drink, to drive fast and to do as they wish.

But with self-restraint people are really much freer. Prohibitions that forbid also legitimize all the other things which are permissible. Limits provide stability and order, both of which are needed for peace of mind.

Here are a few practical ideas helpful to mothers and fathers in developing self-restraint in a child:

1. Determine what your child is able to do at any one time, and set your demands accordingly. Change these requirements as the child grows and becomes more competent. Teach young children how to dress, eat and speak. Spell out basic manners. Establish when dinnertime is and how late they may stay up. Also how much TV watching is enough.

Give the child responsibility for specific tasks around the house and adjust these with age. See to it that each task requires a suitable amount of time and effort. Insist that the child fulfill the assignments as expected and that everything is always done well. But remember that perfection is not attainable and that it is unreasonable to expect it.

2. Explain clearly what your standards are. Be specific. What is acceptable and what is not. A child cannot hear what a fathering parent does not say. Explain until your expectations are thoroughly understood, so there is absolutely no room for excuses. Reasonable and clear explanations can be understood by reasonable and attentive children.

3. Enlist mother's help to make sure that every age-appropriate expectation is met. On time, fully and not sloppily. Do not forget or neglect to follow up. This too must be done in an orderly and timely manner, especially since you also serve as a model. Always try to enlist the child's willing cooperation if possible, but insist that the standards be fully met, even if reluctantly.

4. Punish appropriately. This means only as necessary. Do not accept any failure to meet deadlines or to accomplish tasks responsibly and well. No halfhearted attempts are acceptable. If they are to become competent adults, your children must learn early in life that they are always expected to do their best. But also do not be a stickler for every last little detail.

Punishment should be severe enough to make the point that meaningful consequences follow chronic forgetfulness, resistance or defiance. It must be light enough to remain reasonable, fair and just.

5. Teach your children to budget all their assets, including time. Give your children an allowance that is appropriate for their age, thus enabling them to use some money for immediate spending and to save some for the future.

Encourage your children to earn a little by doing tasks that are real and useful to others. Insist that they discharge these responsibilities in a way that enhances their self-esteem. Guide them in managing their money but remember that it is theirs. In extreme situations you are justified in freezing the child's funds, but make sure that the situation is indeed extreme if you do.

6. Teach your children to value what they own. Do not allow them to discard or destroy any of their belongings just because they want to have something different or new. Never buy a new toy, jacket or coat that the child badly wants because they just "lost" the one they had. Do not allow careless waste of anything. Every paper tissue is made from a tree. All resources are limited and many are scarce.

But remember that preserving resources is not an excuse for stinginess. And be careful not to raise constricted kids who are unable to enjoy the rich bounties of Earth.

7. Praise your children for good performance and help them to achieve it, but only to the extent that such help is objectively needed. Do not accept excuses but notice real difficulties that each of your children has in learning to master new tasks. Offer your help in such cases generously and openheartedly, even when it takes time and special effort on your part. After all, devoting enough time and effort is what you expect from your child too.

8. Patiently explain why you forbid your children to do certain things that they want to do. Explain in terms children can understand, even if such explanations are not complete. Do not distort the truth at any time, but the whole truth need not necessarily be spelled out. Youngsters cannot understand concepts beyond their capacity.

Avoid being arbitrary or even sounding this way, and don't get impatient too often or too soon. Sometimes this is unavoidable, so don't kick yourself when it happens. But always make sure that your impatience is related to the child, not to other circumstances in your life.

Beyond all the protests, an emotionally healthy child must eventually agree that your demands and standards make sense. Only then will youngsters incorporate them and make them their own.

9. Above all, be a good model of self-restraint. All your efforts will not bear fruit if you are self-indulgent, thoughtless, loose or disrespectful of yourself or others. Such a thing may happen on a rare occasion, but it will always make your task much harder. Having to father your children may thus have an important side benefit: it may help you in fathering yourself and in developing more of your own self-restraint.

Laws cannot regulate everything. In the last analysis, civilizations are best protected by the civilized nature of the individual citizens who make them up. Without self-restraint Capitalism becomes a wild jungle. Such terms as love-of-country, loyalty, patriotism and personal integrity have no meaning for those who live mostly by what comes easy and feels good. Without self-restraint people are only out to advance themselves and greed is king then, even a god. The expectations of the "me" generation then become the norm, the communal good is ignored, and the public interest is overlooked if not corrupted. We are already seeing some of these dangers prevailing in many situations we face.

Families and societies fail in the absence of self-restraint. Fathers who instill it are in a very real sense the trustees of civilization, and they hold its future in their hands.

26

Battle Self-Indulgence and Instill Self-Discipline

*Self-indulgent people are often infuriating...
because they use their condition as an excuse
and demand special rights or privileges p. 195*

*We gain self-control and self-discipline only
slowly and only painfully, if at all. And to
do so we need the help of a steady, consistent
and firm enough fathering parent to remind us,
push us, and leave us no other choice but to do
whatever we can do for ourselves p. 196*

*Even very good mothering does not establish
self-control or self-discipline. These develop
only in a crucible of no-choice where unruly
behavior is controlled by competent fathering p. 201*

E arly in the process of growing up everyone needs a reasonable and consistent external voice of authority to define right and wrong. This is what good fathering provides. Under such patient but unyielding influence we slowly develop an internal voice of authority which is our conscience. A sense of personal responsibility comes with it too. Without enough fathering we continue to insist that we must have what we merely want to have, and we do not yield our claim that we are unable to do what we simply don't want to do.

As babies we all wanted whatever we wanted immediately and without delay. Babies settle for nothing less and neither do they settle down otherwise. They demand instant gratification. And some grownups still expect the same and they also act as if they had an unlimited license to get whatever their heart is set on. If they are VIP's they may even succeed for awhile, but this is no bargain. Many become victims of such a self-indulgent existence.

Self-indulgence not only limits an individual's own achievements and dignity but also those of husbands, wives, children and coworkers. Friends are not listed because self-indulgent people usually don't have many real friends. It is practically impossible to be a friend on this basis. Relationships usually deteriorate even if the fear of being abandoned glues them together for a while. Self-indulgent people repeatedly anger and hurt those who are involved with them, and their spouses and coworkers must eventually make a painful choice: leave or see their own lives also become disorganized.

How do we recognize self-indulgence? By noting that such behavior and habits are changeable by will. With effort of course. But the same behavior and habits are not self-indulgent if they are a shield against anxiety. Then they cannot be given up willingly. The push away from fear and dread supersedes everything.

Self-indulgent children and adults expect others to do for them things that they are able to do for themselves. Every wish of theirs is claimed to be an urgent need, and false claims of incompetence are common. In effect they try to force others by manipulation to yield to them, to give them and to do for them. By the time such children grow up, self-indulgence is so tightly woven into their character that they really believe that their claims are true.

Self-indulgent people are often infuriating not only because they use their condition as an excuse and demand special rights or privileges. But lacking self-discipline and self-respect, they are also grossly disinterested in the many hardships they cause others. Theirs is a chronic and seriously debilitating condition which robs them of dignity, income, position in life, education, relationships and happiness.

Because self-indulgent people are often so good at manipulating others they commonly fail to change or to get well. Even parents, teachers and potential therapists are often manipulated and sucked in. Others usually give up, yield or leave the manipulators alone instead of standing firm. It takes less energy to do so. Many self-indulgent children and adults therefore never have a chance to discover their real competence.

Self-indulgence is ours by nature since we all slip into it after infancy. Nobody gives up freely the privilege of demanding unreasonably. We gain self-control and self-discipline only slowly and only painfully, if at all. And to do so we need the help of a steady, consistent and firm enough fathering parent to remind us, push us, and leave us no other choice but to do whatever we can do for ourselves.

Fear causes nonswimmers to hold on tightly to the sides of deep swimming pools. But later on, after they have learned to float and to be safe in the water, some still continue to hold on. They never let go, never venture into the middle and never become swimmers. Even when they are not afraid anymore they still act as if they are, claim that they are and believe that they are.

The memory of old fear holds such people captive. As children, both being fearful and claiming to be fearful were equally allowed to determine what they did and did not do. The claim of fearfulness has thus become a mode of existence, useful in getting their way. Only firm fathering can force such nonswimmers to discover that swimming can be not only safe but also fun. By nature we are not self-starters. Similarly, self-reliance does not come to us without a struggle.

With the help of good fathering we eventually replace self-indulgence with self-discipline. We then push ourselves to take reasonable risks that we prefer not to take but know that we should.

Children and adults only do what they must before this point is reached, both in school and at work. And only for as long as someone else forces them to do so. Such people do not generally attempt anything beyond their safe routines and hardly ever do they invest much of themselves in any job or situation. They lack an inner drive to explore and to discover new things that lie outside their past experience.

Youngsters without much self-discipline approach many of their daily chores with resentment. They often experience even self-care as an imposition from the outside. As grownups at home, where no parent, teacher or boss can tell them what to do, they typically neglect their affairs and themselves and just let go. They usually even believe and claim that this is their free choice: they simply like to relax and to take it easy. But it obviously is not something under their control since such a lifestyle characterizes everything they do even when it is patently inappropriate. They repeatedly find themselves in all sorts of trouble because they live as if self-discipline and self-respect are unimportant qualities that they can well do without.

Self-indulgent people can thus be easily recognized by the way they dress, by their mumbling speech and loose manners, and by their undisciplined attention to time and to money. They are often late and they tend to pay their debts only when they can no longer postpone doing so. Without self-discipline there also cannot be much self-respect. Pain, hurt, anger, irresponsibility, money troubles and broken lives are common.

Fathers or mothers are the ones who must discipline their children when they are young. This literally means that they must make their children into disciples who will follow their rules. But no pupil can learn rules from someone who has not mastered them yet. And by now many parents of young children are themselves the products of inadequate fathering. They are therefore not sure of what to do or how to discipline. They themselves have not experienced it enough. They need help.

So here are a few suggestions. The nine points at the end of the

198 EVERY FAMILY NEEDS A C.E.O.

previous chapter all apply here too. What instills self-restraint is also useful in combating self-indulgence. Here are a few more points that are specifically helpful in the effort to discipline:

1. Again, assess and re-assess the growing competence of the child and demand that age-appropriate tasks be completed. Even if they require more than a little effort. Don't ever accept "I can't" unless you are sure that such a claim is justified. Volunteer to do a difficult task together with your child but never for the child. Patiently explain what you do step by step. Do so once, twice or even three times. But then demand that the child try it alone. Do not permit your child to give up just because something is difficult. It is natural for all of us to get discouraged at times when we learn new things.

2. Openly welcome and praise good performance, but only to the degree that it deserves praise. With increasing competence children will learn to reward themselves with justified self-praise. Virtue ought to be its own reward.

3. It is in everyone's interest that your child succeed. Make sure that any failure to complete a task properly is not because it was beyond the child's capacity. Be very careful not to set the child up for failure. One failure often breeds others.

4. Try to gain the child's cooperation. Great efforts require a willingness to make them. Insist when you encounter stubborn unreasonableness and punish any outright refusal to try. But it is best to create an atmosphere where such situations will not occur often.

5. Push gently at first, harder if this is not enough to get the child going. But push. And don't relent because of protests, tears or charm.

6. Teach the child to live by the principle that if any effort has not produced the desired result it is because it was insufficient. Even if much energy and time have been spent. Obviously, no one can always achieve whatever they set their heart on, but living by this principle will double your children's efforts before they give up.

Also, live by this principle yourself. Not only will you be a good model but you may discover that it also advances your own interests in an important way.

7. You must rid your children of self-indulgence, and the sooner the better. But be extremely careful not to break their spirit, and don't damage their ability to pamper themselves lovingly when this is appropriate. Also guard the child's initiative and good will.

Do not blame yourself when you don't do it right each time. This is an extremely difficult task. But correct your errors quickly and openly. It is often useful to discuss the difficulties of fathering with a thoughtful youngster, but not in the midst of a confrontation.

8. Acknowledge your errors openly. It is human to err and nobody is perfect. Apologize when called for but don't grovel in guilt. Remember that children can be right too. They must know that you know it.

9. Recognize real effort even when you don't accept the results. Demonstrate respect even to little kids by never talking down to them. Stay away from baby talk even when you address toddlers. Many kids under five experience it rightly as an insult.

10. Punishment must always be related to the child's age, maturity and personality. Never punish harshly. Small transgressions deserve only minor penalties. Always remember that it is best if you never need to punish at all. A brief, disapproving look should ideally be more than enough for kids who understand its meaning.

Remember that you are very powerful in the eyes of little kids. Even minor disapproval by you can cut deeply. Live in such a way that your children will look up to you even when they are bigger. Respect yourself, your promises and your words. This is the only way to command respect.

If necessary, withdraw privileges but not too many or for too long. It is damaging to your authority if you must reduce a penalty because it was harsh. See chapters 6 and 7 for other specific suggestions about spanking and other matters.

It is difficult for children to learn to moderate themselves when they have the freedom to abuse themselves with excess. This is how the blessing of affluence has often ended up as a curse. Self-indulgent people never have enough. They don't stay with anything for long and tend instead to be distracted easily, always in pursuit of some new quick "fix." Such are the results of not having been disciplined properly, sufficiently or in time.

But nobody likes to be disciplined, and by now many parents even reject the idea of having to force anyone. Can we not teach children to accept reality in any other way? Why must coercion or force ever be used?

Because no one gives up privileges without resistance and many fights. This is as true in the raising of children as it is in national and international affairs. Though we all wish it were otherwise, reason is not powerful enough to win the day against unreason, impulsivity and temper tantrums. Every parent has plenty of evidence that validates these observations. Such evidence also exists everywhere else around us.

Fathers must be ready therefore to incur the wrath of their children when they are stubborn, and nevertheless stay with them and stop them. And fathers must be capable of tolerating being experienced from time to time as unjust despots. This is not easy for anyone. For some fathers it is an impossible task and they mother their children instead. They give and endlessly explain, reassure, allow and grant almost anything that the child wants. Naively they hope that the child will thus become reasonable.

But even very good mothering does not establish self-control or self-discipline. These develop only in a crucible of no-choice where unruly behavior is controlled by competent fathering.

The average child will eventually incorporate the standards enforced by a fathering parent if they are fair and consistent, and if discipline is administered reasonably. This is how *self*-discipline eventually develops. With it children become thoughtful and able to think critically. They have the needed tools then to resist the powerful pull and push of feelings when they make no sense.

27

Help the Child Express Hurt but Don't Overprotect

Feeling hurt in itself causes no real damage.
It is painful but not dangerous and is easily
tolerated, especially by adults p. 203

Many people carry enormous quantities of [hurt]
in their chest, often experienced as actual physical
pressure. It also shows in their constantly hurt
eyes and in the dark circles under them p. 204

Growing pains are unavoidable. The fathering
parent's task is so difficult because the job
requires that such pain be elicited at times for
the child's long-term benefit p. 206

Fathers who do their job well often provoke not only anger but also much hurt. Children are unavoidably disappointed whenever they're prevented from doing what they want to do. But it is impossible to civilize a child without such disappointments. It is easier to domesticate an animal, but even this does not happen without many struggles.

But most people find it extremely hard to be the cause of hurt in anyone who is important to them. They usually distort themselves in order to avoid doing so, frequently to the point where they harm themselves and others. Hurt can bring about rejection, and almost everyone is afraid of it and tries to avoid it. Seeing one's own beloved little child crying in hurt is doubly painful. Surely a child's deep disappointment is often much more painful to the parent than it is for the youngster.

And yet, children who are protected too much from feeling hurt suffer more as adults. They are stuck for life with the impossible expectation that life without hurt is possible. Typically they withdraw into themselves when someone or something displeases them and hurts their feelings. They are too sensitive. They end up hurting too much and too often.

Such people never discover that hurt is only a feeling and, like all feelings, it too has a short life. Feelings come and go in quick succession unless we intentionally hold on to them or even nurse them. Feeling hurt in itself causes no real damage. It is painful but not dangerous and is easily tolerated, especially by adults. And most importantly, hurt is unavoidable in any relationship and in many situations. It is a common human experience that should be expected from time to time.

The fact that we feel hurt does not prove that someone has actually hurt us. Much hurt is self-produced. It results from unfulfilled expectations that may have been unrealistic to begin with.

Being very sensitive is a blessing, but only if we can remember that hurt is no more than a fleeting feeling. Sensitive people enjoy sunrises and sunsets more. They can smell the flowers and respond to beauty and to love. Their psychological skin is not so thick that it blocks out pleasure as well as pain. On the other hand, people who were overprotected from hurt in childhood tend to develop only paper-thin protection. Everything hurts them. They're crippled by their sensitivity. They have not been fathered well.

Why is this a job of fathering rather than mothering? Because the child must be prevented from withdrawing into silence when hurt, or from retreating into their corner or room. Potentially this is a conflict situation and, by definition, conflicts always belong in the fathering department. Since everyone's natural tendency is to withdraw when hurt, an active, firm, supportive, but non-nurturing intervention is called for to prevent it. Stopping the child may require the use of a loud voice. Or some other form of firm insistence. This is fathering. Even when mother performs this task.

But fathers and mothers must also help their children to express their hurt by allowing such expressions. Tears ought to be welcome. And also a few quiet moments of solitude in which children have a chance to "lick their wounds" in private. But withdrawal beyond that is not welcome. It allows for the development of inner distortions, in particular self-righteous indignation. And hurt that remains unexpressed and hidden inside is also damaging for another reason: its residues slowly accumulate. Many people carry enormous quantities of it in their chest, often experienced as actual physical pressure. It also shows in their constantly hurt eyes and in the dark circles under them.

Normally, people tend to hide their hurt. We are all more vulnerable in that state and naturally wish to hide this vulnerability from potential enemies. And since fear and distrust of others are common, people generally pretend that they are not hurt, even when they are.

But sensitive and loving eyes can see hurt in others even if they prefer that we do not notice it. Generally it shows. In the sudden change of muscular tension in the face, in the quivering chin, in soft teary eyes and in a lowered head. Its presence is also noticeable in the choked voice and in the tendency to withdraw. Sensitive parents make room for expressions of hurt by noticing its presence and by inviting and welcoming the child to not remain quiet about it. A gentle reassuring hug is even better. Grownups often need the same treatment in similar situations. They are often even more choked up, having constricted themselves for much longer.

Fathers are especially prone to do the opposite. They often forbid open expressions of hurt. Many have been wrongly led to believe that hurt is a sign of weakness rather than an expected and normal human reaction. Especially "macho" fathers want their children to be "strong." So they typically ignore the child's hurt and sometimes they even belittle hurt children, to shame them out of being this way. Such fathers may laugh when the child is hurt or even get angry about it. This only increases the pain and pushes it even deeper into hiding. From its hiding place it will often sabotage these children even many years later when they become adults.

But hurt should not be rewarded. Ever. Otherwise it may become a means to get things, a technique to gain sympathy. A lifestyle. Such youngsters always feel hurt as adults even when no one has hurt them. But they suffer greatly nevertheless because other people get tired of them and often refuse to give them what they want. And some get themselves into real difficulties in order to substantiate their claim of being hurt. For them feeling hurt is like having money in the bank. This troublesome condition is preventable by consistent fathering and not in any other way.

It is easier to see now why feeling hurt should not give a person any special rights or privileges. This must become self-evident to the child very early in life as a result of firm fathering. Surely by the time the child reaches its second birthday it should be clear that not much can be expected as a reward for hurt. Children who have been indulged when hurt quickly become angry and indignant when they are denied. As adults they run into trouble at work and in close personal relationships. Such people often end up emotionally bitter, battered and broken. Friendless and all alone.

Children who have not been overprotected from hurt are also better off because they learn early that reality is sometimes unpleasant and painful, but tolerable. Life is not always a bowl of cherries but it can be good nevertheless. Recognizing early that hurt is a common occurrence highlights the need to learn to navigate the rapids that are inevitable in everyone's existence. We drown quickly if we are unable to float when the waters become turbulent and not only when they are calm.

But for reasons that are obvious now, many loving parents try to protect their young children from painful struggles anyway. And they also try to shield them from harsh facts and from unpleasant realities. Yet even if propelled by love, overprotecting the child produces an adult who always expects to be shielded. Such oversensitive people treat themselves as fragile, and they are mostly concerned with their own prissy welfare. They usually lack any sense of obligation to anyone or anything outside themselves. For instance, such people tend to litter with self-righteous disregard for the common good. In extreme cases, when they believe that they have really been shortchanged and wronged, some even steal, rape or kill to get even.

It is no longer obvious to many, many people that nobody can always get what they want, even if hurt is the result. Such people are the products of chronic parental overprotection. Whole groups of such people now organize themselves to march in protest because some painful reality has not been eliminated.

Such people continue to think and to act unrealistically, like little children. Naively they always expect happy endings. They quickly get angry when a disaster hits and when "the government" or someone else in a position of power and authority does not instantly fix everything. They see evil intentions, or even a conspiracy, in the absence of easy or quick solutions to serious problems. Surely somebody can always do something to set things right. They refuse to accept the fact that accidents happen. And that tragedies are an inevitable part of life.

But growing pains are unavoidable. The fathering parent's task is so difficult because the job requires that such pain be elicited at times for the child's long-term benefit. Even so this is hard to do. Father must take positions that give rise to hurt. His love must at times be expressed by firmly saying no. By forbidding. Even by punishing. Young children generally do not understand the motives behind such acts. They just resent the limits and the one who imposes them. In the short run at least, father's love is often returned with hate.

28

Challenge the Child's
False Claims of Competence
and Incompetence

*To become reasonable beings we all had
to accept the bitter fact that forces more
powerful than any of our wishes operated
in the universe. We really do not have the
freedom to always have our way p. 208*

*Even though people normally protest any limits
imposed on them, youngsters will often also welcome
them. Limits are reassuring. They lessen anxiety
because they imply that someone knows what is safe
and good, and what is not p. 209*

*It is actually cruel and not at
all kind to give handouts or help
to those who don't really need it p. 212*

Healthy babies express their wishes powerfully and with
much insistence. This is how babies summon their caretak-
ers, except for those who are too weak or sickly to demand
in such a manner. They sometimes die quietly in their sleep.

Everyone reading this is thus truly a survivor. We are the ones
who somehow knew to make our needs known and we had the

stamina to scream loudly enough to be heard. Learning to think and to reason came only much later. We learned to crawl long before we understood where we were going. None of us was aware then of what we did, nor of the trouble that we might have gotten into. Toddlers do not understand yet that real dangers lurk all around them. Unsupervised, they are unsafe.

Like other little animals lacking in judgment to protect themselves, toddlers sometimes drown in pools or get killed in traffic. But even so, no child ever wants to be stopped. Little kids can become ferocious fighters to get what they want. To prevail, they will resist the demands of others, have temper tantrums and also claim competence that they do not yet have. They will argue and try to reason long before they are able to make much sense. For their own safety and well-being they obviously cannot be allowed to win these battles.

More than physical safety is involved. To become reasonable beings we all had to accept the bitter fact that forces more powerful than any of our wishes operated in the universe. We really do not have the freedom to always have our way. For instance, other human beings also exist and they have rights too, no less valid than our own. We also cannot simply take the things which do not belong to us. Fathering begins when a youngster first yields to a firm "no" in situations such as these.

Good parents are thus in effect the ambassadors of reality. For this reason above all their realistic demands must prevail. Even the most stubborn wishes of youngsters (and of everyone else) must take a back seat to the unbending dictates of reality. Regardless of anything else, it always comes first.

But toddlers barely understand any of this, and they invent fantastic stories to try getting what they want. They cannot yet distinguish well between fantasy and fact. They will claim, for instance, that they can have more chocolate, ice cream or cookies and still eat their dinner. But then they don't even touch the food. Their charming innocence is so lovable that it almost is convincing. Young children also cannot see distant consequences very well.

They generally see only what's right in front of their eyes, since they think concretely. But even so they claim that they see well ahead. Even first-graders often argue that they have carefully checked out everything and that all their wishes make excellent sense.

The one who fathers must firmly if gently deny and reject all such false claims. Healthy kids will powerfully protest such rejections and, though protesting is legitimate, the false claims must still be rejected.

But such rejections should always be accompanied by patient explanations, even though feelings don't yield to reason at any age. The explanations mainly serve to introduce an attitude of reasoning. This must be done from early on. While they are still soft and very young children must begin to notice that parental prohibitions are not arbitrary. Instead, they are based on what makes sense. Even before toddlers are fully capable of understanding what this means, they must already sense that the parents too are committed to acting reasonably. And that they adhere to such a system at all times.

Even though people normally protest any limits imposed on them, youngsters will often also welcome them. Limits are reassuring. They lessen anxiety because they imply that someone knows what is safe and good, and what is not. They also lessen disappointment and hurt. When the limits of permissiveness are well known, it becomes less necessary for the child to get involved in the painful process of testing where they are.

Reasonable and fair prohibitions indicate the presence of rules that can be learned and understood. Events are predictable. This always provides tremendous relief, especially to youngsters who can only barely see the outlines of their confusing surroundings. They don't have to discover everything by trial and error. Clear limits imposed by good fathering make life easier, and most children eventually come to realize that this is so.

Why do children claim more competence than they have? To be allowed to do the things that they like to do. And they will falsely claim incompetence to avoid doing other things that they don't like.

Without firm fathering "I don't know" or "I can't" soon become self-fulfilled prophesies.

The best way to combat such false claims of competence and incompetence is to elicit the children's willingness to examine each claim in the light of their real capabilities. But this is often an impossible goal when it is needed the most, because strong feelings then interfere the most. Reasonableness does not survive well in the heat of emotional storms and other approaches must then be tried.

Shaming children must never be one of these approaches. Shame damages the development of good self-esteem because it evokes the terrible fear of abandonment. Especially when shame is used by the all-important mothering parent. Inducing guilt is even worse. Guilt is an internalized accuser who is relentless, unforgiving and harsh, and from whom there often is no escape. It damages not only self-esteem but also self-confidence. People raised with much guilt typically punish themselves on a regular basis for all the crimes they have not committed. In their own eyes they are guilty nonetheless. Thus, guilt is destructive and it puts a powerful damper on real achievements.

But shame's first cousin, embarrassment, is a useful and sometimes necessary tool for forcing issues when reason does not prevail. It often is also helpful in debunking the false claims of competence and incompetence. Unlike shame which condemns the whole person and holds the threat of rejection, embarrassment passes negative judgment on specific acts or qualities only. To preserve self-esteem and dignity the child is thus forced to put such acts or notions aside and give them up. Because embarrassment and shame produce opposite results, it is incorrect and confusing to refer to the first as a healthy form of the second, as many writers still do.

The pain and fear of shame were always so terrible because shame was associated with dishonor and disgrace and it often led to being shunned. Modern psychology has successfully diminished its use in child-rearing practices. It no longer is a legitimate tool for enforcing society's moral codes. But the fear of shame also used to be the most powerful single force helpful in preserving the standards that maintained civilized behavior. Although as individuals we are much better off without shame, as a society we have become exposed and vulnerable to many other destructive influences.

By now almost anything is acceptable and almost nothing is shameful. Kids committing hideous crimes often show no remorse, and lesser offenses that in the past were obviously outside the pale are now being tolerated without revulsion. Bankruptcy is a common solution now for financial difficulties. Living off handouts and refusing to work is widely seen as a clever lifestyle used to "get by," or as a handicap at worst. And greedily suing for profit is one way to get rich quick. Even larceny, theft and blatant lying are now often considered to merely be shameless pathologic deviations from acceptable behavior. Shame no longer protects civilization enough. And by extension many parents even refuse to use embarrassment, though it has the power to help growing children restrain themselves.

Above all, parents now typically want to make their child "happy," without disappointments. False claims of competence and incompetence are allowed to prevail. As a result, many kids grow up to be brazen, brash and impudent, and they are the ones who often set the tone in homes, schools and neighborhoods. Popular art, music, movies and TV reflect this dangerous shift in values. Comedians sometimes make fun of such improper "cool" behavior, but in the process the sense of outrage about it is being dulled. Such behavior is fast becoming normal and our new, acceptable mode.

It is more common for children to claim false incompetence than false competence because the wish for more and better mothering is almost universal. Those who have been mothered too little or not well enough obviously seek more nurturing to feel more secure, and the others who have been babied too much want more mothering for the opposite reason: they have become addicted to it. Even as grown-ups they still want to be cared for, and they refuse to care for themselves until they are given no other choice.

Such claims of incompetence are more often made behaviorally than in words. Children (and adults) often assert their "right" to be looked after by being sickly, needy, confused and helpless. And such children often really end up being less than competent because their false claims are repeatedly treated as real. This is why it is much better to challenge false claims of incompetence as soon as they are made. It is actually cruel and not at all kind to give handouts or help to those who don't really need it. They often regress physically, emotionally, economically and socially as a result. Good fathering cannot eliminate a real need for mothering but it can and must limit addictive behavior that often is destructive to the receivers. The implications for public policy are obvious.

Children who have been mothered well make false claims of incompetence only infrequently, mostly when they are frightened or sick. Then they yearn to run back to mother's protective lap. But at other times they generally wish to be independent. They feel reasonably safe even while away from mother and eager to enjoy more and more of the privileges that come with nondependent living. And if they have also been fathered well they don't make many false claims of competence either. Relatively secure and reasonably realistic about the limits of their capacity, they are generally also not self-indulgent.

The push of good fathering is even needed by, and helpful to, well-mothered children. Even they often wish to postpone leaving mother's apron strings, though they feel safe enough without her. Like the young in any other species, so they too may wish to check just one more time whether the moment to venture out of the nest is already at hand. Without enough good fathering youngsters tend to procrastinate and even as adults they do not always exercise their options often enough or quickly enough. Their sense of reality is not reliable. Since they tend to be unrealistic about the extent of their reach, they often succeed and fail in quick succession. Even well-mothered people pay a high price if they have not also been sufficiently steadied by good fathering to stay long enough on any one course.

Here are a few practical suggestions useful in challenging false claims of incompetence. They follow the same general principles of fathering also found in other chapters of this manual:

1. Firmly refuse to do for your children what they can do for themselves. Do not allow the child to turn to other activities before the one in dispute is done and done well. Be physically present or at least not physically and emotionally far away while the child struggles. Frequent contacts with you are especially helpful for young children. They need more encouragement than older ones.

2. Notice with open satisfaction but without glee the completion of a task claimed to have been too difficult. Explain that you and everyone else also encounter difficulties often, and that you don't give up easily. Regularly demonstrate to your child that this is true.

3. Remember that children do not know what they have not yet learned. Incompetence is real before a person becomes competent in any area. Be reasonable. Insist that your children pay attention when you instruct them, but remember that they have a limited attention span, especially when very young. Stretch it within reason and don't forget that nothing can be stretched beyond its capacity.

Try to avoid as much conflict as possible as you try to increase the child's attention span. But do not stop merely because of conflict. Like stubbornness and temper tantrums, conflict is not always avoidable in raising a child.

4. Do not allow the struggles between the child and you to become a test of wills or a power play. You have much more power and this imposes a special responsibility on you. Power must always be used wisely, responsibly and with great restraint.

Remember to never be unfair to your children. Using power wrongly reflects poorly on you and damages your standing as a just authority.

5. A reminder: Do not descend to your child's level when you try to stop temper tantrums and other forms of irrationality. Such behavior cannot ever be allowed to carry the day but you must not become irrationally angry yourself. Remain firm and cool. Resume a reasonable discussion and renew your demands as soon as the child's storm of feelings has passed.

6. If on occasion you accept an improperly finished task explain why you do so. For instance, "I see you're very tired now, so we'll let it go for today. But tomorrow you must try again and surely you'll do better." The principle that everything must always be done well is thus still being upheld.

7. Never distort reality out of love for your child. This pattern can be most damaging and usually is most difficult to reverse. For instance, do not do any part of your children's homework because they are discouraged and angry about the time it takes or how hard it is. Insist that the work be completed, perhaps after a brief pause.

Offer a glass of milk or juice to a discouraged child. This works better than anger. Help by explaining a particularly difficult point, but be careful not to get sucked into doing more than that.

8. See to it that your children develop the habits of assisting around the house, resting as needed, eating proper meals on time, exercising, playing outdoors with other children, reading, and listening to music. Insist on these even when the child angrily refuses to follow your demands. Do not relent when your child claims that you demand too much, but make sure that you don't.

Children will claim inability to do things such as these less often once their work habits have been well-established. Insisting that an eight-year-old boy make his bed neatly every morning is altogether different from suggesting it. And at age 13 it may well be too late even to insist.

Not only making the bed is involved. Children who learn that they have to share in the burdens of the family are also likely as adults to face their responsibilities more squarely. All other things being equal, the boy who made his bed regularly will be a much better husband, father, friend and citizen than the one who had the freedom to do or not to do as he wished.

9. Never ridicule. Never shame even a false claim of "I can't." Instead, disagree openly, firmly and respectfully. Explain why you refuse to accept such claims in a way that youngsters can understand. Remain firm.

10. Push even a shy child to play with other kids, and firmly encourage teenagers who don't do so to start dating. Do not accept excuses. Almost all are thin disguises for fear. So is shyness.

Push hard in a gentle way. Offer your help repeatedly. Recognize hidden embarrassment and address it sensitively, gently but without hesitation. It too is a disguised form of fear and should not determine your child's behavior. Have the child get help from others if your interventions are not enough to overcome this hidden fear. Make sure to balance every hard confrontation with softness, warmth and support. But don't yield. Patient and sympathetic listening is always very helpful.

· · ·

Claims of false competence can be challenged much more easily. Here are a few examples:

1. Let young children try to do what they insist on doing as long as it is not dangerous. For instance, stand by while youngsters try to get dressed before they really can do so. Be patient and don't let the child give up at the first sign of frustration. Encourage further effort. Remind the child without glee of the insistence that was present only a short while before. Then help by showing how you do it, and encourage the child to try again at a later date.

This obviously does not apply when young children want to play with matches or cross the street alone before they can do so safely. And obviously driving the car around the block before the youngster has a license to do so is out.

2. More generally, remember the recommendations made in point #7 above. Do not ever distort reality, even out of love. For instance, do not allow even a "good" child to steer your boat alone before he or she can do so responsibly.

But it is not enough to simply lay down rules or even to insist that they be followed. Explain your reasons even though they may be obvious to you. Children often forget in the presence of strong desire that rules exist for their own protection. Remind them and thus try to elicit their willingness to accept your limits. But remember that children will naturally try at first to reject all rules that inhibit their freedom to do as they wish.

One father who failed to do so was called to the police station one night at 2:00 a.m. His 17-year-old son "borrowed" someone's motorcycle and then sped away without turning on the lights, straight into a tree. His girlfriend on the back seat was killed instantly and the injured son was charged with manslaughter.

Stand firm when it makes sense, no matter how strongly your youngster and others pressure you. Pressure is not a valid reason to change your position. Children are generally not good at seeing distant consequences. For that matter, neither are adults who are caught in the web of strong feelings.

3. While it can be dangerous to let young children do things that they are incapable of doing, remember not to dampen their enthusiasm and curiosity by forbidding too much. Children are better off when they are allowed to experiment with things that are safe and almost within reach. No exact guidelines exist. Every child learns and matures at a different pace. Mastery of various tasks is not merely a function of age, and fine adjustments based on repeated observations are always essential. Be sure to regularly check anew what the child's growing competence is at the moment.

Success breeds success and repeated successes help the child develop a self-image of a successful person. Therefore make sure that the tasks you assign and the demands you make are within the child's reach.

But if the tasks are too easy your child will soon learn that success is possible without trying hard enough. The habit of doing less than one's best can also become a lifelong trait. Always guard against this danger.

4. Errors in judgment about the child's level of competence are unavoidable. Both the youngster and you will make them. Remember that they can be useful in helping to discover the real limits of a youngster's current competence. Be patient so that everyone can learn from such errors.

Twelve-year-old George wanted a hamster after he had chronically failed to care for his dog and it was given away. His parents agreed that having a pet would help him be more responsible. But again he failed repeatedly to feed the animal and to provide for its needs. After many confrontations failed to change the situation, George was told firmly that the matter would be left in his hands. The youngster assured them that he had learned his lesson. The hamster was soon found dead for lack of water.

George not only grieved but was also deeply embarrassed whenever the hamster incident was mentioned. And to elicit this embarrassment it often was. This proved to be an important turning point in George's life. Eventually he graduated from West Point with high honors.

5. Even older children (and many adults) are often grossly unrealistic about money. They may wish to buy on credit without knowing the actual price of an item, only the monthly payment. As grownups such kids are always in debt and often in trouble.

Youngsters will often claim competence in this area in order to be able to buy something that they want badly. Challenge such claims when necessary by going over their income and proposed purchase plan in great detail. And don't just buy for them whatever they wish even if you can easily afford it. Doing so will rob them of an opportunity to learn to budget their resources.

Insist that your children save some money out of their earnings and allowance for future use. Provide help in opening a bank account. Give children an age-appropriate allowance that allows for a little saving and also for buying small items that they need or want. Do not buy those items nor have them freely available around the house. Over time this will demonstrate the value of money much better than any words.

Explain while the child is still young that money and all the bounties of nature are limited resources. And repeat these explanations when appropriate from time to time. Do this even if you happen to be very well off.

6. Children frequently claim false competence in budgeting their time. They typically wish to watch TV, play or visit with other children before they do their homework or other duties.

Using even embarrassment as a last resort, elicit the child's observing powers to gain cooperation in changing such priorities. In doing so you establish the rule that rights are bound up with responsibilities and that work comes before play. But make sure that you do not devalue play as such.

7. Unruly friends are hazardous to your child's health. Sometimes also to your own and to everyone else's, as seen in chapter 3.

You not only have the right but also the responsibility to have a say in who your children's companions will and will not be. And not only when they are little. This responsibility is yours for as long as your children are part of your household or supported by you financially.

Forbid involvement with youngsters who are likely to entice your child to become involved in illegal, immoral or other activities that go counter to your basic beliefs and values. But also remember that young people must experiment and make their own mistakes to become independent and thoughtful adults.

Susan insisted that her "best friend" Bob was a good fellow although he was sloppy, used hard drugs and ran around with a fast crowd. He also dropped out of high school and worked only sporadically. Many bitter and angry confrontations did not convince her to give him up. Both parents suspected that they were still seeing each other on the sly after Bob was barred from entering their house.

Only many years later—when her own son by another man was born—did Susan thank her father for these confrontations. He was right but she could not see it till after Bob was shot dead by a member of another gang. She had been in love and was blinded by Cupid. The pressure at home kept Susan from being completely swept up by Bob's charm. He had almost convinced her to run away with him.

8. Kids often really believe that their false claims of competence are valid. Do not argue with a child at such a time. Hold the line and try to show the child later that you were right. In the meantime your stand prevails.

But be careful not to be wrong too often. It damages your child by lessening your authority and standing.

29

Force the Child to Think and to Live Thoughtfully

*Father and mother must insist that their
children learn by exercising their "thinkery."
The task is exactly the same as exercising muscles
for playing ball or for becoming a good runner.
It takes training. And lots of it p. 221*

*Nourish the child's good will and cooperation,
but this does not mean that you avoid
necessary confrontations p. 223*

*Feelings push children (and adults) away from
reason. Then they may try to go after things
or pursue people who are not good for them. Or
take what is not theirs, do what is
age-inappropriate, or be spiteful p. 225*

Relatively few people think thoughtfully. To do so requires that we stand back and really observe the circumstances or situation we face, as if from behind ourselves. This in turn demands that we slow ourselves down enough to check the details of any issue, along with our options and their relative merits. We must make sure that our decisions indeed are the end product of such considerations, not "gut" reactions merely based upon feelings.

With all these in place it's safe to assume that we are in charge. What we do then makes sense. After awhile this whole process happens almost instantaneously. But it takes lots of practice. Our brain is a wonderfully complex, rapid and efficient computer, and all these steps can be taken in quick succession, almost in a flash.

This ability to think critically is what distinguishes us humans from all other species, although most people tend to react before they think. Normally children (and most adults) do what comes naturally which is what they feel like doing. We thus waste our special gift, our unique capacity to reason.

This capacity of the cortex, our wonderful "new" mammalian brain, must be developed, strengthened, sharpened and perfected by repeated use and by much learning. Even as a physical organ the cortex is not ready at birth. Its nerve fibers do not become insulated (with myelin) until many months later. This is why we don't even know that we exist during the first year or so. And why we have no memory yet.

But even when the cortex is fully developed physically it is not yet ready to do its amazing job. Like a computer it must be programmed. This requires lots of work, yet by nature we like to take it easy and prefer to pass on effort. Why do we need a work ethic? As protection against our natural tendency to "goof off."

Most people do not develop enough of this ability to really think. It is a fathering job to force children to develop this potential. Father and mother must insist that their children learn by exercising their "thinkery." The task is exactly the same as exercising muscles for playing ball or for becoming a good runner. It takes training. And lots of it.

The job, like most other tasks of raising children, falls into the lap of both parents. Since learning to think is difficult, resistance is always encountered, later if not sooner. Ideally, father then serves as the "heavy" while mother continues to support and encourage the child to overcome the difficulties. But no amount of encouraging alone will ever do. Conflicts here are at times unavoidable, and mother's role is to support the child without sabotaging father's efforts. The fathering parent ought never to be contradicted in the midst of a confrontation with the child.

If the demands of the fathering parent appear to the other as excessive or unreasonable it is obviously necessary to intervene in an attempt to change them. But not then and there. An immediate intervention is justified only when the fathering position is unquestionably dangerous and immediately damaging. The child's welfare must always be the primary goal to be kept in mind and it requires, among other things, that the fathering authority be preserved. In many families mother is the stricter parent who fathers, while father is the more permissive and supportive one who mothers. While this arrangement can work, for reasons discussed earlier it is often especially confusing to sons.

One way or the other, two cooperating parents can do this difficult job much better than either one of them alone. Contrary to our current politically correct theories, one-parent families have obvious disadvantages even when the one parent is dedicated, well-meaning and mature, which is not always the case. Even if we may wish everyone to be equal in everything, not all arrangements in family organization are equally effective. But a one-parent family can be a healthier environment for raising children than a situation where two parents chronically war against each other. This worst of all possibilities is often the case just before or after a divorce, as seen in chapter 13.

Here are a few specific suggestions:

1. Remember that children are generally eager to master what their parents want them to learn. But repeatedly getting hurt, disappointed or bitter saps their energy and limits their enthusiasm. Children are discouraged the most when they believe that their efforts are chronically overlooked, and that they are unseen and unheard, unloved and unappreciated. Try to avoid such dangers by being attentive, involved and helpful. And be sensitive at least some of the time.

Explain why sometimes you may be unable or unwilling to be more attentive. You have a life too. Be as candid as makes sense, depending on the child's age and understanding. Explain if such is the case that it is difficult for anyone to love children who repeatedly make themselves unlovable. Demand changes and improvements that are needed. Actively correct the child's distortions on this score, if such exist.

2. Nourish the child's good will and cooperation, but this does not mean that you avoid necessary confrontations. Be sure to explain why you take the stands you do, and don't apologize if they are right. Remain firm. This does not mean that you can't be sympathetic and loving to an agonizing youngster.

3. Remember that learning anything new is really difficult. Learning to think and to be thoughtful is doubly so.

4. Anxiety often interferes with the ability to think. Recognize its presence and try to lower it by lessening the pressure. But don't give up the struggle because of it. The process is bound to be very painful for the child at times, and for you too. But the benefits are clearly worth it. Adults who can't think well are truly crippled.

5. Listen carefully to what your child says. And hear it too. Also try to understand any complaints beyond the words. Young children can't always express themselves well. They also do not know at first the difference between facts and fantasies. Patiently and repeatedly make this clear. Such explanations must often be repeated many times before children really get the point. Don't lose heart. Eventually your words will stick. Start by the time the youngster is two, or at any later time if earlier opportunities have been missed.

6. Never let fantasies or a distortion of reality pass as fact, even when you are busy or the circumstances do not allow for a long discussion. Even then register your disagreement immediately in a word or two, and if this is not possible at least with a gesture. Not angrily. It is hard to learn what is real and what is not. Most people never learn it well enough. Helping the child often helps the parents sharpen their own skills in this area.

7. The previous point (#6) does not mean that you ought to dispel the magic of fairy tales or of Santa Claus too early. They are helpful in developing the child's ability to fantasize. But children should learn while they are still little that these are nice stories and that real life is different. Even Santa should never promise nor "bring" more than what makes sense. Even very young children can and must begin to learn that realistic limits exist.

8. Help children learn from their mistakes. For instance, give a six-, seven- or eight-year-old a small restaurant check and ask the child to pay it and get the correct change. Children will often calculate that they'll bring back $3.35 from the $10.00 dollar bill you gave them to pay the $7.65 check. Count the change together carefully and ask about the "wrong" amount. Why did the cashier give less than the youngster expected? Help the child figure it out. Obviously, don't reprimand.

9. Be patient with age-appropriate efforts of children to reason and to express themselves. They will stumble again and again for years. Correct patiently as long as they do their best. And then correct them again as necessary. But at any age be impatient with stubborn thoughtlessness, impulsivity and the refusal to try.

10. Do not argue with a headstrong kid. Reach a reasonable decision and enforce it. All discussions and interchanges should be stopped cold when a child becomes sassy, whiny, endlessly stubborn or disrespectful. Process always comes before content. Such expressions are common in some families where they have always been allowed. But such expressions are improper and unacceptable. They always are a sure sign that something went seriously wrong in past fathering. Too much permissiveness is harmful. Correct it without further delay whenever you see it. Do not compromise on this and do not descend to the level of a rebellious child.

Your decision stands but the discussion is resumed only after youngsters settle down and become reasonable. And only after they have repaired the relationship with you that they damaged by being disrespectful. Insist that they do so without too much delay. This means that they acknowledge their behavior as wrong and express true regret about it. No room is ever made for disrespect or for disdain as explained in chapter 24.

11. Feelings push children (and adults) away from reason. Then they may try to go after things or pursue people who are not good for them. Or take what is not theirs, do what is age-inappropriate, or be spiteful. Such irrational expressions always have much power behind them and require a powerful counterforce to maintain sanity or even safety. Teach the child how not to yield in such situations.

For instance, young children can usually not be reasoned with in the midst of a strong push to have cookies or ice cream. The time for cookies may be wrong or they may already have had too many, but they don't care. Even adults use poor judgment when their heart is set on something, and they too may fervently deny that this is so until later.

First slow the child down. Sometimes this can only be done by physically holding the child firmly, or by raising your voice. Be sure not to hurt the child by squeezing too hard. This may be an expression of your own anger and it will create a secondary problem. Use any reasonable intervention that is firm enough. A slap on the behind may be the only thing that gets the youngster's attention, and this is the only justification for it. Avoid humiliation.

You too may need to take a deep breath to contain your impatience or growing rage. *Never explode and don't withdraw.* Passing the buck usually spells serious trouble for the child later on, and it often is a source of heartache for the parents. Insist that the storm of feelings be allowed to blow over before more reasoning begins. The merits of an issue cannot usually be seen before then.

12. Commit and recommit yourself to living thoughtfully and according to what makes sense. See to it that all your family members also commit themselves to this same principle. And others in your sphere of influence too. It means that you will try to resolve every conflict thoughtfully. Not on the basis of fear of rejection, hurt, hysterical outbursts or temper tantrums.

Such living requires that we use continuous self-observation. Our own wishes and those of others must pass the test of critical scrutiny. In such a system children learn to reason in order to prevail. To get their way they become experts at seeing what does and what does not hold water.

• • •

With the help of these and similar approaches, children have room to exercise their growing competence to be thoughtful. Their ability to think is sharpened, strengthened and speeded up. This weakens the relative power of their feelings which are then less in control. The visceral brain which controls autonomic bodily responses is slowly forced to yield, and it does so more and more often.

Breathing can be deepened and slowed rather than speeded up in situations of real and apparent danger, when the cortex is in charge. This enables children and adults to focus their attention, and it increases their chances to choose the best way out of a bad situation. It also helps them control their eating, drinking and concentration much better than before. Rational living becomes possible when we somehow arrange to come under the control of the cortex. Learning to think and becoming thoughtful are important necessary steps in this direction.

Feelings help us recognize our wants almost instantaneously.

This is their advantage. But feeling reactions are so quick that they normally leave us no time to think. This is their disadvantage. Room for thoughtful consideration exists only if we succeed in slowing down our spontaneous reactions, actions and "decisions." Under the influence of feelings we can't evaluate our options. We make too many mistakes.

Feelings often mislead us. For instance, as we've seen in chapter 27, hurt often pushes people to leave essentially good relationships. Fearful people are often too scared to break away from impossibly bad ones. Our heart sometimes pines after things that are in fact not good for us. Thinking is generally too weak to protect us when feelings are strong, unless good fathering has forced us to strengthen our thoughtfulness.

The visceral or subcortical part of our brain is independent of its younger neighbor, the cortex. It does not even pay attention to the wishes of this brash, bright youngster. So our thinking and feelings do not necessarily go hand in hand. What we feel is often the opposite of what we think. When this happens, feelings usually win out because people are already used to following their dictates. As babies, feelings alone helped us survive. Our bodies therefore know and trust them. We follow them blindly. This explains much of the mess so many people and societies find themselves in.

Recent Nobel Prize-winning research on brain development confirms that every person's typical reactions and feelings are determined very early in life by chance. Billions of possibilities exist for cells connecting with each other. This is why no two people are ever exactly the same, including identical twins.

Connections that helped us survive soon become preferred pathways. And the more a pathway is used, on earth and in the brain, the sooner it becomes a highway. Generally we prefer to travel on highways because it saves time and lessens the chance of getting lost. Side roads fall into disuse then. This is why our physical habits and typical feeling reactions cannot be changed easily. It is doable, however, but only with good professional help by people who themselves have fought and won such battles.

The fact that we use these well-traveled highways whose course was laid out in early childhood explains why feelings often don't make sense in adulthood. But even so, we generally do what we "feel like" doing, even if upon reflection later on we ourselves don't approve of it. By then it's too late. It's a done deed. By then we are stuck with the results. Just about everyone has been "out of control" this way at one time or another.

But many people don't *ever* think things over enough. Some wake up many years later to discover that they "goofed." So they try to at least save face by claiming that they got what they meant to get out of life. Everyone wishes to be seen as rational, which is why people invent explanations to justify actions that were taken too quickly. Such rationalizations come so easily to us that even those who offer them usually believe them to be true. That's why people defend even rationalizations that are obviously senseless.

We would need to rationalize less if as youngsters we had been helped to be more thoughtful. Our lives would make much more sense then. But learning to think is hard and only children who have repeatedly been forced to slow down master it. The trouble is that even when good fathering is available, the lessons cannot start until long after the child has already acquired firmly established habits and character traits. Our cortex is not ready for learning at birth. We must therefore overcome the previous "knowledge" already established in our bodily reactions. The head has a very hard time taking over from the gut, but this is what needs to be done.

For those still in doubt about the unreliability of feelings, here is further proof: sudden and loud sounds cause every living thing to automatically jump or freeze. They cause us and most animals to want to run away. Animals usually do. And they can be counted on to run away from the direction of the noise towards the traps that we set for them. This explains why we became the best hunters and fishermen of all. Even the biggest, fastest, strongest and most ferocious creatures are our prey. With the aid of thinking and reason we found ways to dominate all other species in nature. But we too get trapped when we don't think. And when we act impulsively instead.

Even now in the age of psychological sophistication, people still marry for love, a feeling. They divorce because of hurt and anger, more feelings. They also make other major life decisions by intuition, feelings again. Nancy Reagan made many of her "decisions" on the basis of astrology. No reasoning here.

The sad results are evident everywhere. We often fail to benefit from our potential ability to evaluate reality accurately. We do not make choices thoughtfully often enough. People generally act impulsively on the basis of "chemistry" or whatever. But we have the potential to anticipate even distant consequences and plan accordingly if we only slow down and look ahead.

Children and many adults prefer to avoid the seeming rigors of critical thinking for the apparent ease of living by feelings. Even language reflects this attitude: "I feel like, or don't feel like, getting up (or going to work, or studying, or anything) right now." That's why fathers must repeatedly force their reluctant offspring to be thoughtful. And why they must stop their young from always doing what comes naturally.

Without such ongoing pressure children remain impulse-ridden. Procrastinating and unmotivated. They always try to get away with the very minimum required of them, even after they become adults. Such people cannot think for themselves and they are swayed too easily by what they hear from others. This is quite common now. In extreme cases, people are easy prey for con men of all kinds or they even get lost in cults. Such people are crippled by their inability to gain control over their lives. They are all victims of insufficient fathering.

30

Teach the Child to be Sensitive and Empathetic

It takes patient fathering to teach children to become sensitive since the normal preoccupation with oneself must be overcome p. 232

Sensitive people indeed get hurt more easily, but such hurt normally has only a short life span. It usually passes quickly and without leaving any emotional scars. And, such people also experience more joy, love and happiness than those who are less sensitive p. 234

Irresponsibility and cruelty are not funny even when they are portrayed that way in plays or on TV p. 239

N o one is born with the ability to empathize with others, and it is not something that develops naturally. It makes no sense therefore to expect a young child to have empathy or to blame it for lacking sensitivity. Kids who have not been helped to become sensitive usually remain oblivious to all but extreme pain in anyone except themselves. Yet without this capacity we are basically no more than trained robots who can perhaps reason and think, but who are emotionally constricted and capable only of superficial human involvement.

Without sensitivity we cannot even take very good care of ourselves. Even our own emotional needs, hurts and joys must be deduced by reasoning, and thus we often misunderstand and misinterpret them. The needs, wishes and feelings of others remain an altogether unexplainable mystery. Insensitive people usually experience life as tasteless and flat, no matter what their other achievements.

Following basic moral principles and having common sense are essential ingredients in the making of a satisfying life, but these alone are not enough. Knowing right from wrong does not provide the quality that is commonly known as a "good heart." Self-esteem, kindness, generosity and the willingness to extend a helping hand, as well as the capacity to forgive and forget, are all products of being sensitive to oneself and empathetic with others. Even simple decency is a function of our ability to see other human beings as real brothers and sisters, which in turn results from empathizing with them and from being able to identify with their position and condition.

But identifying with others is altogether different from over-identifying with them. The first enables us to imagine the real emotional and physical needs of other human beings, their pain and joy. The second is an emotional confusion that causes us to actually feel what others may or may not experience, as if we actually were them. The first is helpful and desirable, the second is pathological, always confusing and often damaging.

People who can identify with others are sensitive to their friends, spouses and children, and to all other living things. Without being told, they "know" what other creatures want or must have. When they are willing to do so they can offer the kind of help, sympathy and solace that others wish for and welcome. Such people also don't usually stand idly by when injustice is done, when hunger or disease take their toll or when other human needs come to their attention. Intimately involved, they have close personal relationships and they actively add to the welfare of mankind.

Not so the people who overidentify. Rather than offer help and solace, they push and try to impose them. Their efforts are basically self-serving. Since they actually experience other people as if they were a part of themselves, their anxiety rises when they can't protect, and when they do not have a chance to give. They are the compulsive do-gooders who typically believe that they know best what other people want and what's good for them.

This tendency to overidentify results from an inner confusion as to where a person begins and ends, what is us what is not. To a small degree such absence of clarity about one's boundaries is almost universal, but in larger doses it is less common and harmful. Over-identifying parents cannot help themselves from overprotecting their children and they are usually driven to help even when such help is not needed, desired or good for the child. Such oversolicitous busyness is usually called "love," but obviously it is not. Over-identifiers get relief from doing what they do, and any benefits to the ones on the receiving end are merely coincidental. Overidentification is an example of gross insensitivity, damaging to everyone involved.

It takes patient fathering to teach children to become sensitive since the normal preoccupation with oneself must be overcome. Toddlers often treat other little kids who are in their way as if they were nonliving objects to be pushed aside. They typically grab whatever toy they want, even if another child is playing with it. One of the first lessons in nursery school is to "share and share alike." We don't know such things before we learn them.

Early in life every discomfort of the baby is expressed by crying. Even later on young children do not yet know how to identify or to name their wants accurately. All they need is "something," and mothers must often guess what it is. But feeding a tired toddler obviously does not stop the complaining. With time kids can learn to identify correctly both their inner and outer needs, which enables them to take better care of themselves in a regular, reasonable and consistent fashion.

The anxiety of loneliness, for instance, is best relieved by human companionship and by careful attention to what one's situation really is. But most people eat, drink, pursue sex, smoke or take drugs instead, or they become addicted to making money or to a variety of other distracting activities. But all these, or even running, golfing and other sports activities still leave the basic loneliness unattended. The gnawing pain persists and returns whenever one rests. In the absence of real sensitivity to one's real emotional needs, children and adults are condemned to endlessly chase after a little comfort, usually without much success. Those who have not been taught to differentially identify their needs have no better choice. They cannot save themselves from much agony and from needless pain.

Children become sensitive by being treated kindly and sensitively. Eventually they also begin to treat other living things in the same manner. By being sensitive to the child but also to themselves, parents serve as good models. Children soon notice that they too feel various emotions. With help they slowly learn to identify them and also what brings them comfort.

Many parents are reasonably good at this task as long as their kids are little. But later on, when the child begins school, even well-meaning parents often become somewhat hardened, perhaps out of a laudable wish to toughen their youngster in preparation for life's battles. Boys especially have gotten shortchanged on this score but girls are not exempt. Shedding tears of sadness, pain or joy is from then on considered "breaking down," which by definition is dangerous and to be avoided.

But life without feelings is barren and empty of the many available comforts and joys that exist for those who are sensitive. To not act according to feelings does not in any way mean that they should not be experienced. On the contrary, it is generally healthier if feelings are not suppressed, hidden or denied. And it is safe to experience every emotion with full intensity as long as we are committed to the principle of not following its dictates with action. It is not risky then to feel anything since we always remain in control of what we do. Many people, including some who call themselves "experts," do not know that such a complete separation between feelings and action is possible. But it is in fact easy to teach children and adults to act responsibly even under the influence of emotional storms. Nothing bad or destructive ever results from feelings alone.

Powerful emotions occasionally bubble up once people discover that they can indeed be in complete charge of everything they do. Even though it is painful at times to feel every feeling, the alternative is much worse. The residue of feelings that are not experienced and expressed openly remains inside. With time it often causes physical damage to the body and much more pain. This pain also tends to last.

Sensitive people indeed get hurt more easily, but such hurt normally has only a short life span. It usually passes quickly and without leaving any emotional scars. And, such people also experience more joy, love and happiness than those who are less sensitive. Moreover, even sadness and pain add a real and useful dimension to life. Wisdom is impossible without them. By insulating and separating feelings from acting and thinking we improve our capacity to benefit from all three: we feel our feelings more strongly, act more rationally, and think more clearly.

Children raised by insensitive parents or in very large families often encrust themselves in layers of psychological deafness, blindness and dumbness. Thus they protect themselves from the lack of sufficient sensitivity in their environment. Anything to lessen the pain of repeated disappointments. But the price of a stunted capacity to experience feelings is a lessened ability to enjoy life and to experience love and pleasure. Besides, the accumulated residue of buried feelings builds up internal pressure which often interferes with thinking and with rational living.

People with very thick layers of such self-protective coverings are virtually isolated from meaningful and intimate contact with anyone. Even when they are with and in the midst of good people, they have a sense that they are all alone and lonely. Hopelessness often reigns within these prisons of solitary confinement. Those who find themselves destined to live in such a space cannot break out without the help of experts with special training and expertise who can get through such otherwise impenetrable walls.

It is much easier for kids who are taught to be sensitive. Not only do they experience their needs but they usually also learn to identify them correctly. They are thus able to satisfy these needs whenever it is reasonable and right to do so. This minimizes the frustration and the emotional hunger which otherwise give rise to bitterness and jealousy at the good fortune of others. Such bitterness is fertile ground in which the seeds of hate often sprout and upon which cruelty and interpersonal conflict are often staged. Here we can often find the beginnings of child and spouse abuse, as well as the roots of racial and religious harassment, discrimination and violence.

The absence of sensitivity to oneself and to the fate of others is therefore not only detrimental to the person involved, but it also is a loss to everyone else. The widespread lack of empathy has even proven to be dangerous at times. Hitler purposefully obliterated it to turn the Germans into Nazis capable of genocide. Without empathy it became relatively easy to avoid getting into the shoes of potential victims. Killing and incinerating human beings indiscriminately as vermin could happen only after the Germans no longer identified in any way with those whom they destroyed.

Developing the sensitivity of children is thus not only a personal need but also a social imperative. Only sensitive people can authentically know and identify with the needs, wishes, rights and aspirations of other living things. Fear of punishment, guilt and shame are not reliable enough to maintain the civilized order. Sensitivity and empathy which have become inseparable parts of the character are far better as guarantors of civility.

A false as-if hypersensitivity often takes over in the absence of real sensitivity. This has become the current norm of public expressions, for instance on TV. Politicians and media personalities who want to sound sincere and genuinely concerned usually exaggerate whatever they say. Such plastic hyperemotionality is now common not only in public expressions but in private conversation also.

Children and adults are often addressed in a singsong, condescend-ing fashion not even befitting young kids. Such phony sentimentality is by now accepted as a way to demonstrate humanity and folksiness. For many such speech habits are already second nature. The chronic lack of attention to teaching children to be really sensitive now also has widespread social consequences.

Learning to be sensitive to ourselves and empathetic with others requires that we master two very difficult tasks:

1. We must be able to leave our own frame of reference, stand back a little and observe ourselves, and

2. We must be willing and able to figuratively step into the shoes of someone else in order to imagine more or less accurately what that other person may be experiencing.

The ability to observe ourselves and others objectively is not only the first step towards developing empathy but it also is an essential requirement for becoming thoughtful. We can begin to correct undesirable traits only after we can see ourselves as we are and as others see us. This capacity for self-scrutiny develops slowly when respected parents repeatedly bring their observations to the child's attention. The wish to please and to be liked will push children to begin observing and correcting themselves also.

The rewards of being sensitive are great, though getting a reward is not the purpose. Sensitive people are emotionally enriched not only by how they treat themselves but also by the many good human contacts they make with others. Having good personal boundaries, they are less anxious and not often lonely. They see, hear and risk more, and respond to life more fully. Attentive to themselves and to their surroundings, they smell the roses and can hear not only the pain and cries of others but also their laughter and song.

So why must children be fathered to become this way? Because the tendency to be autistically self-preoccupied must be overcome first. Kids can learn to attend to themselves and to others sensitively only as this battle is being won.

Here are a few practical suggestions:

1. Do not hide your own feelings. Show affection openly when you are affectionate. It's okay to hug and to kiss your spouse, your children and good friends from time to time. This is very different from giving your child a daily hug out of duty. It is not a sign of weakness to shed tears of sadness, pain or joy.

2. Happiness is a feeling too, and legitimate. Do not hide your enjoyment of your own achievements and those of others, including your children. Anger does not have to be hidden either. But it must never be expressed by violence or by withdrawal.

Help your child discover that even real hurt can be safely experienced and even seen by people who are friendly and who mean no harm. It is human to feel it. Everyone does from time to time. But never forget that experiencing and expressing all feelings is only safe if they remain completely separate from all action. And be sure to teach your children never to forget it.

3. Demonstrate that being sensitive does not make you a sucker or a soft touch. Even very sensitive people can be tough and hard when the circumstances require it. Truman was a sensitive man and a loyal husband and father but it did not prevent him from deciding to drop atomic bombs on Hiroshima and Nagasaki. He reasoned that it would save millions of American and Japanese lives.

4. Be kind to all living things. Be an example and serve as a model of compassion to your children. It's okay to kill mosquitoes and to eat meat if this is your preference. These are acts in the service of self-preservation. So is going to war in defense of liberty and justice. But do not otherwise allow frivolous killing of anything alive. And no torturing ever.

5. Teach your young children whenever it is opportune that other living things also experience pain, although not in the same way that more complex organisms do. Put a mortally wounded creature out of its misery in front of your children if they are old enough to understand. Explain why you do so. It is kinder to give a fish you caught a blow on its head than to let it wiggle until it dies from lack of oxygen. Chapter 19 is an example of the many struggles that you must get involved in to teach these principles.

6. Explain even to very young children why it is wrong to point their finger or snicker at a handicapped person. It is unkind to add insult to their already existing injury. Even some panhandlers who exhibit their misery for gain can get embarrassed. Explain why you may refuse to give anything to a pestering panhandler. Children learn from such situations to step into your and other people's shoes and to identify with others. This is how they slowly learn to be empathetic.

7. Help those who deserve and need your help. Go out of your way to guide a blind person across the street. Come to the aid of a child lost in a crowd. Do not ignore someone who has just stumbled and fallen. The Biblical commandment to aid the widowed, the orphaned, the poor and the stranger has less immediacy in a welfare state, but the principle still applies. Offer your seat to an older person on a bus or a train. Insist if necessary that your children do all these things too.

8. Teach the child that many things they see on television and in the movies are wrong. Stop your children from watching programs that are especially offensive, and explain why you do so. Strictly limit the time devoted to watching TV and exercise some control about the programs youngsters can watch.

It is unkind and wrong to only laugh at people who have gotten themselves into trouble, even if it is portrayed in a funny way. Too much slapstick too early can desensitize children to the suffering of other human beings.

Irresponsibility and cruelty are not funny even when they are portrayed that way in plays or on TV. Correct your children repeatedly when they just laugh on such occasions since it is a hard and important lesson to learn. Young children get much more confused by what they see than may show outwardly. They don't know yet what is real. Keep talking, listening and explaining.

9. Don't just give to charity at the office. Let the child participate and see you when you are involved in charitable giving and doing. Explain why you are sensitive to communal needs and what you do to help others. Explain what is important to you, and why. Insist that your children also contribute a small part of their allowance for the welfare of less fortunate people. In teaching empathy this way you also force the child to learn to be thoughtful.

10. Protect your child from overidentifying with other living creatures, and from having too much sensitivity and too much empathy. No one can be sensitive to others if they ignore their own needs. Do not allow a young child to be vegetarian unless the whole family is. It often is a sign of confusion, not of conviction. We may try to make nature a little kinder but we can't change its ways altogether.

Insist that your children always take very good care of themselves physically and emotionally. Do not permit them to be so sensitive to the fate of others that they forget their own. Explain why you take such a hard-nosed stand. Listen respectfully to what they claim to believe in, but correct their misconceptions without apologies.

Even young children can understand that too much sensitivity and too much empathy are really self-serving, but don't bother to explain such complex concepts as overidentification. Instead, teach them simply about the real perils of existence in nature and in the real world.

Do not overprotect your children. They should attend funerals of close relatives if they are old enough to understand that life begins and ends for everyone. Death should not be a taboo subject in your family discussions. But make sure that information about painful life situations that your children are exposed to will not overwhelm them.

Children must be able to make sense of what they see and what you teach them. Be sure to keep all your explanations on their level.

31

Encourage, Support and Teach Self-Mothering

*The Judeo-Christian tradition has...underscored
the importance of respecting and loving others, but
not the self. Yet the commandment to "Love thy
neighbor as thyself" is meaningless before one learns
to love oneself p. 243*

*The development of self-mothering...requires both good
mothering and good fathering. Good mothering is a model
for learning to satisfy the physical and emotional needs
and good fathering directs the struggle against the natural
tendency to seek instant gratification from the outside.
Neither function is gender-related p. 244*

*Picky eaters are not made in heaven
nor are they born this way. They are
products of too much permissiveness p. 247*

Good mothering consists of attending to the child's physical and emotional needs at the right time and in the proper dosages by a loving, supportive, responsible and consistent caretaker. An inner sense of safety and well-being is the result, and it lasts throughout life if these supplies continue to be available on a regular and steady basis. But we can't mature emotionally if we continue to be dependent on our mothers. Someone else must become the reliable supplier of these essential needs. We ourselves must learn to be that supplier if we are to become emotionally self-sufficient. Self-mothering is thus the basic ability which makes individuation possible.

Most people do not acquire enough of the skills of self-mothering and they continue to look for emotional sustenance from the outside. Others take the place of mothers. People usually attach themselves emotionally to another person when they grow up. They hope and magically even expect that a spouse or someone else will take mother's place as the source of comforting, safety and well-being. Since both marriage partners often have these same expectations, many marriages fail. And trouble also develops when the marriage partners have uneven needs and one partner is able to give much more than the other. Even very loving spouses sooner or later tire of giving which essentially is one-sided.

Not only babies but grownups too need regular well-balanced meals for their physical well-being and they also need rest, recreation and emotional support. But many people fail to take good care even of their basic needs, and stocking up on emotional supplies is much more difficult. Too few people nowadays sit down at a table to leisurely dine in the company of others, except on special occasions. Instead it is more common to eat on the run. Most people eat, sleep, work and play either too much or too little.

It's normal now to lead busy hustle and bustle lives. Father is often away at work or travelling on the job, or he's absent altogether. Mother must often drive the children and run the family without much help. The kids have TV and the personal computer as constant distractions. All these make it much too easy for people to forget themselves and their need for relaxation and companionship.

Many people take more time to exercise their bodies than they do to replenish badly needed emotional supplies. And relatively few of us allocate enough time for friendship with a few good people, to be alone with a book or listening to quiet music. It is not unusual for people now to even become restless when they try to relax and rest. As children they have not been taught to mother themselves and as adults they feel empty when they slow down. It takes encouragement and lots of practice to master real self-loving.

Most civilizations have emphasized the importance of humility to vanquish narcissism in the young. No parents want their kids to become empty-headed braggarts. Self-praise was thus condemned, even as children were taught to praise the desirable traits of others. The Judeo-Christian tradition has thus underscored the importance of respecting and loving others, but not the self. Yet the commandment to "Love thy neighbor as thyself" is meaningless before one learns to love oneself.

Even so, we still look upon self-love with suspicion and do not teach our youngsters to attend to themselves with appropriate self-concern. We also do not encourage them to take pride in their realistic achievements. Hence the enormous and widespread hunger to be seen, recognized and praised by others, and the almost universal wish to be caught in the spotlight even if only for a passing moment. This is why people wish to become VIP's and why they do grossly bizarre things for a little attention. Anything to be lifted out of the gray anonymity that envelops those who have not learned to observe themselves, to see themselves and to love themselves appropriately.

Loneliness is especially oppressive for people who are poor in self-mothering. Daily disappointment is unavoidable when practically all emotional supplies must be gotten from others. To protect themselves such people typically allow no one to come close. Physical intimacy may be desired but no emotional involvement beyond it. It is understandable why people who are poor in self-mothering normally refuse to leave their isolating shells even to make the human contacts they so desperately desire. Many are hopelessly caught in this double trap from which they often see no exit for escape.

Unless they are helped to change, grownups who have not been mothered adequately in early childhood usually also do not mother themselves well later on because:

1. They do not know how to mother themselves, not having experienced it enough. Commonly they neglect their realistic needs for food, rest, and human companionship. The triggering mechanisms that cause others to be alerted to their unsatisfied real needs are underdeveloped.

2. At least some resignation and hopelessness are often built into the core of such people's personality. They expect nothing but disappointment if they ever really reach out to anyone. Since many of their physical and emotional needs remain chronically unsatisfied, they fill themselves instead with self-destructive indulgences. Overworking, overeating, alcohol and drugs are all good examples.

Sensible and appropriate self-care, self-recognition and self-praise, tempered by moderation and good taste, are scarce and urgently needed in our society. Kids stare into TV cameras to make up for this deficiency and scream that they and their team are number one. This is the closest our advertising culture comes to promoting self-mothering. Generally people do not dare to describe themselves seriously as valuable human beings.

The development of self-mothering thus requires both good mothering and good fathering. Good mothering is a model for learning to satisfy the physical and emotional needs and good fathering directs the struggle against the natural tendency to seek instant gratification from the outside. Neither function is gender-related. Most early mothering and fathering is done by mothers since they are the ones who usually provide most of the baby's care.

Specifically, what does self-mothering consist of? First and foremost it includes good attention to the physical needs of the body: balanced and regular meals, enough sleep and regular rest periods and the avoidance of all harmful situations and substances such as tobacco and street drugs. And obviously also regular exercise and physical checkups to maintain health and to prevent illness. But beyond all this it requires intellectual and aesthetic stimulation and involvement as well as meaningful relationships which satisfy the normal need for human companionship.

Children need help to learn to provide these and also to sensibly satisfy their emotional needs for acceptance and praise. This is a particularly delicate and difficult task since such qualities are beneficial only in measured doses. In excess, self-praise and self-love produce self-satisfied windbags, interested only in themselves. But even recognizing this danger, children should be supported in their attempts to look after themselves lovingly. Those who are not embarrassed to praise themselves appropriately for their real achievements do not need so much praise from others and they distort themselves less to get it. The same with love.

The pressure of fathering is often required to actively interrupt the common tendency of children to passively watch "the tube," play video games or be endlessly involved in sports. They ought to be encouraged to explore age-appropriate new life experiences and pushed to study and to work beyond the zone of their comfort. Many children must even be pressured to seek the company of other kids for quiet play.

The normal rough and tumble that in the past immunized the young against the harmful effects of remaining overprotected little kids is often absent in many well-to-do families. Suburban kids do not have a chance to get together with other children in natural environments such as neighborhoods. Here everyone had to fend for themselves in order to survive. Even if latchkey children happen to be affluent they are often emotionally poor and their life is often empty.

Unchallenged, kids tend to end up being soft, spoiled, chronically unsatisfied, forever in need of emotional support and worse. Youngsters always driven to the houses of their friends or to activity centers are not so well off either. Being always dependent on others perpetuates their dependency.

The addiction to emotional support from others is by far more common but recognized much less than the better known addictions to alcohol, tobacco and drugs. They all produce serious damage. Anxiety is usually very high in emotionally addicted youngsters while self-esteem, self-respect, inner contentment and dignity are in short supply. In general, such children are poor in self-mothering and short on self-love.

Here are a few specific suggestions to help parents pursue the goal of inculcating proper love of self in their children. Many of these involve fathering since self-indulgence and endless dependency on others must first be curbed:

1. Praise the child openly for what is praiseworthy. Do so in words and also by not hiding your pride at such achievements, especially when the task required much effort and the overcoming of difficulties. But be careful not to praise excessively. Do not praise and do not reward small things that should be expected. Never infantalize in speech or in any other way. Even very young kids deserve the respect of not being talked down to.

2. Encourage the child to express its joy openly at having overcome hardships in pursuit of worthwhile goals. This specifically includes pride for winning battles over the tendency to procrastinate, to be distracted or to give up when discouraged.

But explain carefully and repeatedly why self-praise and pride must always be expressed in moderation, in good taste and under circumstances that do not in effect put others down. Correct your children when they err in such matters. Support them for patting themselves on the back if it's free of boasting. Insist that your children remain sensitive to others who have less to be proud of.

Some people will always resent anyone who is openly pleased with his or her real achievements and victories, even if they don't toot their own horn. These people experience such an attitude in others as a reflection upon themselves. This is not a good reason for your children to deny themselves what they deserve and need. Teach them that it is impossible to please everyone all the time.

Support your children in doing what is right and best for them, as long as it is done properly and tastefully. Your support in such delicate matters will indirectly also help your children stand on principle at other times and in other matters.

3. Insist from early on that your children eat proper and regular meals, sleep enough and learn to dress and to care for themselves thoughtfully and carefully. Even toddlers can learn to brush their teeth, not just play with their toothbrush. Insist that they wash themselves regularly and that they follow your guidelines even when they don't want to. This includes combing their hair. Show them how to do it and explain briefly, clearly and repeatedly why it should be done.

Restrict junk food, sweets and snacking. Determine fixed bed-times for young children but be flexible when exceptions make sense. Having an orderly regimen and clear expectations will help your children accept the legitimacy of limits and introduce them to the need for self-restraint and self-discipline. Eventually they may adopt such guidelines and make them their own.

4. Picky eaters are not made in heaven nor are they born this way. They are products of too much permissiveness. With a few exceptions the same is true for difficult, cantankerous or rebellious children.

Make your own life easier as you also help your children enjoy theirs more by insisting that they share all the food cooked for the rest of the family. No special menus for youngsters. Everything must at least be tried, and more than once. No new food is ever rejected out of hand. Limit the intake of soft drinks, especially before, during or instead of meals.

You not only lighten the burden of the one who prepares the meals by laying down these ground rules, but you also establish the important principle that you and mother, not the child, are the authority in the family. By the same token you also reaffirm your role and responsibility to limit the youngster's right to choose his or her clothes, toys and even playmates.

Be reasonable at all times. Arbitrariness weakens your moral stature and your power to serve as a just authority. Being arbitrary also makes it easier for youngsters to claim that authority in general is faulty and that it is OK to disobey it. Those who end up with such an attitude cannot become effective in the role of authority for their own children, or for anyone else. The damage is thus multiplied and extended over time. But children who internalize reasonable standards enjoy the dignity of living reasonably.

5. Adopt some dress code for yourself and for everyone else in your household. This is an almost universally overlooked principle these days. Clothes serve not only to cover one's nakedness and to protect the body from the elements. They unavoidably also express a person's basic attitude towards self-discipline, authority and the value of the self.

Sloppiness is not necessary even in casual dress. Jeans can be elegant. The preference for faded clothes or those with tears in them is an expression of protest and rebellion against the Establishment. So are T-shirts with slogans disrespectful to oneself or to others. Disallow wearing them. The same with T-shirts that advertise products. Your youngster is not a billboard and good taste must be acquired early if it is to be acquired at all. As always, welcome and even invite protest verbally but not in deeds.

Teach by example that dressing up is not silly, square or wrong but appropriate for many occasions. It increases the importance of red-letter days, encourages thoughtfulness and solemnity and adds a sense of festivity that is altogether missing in many families.

It also is *not* undemocratic to dress up. Cost is a poor excuse for refusing to do so. The clothes that children prefer, demand and often get these days are much more expensive than the simple but dressier clothes that are sometimes called for. Dressing up does not mean wearing designer clothes.

Ceremonies of celebration are only pooh-poohed as bourgeois by people who do not think enough of themselves and who do not value special events in their lives sufficiently. Be sure not to deprive yourself and your children on this score even if you may have been deprived in the distant past. Do not get discouraged if most of your children's friends will not understand your efforts, and even if you're told that they make fun of them. At first it will all seem artificial, but it becomes natural with time and it will add a valuable dimension to your life, and to theirs.

6. Teach your children to be grateful for the many blessings that they enjoy every day. Even the poorest among us live better than most rich people did a couple of hundred years ago and as many people elsewhere still do. Contentment depends not so much on having more as it does on appreciating what we already have. Most people are much more experienced and quicker in complaining about what they lack than they are in being thankful for what they have.

Remind your children that TV and the computer did not always exist and only a century ago there were no cars, no airplanes, no telephones, no air-conditioning or central heating, no antibiotics, x-rays or even indoor plumbing. Millions died of pneumonia and other infections.

To complain is natural but to be thankful requires the exercise of our powers of observation. The first is a product of feelings, often an expression of old dissatisfactions known as preverbal hunger. The second is the result of thoughtfulness. To always demand more is characteristic of children. The joys of inner contentment come only with maturity. Help your children get there.

7. In spite of all the demands of your job and other preferences you may have, spend enough time with your children. Having more of dad's physical presence is what many children yearn for. But this alone is not enough. Also be attentive to them and make yourself emotionally available.

A family of four consisting of a father, a mother and two

daughters about 10 and 16 was recently seen in an upscale restaurant. Father and the older daughter were involved in an animated and friendly conversation throughout dinner. Mother was quiet. And the youngest daughter was buried in a book throughout, emerging only briefly to quickly swallow her food. Even then, the only eye contact she made was with the items on her plate. No one even tried to address her and she remained totally uninvolved. She even walked out behind the others, as if she were all alone.

Do not allow such withdrawal, no matter what the explanation or the excuse. Reading may be better than being addicted to watching TV, but neither is acceptable at dinnertime. Meals are not only for the consumption of food. They are important times for social interchange, for teaching and for learning, for unburdening and for fun.

Make sure that your family sits down for an unhurried meal together several times a week, even if this cuts into the time available for hockey, ballet or Little League. First things first. Such togetherness is a major tool to foster family ties and values which, in turn, protect the kids from the corrupting influences of the street culture. It is much easier to keep youngsters away from drugs or crime than to try fixing them later on.

8. Encourage your children to be sensitive to all the messages of their body. It has its own language to express its needs and that language should be learned and listened to. There is nothing shameful in the urge to urinate or to defecate, and neither should any other subject be taboo. Display a thoughtful, matter-of-fact attitude in all discussions that relate to the body.

Teach your children to keep their body in good working order. Children at play will typically ignore the call of nature for as long as possible. But repeatedly ignoring the body's call for defecation, for instance, eventually results in chronic constipation. And people who habitually continue to eat when they are full no longer know when they are satiated. Obesity is a common result.

But play down minor or unreal physical complaints. Be careful and see to it that your child does not become a hypochondriac.

9. In general, expose your child not only to new foods but also to new ideas, new experiences, new situations and new people. Everyone prefers what they already know and what they already are good at or comfortable with. Insist that your children expand their horizons in all healthy directions rather than limit themselves to what they know to be safe.

Do not accept shyness as an excuse but be gentle in your firmness. Shyness is merely a disguised expression of fear, and feelings alone should never be the guide for action. But do not ignore the fact that in general new situations really provoke some anxiety.

To succeed, make sure that you are not yourself overinvested in one or another of your child's activities such as hockey, ballet, football, karate or music. You are otherwise likely to err when it is best to limit such an activity in favor of something else.

10. Insist that children not exclude themselves from family visits and affairs even when they prefer to spend time with their friends. As long as they live at home they are part of your family. But remember that growing up is a gradual process that requires youngsters to have an increasing say about their life. Remain reasonable at all times.

11. Most importantly, teach your children to cope with their anxiety, not only when they must face new situations but in general. People normally try to lessen their anxiety by avoiding anxiety-producing situations. This usually determines the limits of their freedom as human beings.

Explain that even extreme anxiety is temporary fear originating in a distant past. It usually passes quickly, or at least it becomes manageable once we stop to notice that it is not based on a current danger. Anger at children because they are anxious makes a bad situation worse. It never helps.

An attractive woman who never dated because she always believed that she was boring and shy finally cried bitterly about her wasted years when she was 45 years old. She would never have children and was desperately lonely. Why had her parents not pushed her 30 years earlier, she lamented painfully.

Yielding to your child's anxiety is obviously not an act of kindness. But the opposite is. Firmly but gently push your growing children to care for themselves in an age-appropriate manner. Do not relent even when this provokes anger.

Be patient. Teach the child to sit tight and to take a few deep and slow breaths when anxiety is high. Stay physically nearby. A firm but supportive physical touch is most reassuring. Do not allow the youngster to retreat from the task at hand because of anxiety alone. Urge your child to proceed as soon as possible once the peak of the storm has passed.

This probably is the single most important lesson that parents can teach their children. It is useful for adults too. Everywhere. Always and throughout life. Remember that at first no one dares to face anxiety without the consistent support and presence of a dependable, trustworthy and loving helper.

12. Encourage your children to really relax after they have done a good piece of work. As always, the best teaching is by example. Vacations that are too busy with the pursuit of recreation and fun are not relaxing. This is why people often need a vacation after their vacation.

To re-create our strength and energy we need to let go of being busy and active. Hard play is good exercise and often enjoyable, but it does not satisfy the need for relaxation. Many people never slow down because they get anxious whenever they even try to let go. That's why they always watch TV, listen to loud music or play video and other games. These are all no more than distractions. Only the large muscle groups relax. Teach your child to enjoy moments of doing nothing except enjoying.

Arrange for vacations that allow for quiet walks in the woods, for being together in a relaxed way, for an occasional nap and for non-competitive sports and play. Insist that your child make time for reading, quiet music, nonhurried sightseeing and leisurely dining with the family. And for appreciating and enjoying the glories of nature.

Read to your children especially when they are young. Tell them about your own life and let them get to know you. Listen to them and get to know them as they grow up. Don't remain strangers.

Before they discover the joys of relaxation and its power to rejuvenate, children also get antsy when they are not busy with activities. Stay with them and insist that they slow down and stop from time to time, even though they will resist at first. The gift you give them in doing so is priceless and will last for life.

32

Demand Excellence, Instill Values and Develop Respect for Life and for Learning

*Little boys and girls can learn
to stand tall almost from the time
they learn to stand up p. 256*

*An important job of fathering is to support the children
in not yielding to the values of the kids' and street
culture. Being labeled as square is less damaging in the
long run than growing up in emotional confusion without
enough clarity about right and wrong p. 257*

*Conduct your own life in a way that makes formal
teaching of excellence less necessary. Demonstrate
thoughtfulness and self-control in the way you eat,
drink, dress, speak and think p. 259*

Children are naturally hungry to be taught. They need and seek guidance and they are grateful if they get it, even if sometimes they object vigorously to being pressured. They become bitter mostly when teachers are unreasonable and harsh, and even more so when no one cares enough to be around to show them, to check on them and to teach them.

The guidance kids want and need consists of much more than

merely getting facts. Youngsters want to know what life is all about, which is why they ask so many questions. But their attention span is short and they tire easily and want to give up. They must therefore be pushed to do their best and to not settle for less than that.

The quest for excellence eventually becomes part of a child's character, but only after demands for it have been made reasonably and consistently for a long time. And also, provided that excellent performance was recognized, appropriately praised and rewarded if outstanding. Then the expectation of excellence becomes incorporated and part of the self, an inner yardstick.

Fathering for excellence thus requires an ongoing commitment to be actively involved in the raising of the young. For many people this is a self-evident requirement of good parenting, but in practice it often is no longer accepted as true. The emphasis now is on individual rights and many children along with their well-meaning parents interpret this to mean that no one should interfere in somebody else's business. Not even parents. Surely it is not uncommon now for school-age youngsters to protest any adult interference in their affairs.

Many kids claim the right of self-determination long before they are able to exercise it responsibly. It gets much worse when youngsters are a littler older. Confusion has spread like wildfire. Grown teenagers unwilling to support themselves and refusing even to thoughtfully look after themselves nevertheless object self-righteously to any parental direction. Such attitudes always suggest that too little fathering and too much permissiveness were present in the past.

Parental authority is now also widely challenged by self-appointed advocates and "defenders" of children. They presume every child to be a likely victim of abuse. Youngsters are even publicly invited to report parental harassment and to seek legal aid and Protective Services assistance. Enlightened people everywhere reacted with revulsion when Hitler urged the youth of Germany to report parental disloyalty to the authorities, but we are fast creating a similar atmosphere of distrust. With so much suspicion all around them it is no wonder that timid parents are fathering even less than they did in the past. It is also not surprising that so many kids get away with so much. We have more and more troubled, anxious and unruly kids as a result.

Historically we are in the midst of a powerful reaction against the autocratic, harsh and unjust fathering of past generations. A large and influential segment of the population idealizes a life without any rules, which by definition is anarchy. Hardly anyone would thoughtfully defend such a position, but this attitude nevertheless is responsible for many of our chronic crises in the family and in our society.

Many parents and even many of their older children increasingly realize that those who can will have to save themselves, regardless of what happens to others. There is a rising clamor for a sensible code of behavior to be imposed on the young by reasonable fathering. Its specific content and values will vary from family to family, but common to all is the recognition that thoughtfulness, not impulsivity, must be the basis of any action.

No good life is possible unless impulsivity in children is halted from an early age, soon after kids begin to walk. This also is the time to gradually start insisting on the development of responsibility and self-restraint. Little boys and girls can learn to stand tall almost from the time they learn to stand up.

Such important lessons are not learned from listening to lectures. Self-respect, human dignity and good citizenship only develop when proper parental guidance and supervision are consistently present in the many small matters of daily living. Little children who are regularly expected to look after their clothes and toys and to wash and comb themselves without making excuses will more readily accept reasonable regulations concerning TV, homework and the handling of money when they are bigger. Such children will also have learned that they cannot reject the family's values, habits and practices without good reason.

Newborns always join an existing family and it makes sense that they learn to fit into it, not the other way around. But the physical needs of babies do not follow reasonable timetables. Instead, parents must adjust to them. In many families this pattern is never reversed even later on, though no fathering can take place in child-centered households. This is why parents must again become the authority in the family as soon as infancy is over.

The principle that children must adjust to the family culture and values must be established early. Only then can parents succeed in educating their young. Later on, when the children grow up and become independent they may decide to reject what they were taught at home and choose their own way, but not before. Until then all rejections must be limited to protesting alone, except for children who are really in danger of abuse and who really need and deserve society's protection.

It is a shame that in affluent societies some poor people have to wear torn clothes, but wearing such clothes is not shameful in itself. But why do youngsters from well-to-do families wear such clothes? And why are they often unkempt and slovenly in private and in public? It is surely not an expression of a noble wish to identify with the poor. The wearing of badly torn jeans is a rebellious challenge to orderliness in general. To allow it is to accept disorder and order as being at least equal in value, and the absence of effort and self-discipline as no worse than their presence. The lack of unequivocal objections by a fathering parent to the adoption of such a style has profound implications in areas other than dress and personal appearance.

An important job of fathering is to support the children in not yielding to the values of the kids' and street culture. Being labeled as square is less damaging in the long run than growing up in emotional confusion without enough clarity about right and wrong. Such fathering interferes with the natural tendency to take it easy and to always have fun, and it promotes excellence, responsibility and thoughtfulness. With such qualities children become able to pursue difficult but important goals. Not many achievements are reached without them.

Even good teachers often fail with students who have not been trained at home to discipline themselves for the rigors of learning. Mastering requires lots of practice and this often is boring. But boredom is not a good reason to quit. Those who are allowed to do so whenever they are discouraged typically become characterologic quitters. Many of these children never learn to read, write or do math properly. They also earn less, know less, enjoy less and experience fewer of the good things that life has to offer. They do not realize their potential. Some end up in crime. The lack of enough fathering is at the root of their lifelong troubles.

Kids who enjoyed too much permissiveness also cannot usually think critically and hardly ever do they stand up for principle. Nothing but their comfort is important enough. It takes guts and self-respect to have principles and to be ready to defend them. Consequently, as grownups such people tend to be poor citizens, unable and unwilling to be counted on even in the defense of liberty. This more than firm convictions pushed many of the antiwar, anti-Establishment protesters during and ever since the Vietnam years.

Youngsters from permissive homes typically have an immediate and strong reaction against anyone or anything that makes demands upon them, as if this were always necessarily wrong. They see themselves as potential victims. In this framework it is impossible to trust or to believe in the goodness of people. It is much easier and more natural to expect all kinds of abuse and injustice coming from every direction. A large and increasing minority of our population now has such attitudes. This is how the absence of enough fathering in the family is endangering the future of our society.

Achieving is the opposite of taking it easy, and excellence is never reached with a slovenly approach that yields to hardship. Sustained fathering pressure is needed even for mastering technical skills, but much more is required to stimulate intellectual curiosity and respect for knowledge, for ideas and for learning itself. These develop only with good modeling in a setting that rewards and recognizes wisdom, moderation and good taste.

Here are a few specific suggestions for parents eager to bring out the best in their youngsters:

1. Conduct your own life in a way that makes formal teaching of excellence less necessary. Demonstrate thoughtfulness and self-control in the way you eat, drink, dress, speak and think. Children who see their parents read are more likely to become thoughtful and involved with ideas. You cannot teach any lesson that you yourself have not yet mastered, but you can encourage your children nonetheless by showing them that you value it highly.

2. The above applies to any and all areas that you consider important. You cannot teach good citizenship if you don't vote regularl;. As soon as they are old enough, take your children with you to concerts as well as to football games. Teach loyalty, responsibility and helpfulness by being loyal, responsible and helpful within your family and within your community.

3. Your children will repeatedly accuse you of being wrong and square if you do your job right. They will tell you that other fathers are "nicer" and "more reasonable" because they demand less and because they hardly ever interfere with what their children want to do. You may get hurt but don't give up on this basis. Also, don't lose your cool too often by getting unreasonably angry.

Remember that your children are growing up in a society that is confused about many of these issues. They cannot but reflect this confusion. Explain patiently, correct wrong notions repeatedly and stand firmly for what is right. From their limited point of view it makes sense for your children to complain about you. The job of fathering is indeed hard.

It has always been difficult to civilize the beast within the growing child and it is much more difficult now. But the job must be done. Explain, insist, and then explain again. But don't expect your explanations to have an immediate effect. Let them sink in. Be patient and persistent. Help yourself by remembering that nothing is lost in the universe, not even your fathering efforts.

4. Humor is useful in defusing tension but it must be good-natured and respectful, not vicious. Those who are the butt of laughter should not be humiliated. Do not just laugh when irresponsible behavior or disdain is portrayed as funny, and help your children understand why such jokes or comedy situations annoy you. Without intending it, such humor condones irresponsibility and disrespect for people and it lessens your children's chances of treating themselves and others with dignity.

5. Red-letter days are stations in time that add color to the grayness of everyday life. Develop a family culture and family traditions that include special festivities and celebrations if such customs are not already part of your life. It will appear artificial and awkward at first to prepare special dishes and to learn a few specific songs for each occasion, but everyone will look forward to meeting them again when they come back, like old friends, year after year.

Have your young child help you in raising the flag on the 4th of July, and explain why you do it. Charge the older ones with such tasks later on. Don't expect anyone to dress up for a Labor Day picnic, but insist on dressing up for Thanksgiving, Christmas, Passover or other holidays. And even for lesser occasions in public. Speak a few thoughtful sentences to all those assembled on birthdays and during other celebrations and invite others to say a few words too. Eventually urge and possibly even insist that they do. See to it that the house and the table are decorated in a festive way on such occasions, since ceremony and thoughtfulness make a celebration special.

This task is easier if you have acceptable ethnic or religious traditions in your background. But in their absence, create your own. You are the one who must hold the line until the snickering stops and the fruits of such efforts begin to be harvested. Such practices foster family ties and group loyalties and build a sense of belonging. National and group pride and identity are also helpful in developing self-esteem. Betting on your favorite football team and cheering it on is not enough.

6. Spirituality is not mouthing clichés about God or goodness but having a deep inner sense of awe and gratitude for our many gifts and the marvels of existence. Whether you believe in a god or not, allow yourself to be touched by the beauty of cathedrals, by the rising notes of music and prayer and by the silent sounds of a new dawn. Expose your children to such experiences.

A needed sense of proportion comes from appreciating the endless wonders of our universe. Developing such an attitude will help your child experience appropriate thankfulness, grace and humility.

Children and adults are helped by having deep emotional roots. They maintain a sense of balance in the midst of our fast-changing mores, values and habits.

7. Values are not teachable in the abstract, which is why most people do not change as a result of sermons. Use real life situations as examples to make a point. Recall memories of your own father and mother that stuck with you throughout the years and tell them to your children. Even a painful past can teach important lessons and it can be a stimulant to doing better.

Start instilling values while your child is still very young. Even toddlers can understand why it is unkind to laugh at a physically or emotionally handicapped person. It is similarly easy to explain why you pick up a banana peel that someone discarded on the sidewalk.

8. Remember that you are very important to your children. What you do and say often leaves lasting impressions. Therefore measure your interventions carefully. Being gentle is not necessarily a sign of weakness.

9. Even if you can't fix the whole world you still are not exempt from doing what you can. Let your children notice that you always mean to leave the world a little better than you found it. For instance, plant more trees than you caused to be cut down in your lifetime. Don't just be cynical about politics and politicians. Instead, be angry when this is called for and remain involved. It proves to your children that you give a damn and that action is what counts, not feelings.

10. Civilized existence is based on absolute principles of right and wrong. It is best if they are adhered to because they make sense and because they have become part of a person's character, not merely out of fear of punishment. One way or another, it's your job to inculcate such values in your children.

A PERSONAL NOTE
FROM THE AUTHOR

Berlin was a thriving city in 1927, alive with music and art, commerce and industry. The hub of the Western world. I was born in a busy metropolis, a city resembling New York in its best days. A magnet for intellectuals and a necessary crossroads for business. But within 20 short years it was a shambles. Hitler's seat of power was bombed, burned and in 1945, after the war, it was also divided in half.

After the humiliation of defeat in 1918, Germany was politically, economically and psychologically in disarray. The despair was so profound that the Germans democratically offered Hitler the chance to rule. Anxious and lost people always look for strong leadership, and the Fuehrer pledged to bring them bread and honor. Chronic disorder creates a vacuum that makes room even for thugs who promise order, no matter what the cost. Fascist and Communist dictatorships have often arisen at such times. Authoritarian rule is indeed a dangerous and abusive form of fathering, whether in societies or within the family, and it often is destructive.

I also witnessed good fathering. It will remain forever an enigma who in my family was mostly responsible for the courageous decision in 1934 to just get up and go, leaving Germany and practically all our possessions behind. My sentimental and somewhat dreamy father was not German by birth and on this score he may well have had clear vision, unlike my C.E.O. mother who came from Nuremberg and who saw herself largely as German. But whatever the combination of circumstances, strong leadership saved our family. It may have been a most difficult decision but one that turned out to save our lives.

It was not easy to believe that the highly civilized and cultured German people could become much worse than crazed packs of wolves in the pursuit of innocent people. After all, the Germans loved Mozart, Schubert, Beethoven, Goethe and Schiller. It was impossible to forecast the Holocaust, yet for lack of such foresight six million Jews and millions of non-Jews perished. They lingered in false hope when there was still time to escape.

Thus I personally experienced the extreme consequences of both bad and good fathering. I know the subject not only academically. The lessons are deeply and lastingly imprinted on the core of my being. I'm alive!

Years later I saw again the profound opposite effects of the two kinds of fathering. I was barely 20 in the months before the establishment of Israel, and my duties involved contacts with David Ben-Gurion. Like a loving father, the "old man" was consumed with the fate of the new state about to be born on May 14, 1948. He hardly slept trying to ensure that it would not be destroyed just as it came into being. Seven invading Arab armies began their advance towards Tel-Aviv one minute after midnight, the official time of Israel's birth.

Ben-Gurion was a short man but great in stature. His vision, more than anything else, overcame the doubts and fears of many who advised caution and waiting. In spite of his age he personally always accepted the challenge of "the route of greatest difficulty," the opposite of doing what comes naturally. His indomitable spirit changed the map of the world and the history of the Jewish people, even as it created a national home for those surviving the Nazis, and for many others.

On the other hand, the Mufti of Jerusalem at the time, Haj Ameen el Husseini, was a prime example of poor fathering. The religious and political leader of the Palestinians used hate to achieve his goals, like Hitler his mentor. Inciting false fears, he caused hundreds of thousands of peaceful Arabs to leave their safe homes, figuring that refugees who have nothing to lose would fight the "Zionist enemy" more willingly. The tragic long-term effects of such leadership are beginning to heal only now, 50 years later.

So, long before I went to medical school and long before I became a psychiatrist I already knew a lot about good and bad fathering. In the family and in society good fathering is often literally lifesaving. Its absence commonly leads to tragedy.

My intensive psychotherapy work with hundreds of patients over the last 30 years has only confirmed these observations. Good mothering is needed first and foremost to heal depression and eliminate anxiety, but mental health can only be achieved if sufficient good fathering is also present. The requirements spelled out in this book have come into sharp focus by now, and they are no longer in doubt. The lessons of historical events and my own life are obvious and self-evident. In varying degrees, the dangers and opportunities that I encountered are also part of every other life.

Berlin exists but it has never regained its glory of old. The Germans live very well, but Germany paid and is still paying a horrible price. Its shame persists. Civilizations decline and die, just like individuals.

America will surely survive even if it is on the way down, as many claim. But to remain a powerful Beacon of Liberty, and for us even to live safely in our homes, we must raise children who know right from wrong. Democratic institutions cannot exist for long without citizens willing and ready to stand up for the cause of justice. It is dangerous to take our many blessings for granted. As stated in chapter 25, in a very real sense fathers are the trustees of civilization and they hold its future in their hands.

ACKNOWLEDGEMENTS

Many more good people deserve to be thanked than space permits. I was blessed with a lot of friendship, encouragement and helpful cooperation as I was writing this book, and am sincerely grateful to all those who extended these to me so generously. They cannot all be mentioned by name but Mandell Berman, The Honorable Vanesa Jones Bradley, Brian Dickerson, Maureen and Wayne Doran, Robert Fenton, Jane Froslie, Raya Goldenberg, Norma HarPaz, Susan Kaufman, Drs. David Fogel, Harvey Minkin, Craig Neuner, and Christopher Wilhelm, Bernard Mazel, Alex Moore, Paul Nathan, Judith Pizzuti, Rabbi Daniel Polish, Theron Raines, Maxine Reynolds, Charles Soberman, Lea Stanton, Jeremy Tarcher and Koji Watanabe must be mentioned specifically. Their suggestions and questions have been more helpful to me than some of them may realize. Their encouragement is gratefully acknowledged.

Natan HarPaz and the Honorable Ralph Guy have consistently urged me on and supported this effort. They freed precious time from very busy schedules to make themselves available to counsel me whenever this was needed. I am complimented by their friendship and thankful for their help. And I'm most of all grateful to Pamela Torraco, my wise and patient editor, and to David Baker, my diligent publications manager. They brought limitless goodwill to the tedious task of correcting the manuscript errors and of arranging the details of production. Any oversights that remain are the result of last-minute changes and are my responsibility alone.

Finally, this book would not have been created without the devoted and conscientious help of my secretary, Maria Attard, who typed and retyped the manuscript and carefully watched over it as it evolved into becoming this book. Her dedication made this creative effort almost seem easy.

It truly was a team effort. I'm fortunate and very grateful to have had such pleasant, willing and eager teammates. They all deserve to share much of the credit for whatever good this book produces in the world.

BIBLIOGRAPHY

Aronson, E. (1980). *The social animal* (3rd ed.). San Francisco: W. H. Freeman.

Bar-Levav, R. (1976). Behavior change—insignificant and significant, apparent and real. In A. Burton (Ed.), *What makes behavior change possible?* (pp. 278-303). New York: Brunner/Mazel.

Bar-Levav, R. (1976). Life without father. *Detroit Medical News, 66* (47), 6-7.

Bar-Levav, R. (1977). Legislating character. *Detroit Medical News, 68* (26), 6-7.

Bar-Levav, R. (1977). Swastikas on chopped liver. *Voices, 13* (1), 29-37.

Bar-Levav, R. (1988). *Thinking in the shadow of feelings.* New York: Simon and Schuster.

Belsky, J. (1993). Promoting father involvement; an analysis and critique: Comment on *Silverstein. Journal of Family Psychology, 7* (3), 287-292.

Bettelheim, B. (1950). *Love is not enough: The treatment of emotionally disturbed children.* Glencoe, IL: Free Press.

Bowlby, J. (1979). *The making and breaking of affectional bonds.* London: Tavistock.

Bozett, F. W., & Hansons, M. H. (Eds.). (1991). *Fatherhood and families in social context.* New York: Springer.

Bronstein, P., & Cowan, C. (Eds.). (1988). *Fatherhood Today.* New York: Wiley.

Butterworth. D. (1994). Are fathers really necessary to the family unit in early childhood? *International Journal of Early Childhood, 26* (1), 1-5.

Colant, M. (1992). *Finding time for fathering.* New York: Fawcett Columbine.

Collins, A. W. (1993). Father-adolescent relationships: From phase one finding to phase two questions. *New Directions for Child Development,* (No. 62), 91-96.

Crockett, L. J., Eggenbeen, D. J., & Hawkins, A. J. (1993). Father's presence and young children's behavioral and cognitive adjustment. *Journal of Family Issues, 14* (3), 355-377.

Demick, J. (Ed.). (1993). *Parental development.* Hillsdale, NJ: Erlbaum.

Dershowitz, A. L. (1994). *Abuse excuse: Cop-outs, sob stories, and other evasions of responsibility.* Boston: Little Brown.

Dobson, J. (1982). *Dare to discipline.* New York: Bantam Books.

Dobson, J. (1983). *Love must be tough: New hope for families in crisis.* Waco, TX: Word Books.

Edelman, G. (1992). *Bright air, brilliant fire.* New York: Basic Books.

Erikson, E. H. (1963). *Childhood and society* (2nd ed.). New York: Norton.

Erikson, E. H. (1968). *Identity, youth, and crisis.* New York: Norton.

Forehand, R., & Nousiainen, S. (1993). Maternal and paternal parenting: Critical dimensions in adolescent functioning. *Journal of Family Psychology, 7* (2), 213-221.

Freud, S. (1936). *The problem of anxiety.* New York: Norton. (Original work published in 1926)

Garbarino, J. (1992). *Toward a sustainable society: An economic, social and environmental agenda for our children's future.* Chicago: Noble Press.

Garbarino, J. (1993). Reinventing fatherhood. *Families in Society, 74* (1), 51-54.

Greenacre, P. (1960). Considerations regarding the parent-infant relationship. *The International Journal of Psycho-Analysis, 41* (6), 571-584.

Greenspan, M. (1983). *A new approach to women and therapy.* New York: McGraw-Hill.

Hewlett, B. S. (Ed.). (1992). *Father-child relations: Cultural and biosocial contexts.* New York: De Gruyter.

Hogan, D. P., Hao, L. X., & Parrish, W. L. (1990). Race, kin networks, and assistance to mother-headed families. *Social Forces, 68* (3), 797-812.

Izard, C. E., Haynes, O. M., Chisholm, G., & Baak, K. (1991). Emotional determinants of infant-mother attachment. *Child Development, 62,* 906-917.

Jersild, A. T., & Holmes, F. B. (1933). A study of children's fears. *Journal of Experimental Education, 2* (2), 109-118.

Kimmel, M. S., & Messner, M. A. (1992). *Men's lives* (2nd ed.). New York: Macmillan.

Krampe, E. M., & Fairweather, P. D. (1993). Father presence and family formation: A theoretical reformulation [Special issue]. *Journal of Family Issues, 14* (4), 572-591.

Lamb, M. E. (Ed.). (1987). *The father's role: Cross cultural perspectives.* Hillsdale, NJ: Erlbaum.

Lansky, M. R. (1992). *Fathers who fail: Shame and psychopathology in the family system.* Hillsdale, NJ: Analytic Press.

Lasch, C. (1978). *The culture of narcissism: American life in an age of diminishing expectations* (1st ed.). New York: Norton.

Louv, R. (1993). *FatherLove: What we need, what we seek, what we must create.* New York: Pocket Books.

MacDonald, G. (1977). *The effective father.* Wheaton, IL: Tyndale House.

Mahler, M., Pine, F., & Bergman, A. (1975). *The psychological birth of the human infant.* New York: Basic Books.

Mandler, G. (1975). *Mind and emotion.* New York: Wiley.

Manninen, V. (1993). For the sake of eternity: On the narcissism of fatherhood and the father-son relationship. *Scandinavian Psychoanalytic Review, 16* (1), 35-46.

Marsh, P., & Campbell, A. (Eds.). (1982). *Aggression and violence.* New York: St. Martin's Press.

Marsiglio, W. (1993). Contemporary scholarship on fatherhood: Culture, identity, and conduct [Special issue]. *Journal of Family Issues, 14* (4), 484-509.

May, R. (1950). *The meaning of anxiety.* New York: Ronald Press.

Minirth, F., Newman, B., & Warren, P. (1992). *The father book.* Nashville: Nelson.

Mitsherlich, A. (1969). *Society without the father.* New York: Harcourt, Brace, and World.

Munseh, R. (1986). *Love you forever.* Willowdale, Ontario: Firefly Books.

Nelles, W. B., & Barlow, D. H. (1988). Do children panic? *Clinical Psychology Review, 8,* 359-372.

Nugent, J. K., & Brazelton, T. B. (1989). Preventive intervention with infants and families: The NBAS model. *Infant Mental Health Journal, 10,* 84-99.

Ofari, C. (1992). *Black parenting: The guide to male parenting.* Inglewood, CA: Impact.

Ofari, C. (1994). *Black parenting II: Black women talk about their men.* Los Angeles: Middle Passage Press.

Phares, V. (1993). Father absence, mother love, and other family issues that need to be questioned: Comment on *Silverstein. Journal of Family Psychology, 7* (3), 293-300.

Piaget, J. (1954). *The construction of reality in the child.* New York: Basic Books.

Reedy, G. (Ed.). (1984). Fathers. *Feasts and Seasons, 3* (3).

Renouf, E. M. (1991). Always on your mind but not always on your hands: Perspectives on parenting, particularly fatherhood. *Australian Journal of Marriage and Family, 12* (1), 39-45.

Ritner, G. (1992). *Fathers' liberation ethics: A holistic ethical advocacy for active nurturant fathering.* Lanham, MD: University Press of America.

The role of the father in child development (2nd ed.). (1981). New York: Wiley.

Ross, J. M. (1994). *What men want: Mothers, fathers and manhood.* Cambridge, MA: Harvard University Press.

Rustica, J. G., & Abbott, D. (1993). Father involvement in infant care: Two longitudinal studies. *International Journal of Nursing Studies, 30* (6), 467-476.

Sayings of the fathers/Pirke aboth. (1945). (Hertz, J., Trans.). West Orange, NJ: Behrman House.

Scull, C. S. (Ed.). (1992). *Fathers, sons, and daughters: Exploring fatherhood.* Los Angeles: Jeremy P. Tarcher.

Schulman, S., & Collins, A. W. (Eds.). (1993). *Father-adolescent relationships.* San Francisco: Jossey-Bass.

Selye, H. (1950). *The physiology and pathology of exposure to stress.* Montreal: Acta.

Silverstein, L. B. (1993). Primate research, family politics, and social policy: Transforming "cads" into "dads". *Journal of Family Psychology, 7* (3), 267-282.

Spock, B. (1957). *Baby and child care.* New York: Pocket Books.

Sugarman, A. (1994). *Victims of abuse: The emotional impact of child and adult trauma.* Madison, CT: International Universities Press.

Thevenin, T. (1993). *Mothering and fathering: The gender difference in child rearing.* New York: Avery Publishing Group.

Turgenev, I. (N.D.). *Fathers and Sons.* (G. Reavy, Trans.) New York: New American Library. (Original work published 1862)

White, M. (1987). *The Japanese Educational Challenge.* New York: Free Press.

Winnicott, D. (1960). The theory of the parent-infant relationship. *The International Journal of Psycho-Analysis, 41* (6), 585-595.

INDEX

Aaron, Hank, 82
Abuse of children. *See* Child abuse
Achievement by child
    black models for, 83
    and claims of incompetence,
        213
    and effort, 199
    and excellence, 258
    father's pride in, 246
    father's role to push toward, 23
    insistence on, 214
    praise for, 167, 192, 198, 245,
        246
    relaxation after, 252-53
Addiction, emotional, 245-46
Africa, and fatherlessness, 86-87,
    88
Aggression, vs. anger, 174, 187
Aid to Families with Dependent
    Children, 79, 87
Allowance (money) for children,
    191
Andrea (story), 102-3
Anger of child, 26, 42, 97, 171
    vs. aggression, 174, 187
    and disdain, 180, 182
    examination of reason for, 173-
        74, 182
    expression of, 50, 151, 171-73,
        175-78
    as frightening, 28
    overtoleration of, 175
    and respect, 23-24, 175, 182
    suppression of, 172, 173, 177
    as transient, 49
    See also Feelings

Anger of parent
    over child's anxiety, 251
    expression of, 152, 237
    need to contain, 225, 259
    and punishment, 53
    over social conditions, 262
    and urge to get even, 52
Anxiety, 45, 251-52
    of father, 49-50
    "fun" as relief from, 32
    from insufficient mothering, 45
    and loneliness, 233
    and new situations, 251
    and self-indulgence, 195
    and suicide, 45
    and thinking ability, 223
Apologies, 183
Arbitrariness, 192, 248
Archer, Dennis, 83
Ashe, Arthur, 82
Asian-Americans
    and success qualities, 83
    work ethic among, 21
Athletes, as role models, 80-81
Authoritarian fathering, 13, 46, 51-
    54, 58-60
    in story of Tom, 132-33
Authoritative fathering, 59
Authority
    and acts of violent youth, 34
    and challenges to parents, 255
    and children of authoritarian
        parents, 60
    distrust of bred by mini-abuse,
        64
    in fathering, 20-22, 39, 183, 194

273

Authority *(cont.)*
  fathers' loss of, 38
  and parents' errors, 219
    failure to admit, 63
  vacuum of, 34, 54, 111

Baby talk (infantalization), 167, 199, 246
Beauty, openness to, 261
Bedtimes, 247
Ben-Gurion, David, 264
Berlin, post-1927 fate of, 263, 265
Bettelheim, Bruno, 188-89
Bisexuals, 128
Black babies, born to single mothers, 11
Black Power movement, 82
Black youngsters
  and crime, 90-91
  fatherlessness of, 85-89
  and quality of character, 83-84
  role models for, 80-83, 89-90
  and story of Z, 75-76, 77-83
  tiny minority of dangerous, 90
Bob (story), 70-73
Boredom, 258
Brain development, 221
  and character traits, 227-28
Bribery, 168
  in divorce situation, 98, 99
  and teaching of responsibility, 27
Budgeting by children, 191-92, 218

Car accidents, and narcissistic attitude, 180
Central Park "wilding" attack, 31-32
Ceremonies of celebration, 248-49
Chamberlain, Wilt, 80
Changing your mind, 63

Character, and observation of parents, 117
Character change, 53
Character education, 11, 13, 15. *See also* Values
Character formation, by fathering parent, 21-22
Charitable giving, 239
Child abuse, 62, 64
  bitterness as source of, 235
  and challenges to parental authority, 255
  Jodie's charge of, 100, 104
Childbearing, training not required for, 46-47
Child-centered households, 257
Children's Defense Fund, 90
Chores (tasks)
  assignment of to child, 190-91
  as joint projects, 165
  and self-discipline, 197
Christian, Spencer, 83
Civilization
  possible death of, 13
  and self-restraint, 193
  sensitivity and empathy needed for, 235
Cleaver, Eldrige, 82
Closeness, and effects of mothering, 44
Clothes
  and authority, 248, 257
  and self-care, 260
Cocaine-addicted mothers, 89
Comforting, excessive pursuit of, 166-68
Compassion
  from fathering, 33, 237
  teaching of, 138
  See also Sensitivity
Competence, false claims of, 208-11

Competence, false claims of *(cont.)*
  challenging, 215-19
Compliance, vs. cooperation, 60
Confidant of mother, son vs. father
  as, 169
Conflict
  and fathering, 48, 203-4
  need to reveal, 152
  unavoidability of, 97, 213
Conscience, 194
Control, fears of losing, 172
Cooperation, vs. compliance, 60
Courts
  and children of divorce, 101,
    104
  and insanity defense, 156, 173,
    174
Crime or criminality
  as absence of self-restraint, 187
  and black community, 83, 90-
    91
  and disdain or arrogance, 181
  and gangs, 188
  shame absent from, 211
  widespread concern about, 15
  See also Violence; Youth vio-
    lence
Critical thinking, 221
  and father as authority, 21
  vs. permissiveness, 258
  preference for avoiding, 229
  from self-discipline, 201
  See also Reasoning; Thought-
    fulness
Cruelty
  to animals, 137-38, 177
  of authoritarian fathering, 58-
    59
  and human nature, 32
  and punishment, 62
  teaching against, 237, 239
Curiosity, need to promote, 216

Cynicism, about politics, 262

Dads, 26
  vs. fathers, 26-29, 49, 125
  and homosexuality, 127
  unconditional acceptance from,
    125
Dating, 215
Daughters, 113, 160-61, 164
  and aging fathers, 69
  and divorce, 169
  and fathering, 41, 127
  and identity, 166
  See also Father-daughter rela-
    tionship
Davis, Angela, 82
Death, as subject for discussion, 240
Democratic institutions, and justice,
  265
Dependency
  emotional, 141-42
  of welfare recipients, 87
DeRamus, Betty, 82
DeYoung family, 30-31, 34-35
Diary of father, entry in, 137-40
Disagreement, need to reveal, 152,
  215
Discipline
  dislike of, 200
  and self-discipline, 201 (*see also*
    Self-discipline)
Discouragement of child, 214, 222
Disdain, 50, 153, 175, 176, 180-82
  and discussions, 225
  guidelines for battle against,
    182-84
  and hate, 97
Dismissal, 176, 180, 181, 184. *See
  also* Disdain
Divorced parents, 97-104, 169-70,
  222
Dress code, 248, 260

Drug use
  from anxiety, 45
  family ties as preventing, 250
  and father's actions, 62
  and loneliness, 233
  by Marie, 77
  by new fathers, 143, 145
  vs. self-mothering, 244
  and self-restraint, 187
  in story of Joel, 143-44, 145
  as suppression, 155
  from unsatisfied needs, 244
  widespread concern about, 15

Educational psychology, antiauthority
  "value" in, 65
Embarrassment
  vs. shame, 210
  over social backwardness, 215
  See also Shame
Emotional dependency, of husbands
  on wives, 141-42
Emotions. *See* Feelings
Empathy, 230-31, 235
  lack of, 235
  vs. overidentification, 231-32,
    239-40
  teaching of, 238, 239
  See also Compassion; Sensitiv-
    ity
Errors by father
  admission of, 51, 63, 182, 199
  authority lessened by, 219
  and child's level of competence,
    217
  and inconsistency, 63
Ethnic groups, fathering in, 21
Excellence
  black models of, 83
  father as promoting, 22, 24, 257

guidelines for encouraging, 259-
  62
  quest for, 255
  requirements for, 258
Expectations
  toward child, 50
    clarity needed in, 62
    of excellence, 255
    and legitimacy of limits, 247
    need to have met, 191
  child's unrealistic, 179, 186, 203
  in marriage, 242
  of "me" generation, 193
  raised by welfare programs, 88
  of teenagers, 189-90
Explanations to child, 15, 50, 191
  as insufficient by themselves,
    33
  and level of understanding, 152,
    240
  limitations on, 192
  need for, 223
  rejection to be accompanied by,
    209
  of standards, 191

Fabrication, by children, 53
Face saving, by child, 184
Failure by child, need to avoid, 198
Family culture, 260-61
  children's adjustment to, 257
Family ties and values, 250, 260-61
Family visits and affairs, 251
Fantasies
  need to distinguish from facts,
    223-24
  need to limit, 35
  sexual, 158
  and toddlers, 208

Father(s), 110-11
    after birth of child, 141-47
    vs. dads, 26-29, 49, 125
    discouragement and defeat of,
        39-40
    in divorce situations, 102
    dwindling supply of, 42
    and mothering, 46, 127-28, 200-
        201, 222
Father-daughter relationship, 113-
        14, 117-19, 120, 161
    and daughter's attitudes toward
        men, 118-19, 120-21
    and daughter's sexual develop-
        ment, 116-17, 118, 120
    in story of Maryanne, 114-16,
        117
Fathering, 19-24
    injurious, 11, 14, 41, 121, 265
    authoritarian, 13, 46, 51-54, 58-
        60, 132-33
    in author's family, 263
    by Ben-Gurion, 264
    by black grandparents, 91
    by divorced parents, 97-104,
        169-70
    and acquisition of habits and
        character traits, 228
    and thinking ability, 221-22
    and claims of incompetence,
        212
    and male homosexuality, 123-
        25, 126
    difficulties of, 39, 41-42, 206
    discussion of with youngster,
        199
    guidelines on, 55-56, 222-25
        if overly demanding, 51-54
        if overly distant, 54-55
        if overly lenient, 49-51
    guidelines on how not to do, 61-
        63

insufficiency of through genera-
        tions, 38-39
    lack of, 77
    lack of skills in, 14
    mothering necessary to, 13, 24,
        43
    by mothers, 12, 19, 37-38, 222
    mothers' interference with, 165,
        168
    by Mufti of Jerusalem, 264-65
    nurturing outside of, 19, 24
    and parental division of labor,
        25
    and responsibility, 156
    restrictiveness required in, 48
    and self-mothering, 244, 246
    and son's relationship with
        mother, 161
    and states of mind, 84
    and youth violence, 33, 34, 35
    See also Manual on fathering
Fatherlessness, 14
    among blacks, 85-87, 88
    and criminality, 188
    damage from, 36
    in intact families, 11
    and welfare programs, 88
Father's Day, telephone calls made
        on, 110
Father-son relationship
    misunderstandings and insen-
        sitivity, 92-96, 111, 132
    reconciliation, 69-75
    Simpkins' story on, 134-36
    in story of Gene, 109
    in stories of Joel and Johnny,
        145-46
    in story of Tom and family, 132-
        33
    and suiciding, 46-47
Fear
    continued claim of, 196

Fear *(cont.)*
    shyness as, 215, 251
    and social backwardness, 215
    use of, 60, 61
Feelings, 153-54, 226-29
    vs. actions, 151, 153, 155, 173-
        174, 233-34, 237,251
    as basis of relationship, 152, 153
    and brain pathways, 227-28
    children hardened to, 233
    expression of, 151, 155-56, 172,
        233, 237
    as passing quickly, 203
    and reality, 51
    vs. reason, 225-26
    suppression of, 154-55, 175, 234
    See also Anger of child; Anger of
        parent
Feminism, 127-28
Fire-setting, 177
Firmness, vs. harshness, 52, 59
Food
    new, 251
    and self-mothering, 247
    See also Meals
Force, use of, 59, 183
Freud, Sigmund, 117, 155
Friends of children, parents' judg-
    ment on, 218-19
Frustration tolerance, 190
Funerals of close relatives, 240
Future of children, concern
    about, 54

Gangs, teenage, 188
Gene (story), 105-9
George (story), 114-16, 117
Germany under Hitler, 181, 235,
    255, 263-64, 265

Getting even
    with authoritarian father (ex-
        ample), 60
    urge toward, 52
Girls. *See* Daughters
"Good cop, bad cop" combination,
    25
Grandmothers, black, 91
Gratification, immediate, 23
    self-gratification, 14
Guilt, 62, 152, 210
Gumble, Bryant, 83

Harding, Tonya, 13
Harris, Eddy, 84
Harshness, 52, 59, 61
    of authoritarian rule, 58-59
    in fathering of homosexual-to-
        be, 124
    vs. firmness, 52, 59
    from teachers, 64-65, 254
Hate, 63, 175, 180, 206, 235
Hispanics, increase in doctorates
    earned by, 83
Holocaust, 235, 264
Homework, 165, 214
Homosexuality (male), 125-27, 128-
    29
    increase in, 125
    of Jonathan's grandson, 164
    origin of, 41, 122-25, 126, 127,
        128
Household routines, insisting on,
    214-15
Human nature, as kind or cruel, 32
Humiliation, 152, 225
Humility
    and appreciation of universe,
        261
    and narcissism, 243

Humor, 260
Hunter (police officer), 78-80, 83, 89, 91
Hurt, 49, 97, 171, 202-6, 227, 237
el Husseini, Haj Ameen, 264

Identifying with others, 231
Identity, male, 117, 165-66
Immigrants, hard work and loyalty of, 21, 83
Impulsivity in children, 22, 256
Incompetence, false claims of, 210, 211-12
  challenging, 213-15
Inconsistency, 63
Incorrigible kids, 61
Indignation, self-righteous, 177, 204
Insanity defense, 156, 173, 174
Insults, 153, 176-77
  baby talk as, 199
Intimacy, and effects of mothering, 44
Irrationality, battle against, 29. *See also* Reasoning
Israel, establishment of, 264

Jackson, Jesse, 83
Jackson, Michael, 80, 81-82
Jealousy, 126
Jefferson, Thomas, 165
Jerry (story), 102-4
Jewish people
  establishment of Israel, 264
  in ghettos during Middle Ages, 86
Jodie (story), 98-101, 104
Joel (story), 143-46
John (story), 92-96
Johnny (story), 144-45
Johnson, Magic, 80, 81

Jonathan (story), 162-64
Jordan, Barbara, 83
Jordan, Michael, 80
Justice
  commitment to, 174
  and democratic institutions, 265
Kerrigan, Nancy, 13

Larry (story), 74-75, 77, 100
Learning to think, 221-26
Legal system, and children of divorce, 101, 104
Limits, setting of, 22, 185-86
  accepting legitimacy of, 247
  child as welcoming, 209
  on TV watching, 190, 238
Loneliness, 159, 243
  anxiety of, 233
Lying
  accusation of (Margaret), 64
  and teaching of responsibility, 27

Manual on fathering
  anger of child
    examination of reason for, 173-74, 182
    expression of, 171-73, 175-78
  child's feelings to be expressed, 151
  disagreement to be matter-of-fact, 152
  disdain to be disallowed, 180-84
  empathy and sensitivity to be taught, 230-40
  excellence and values to be taught, 255-62
  false claims of competence or incompetence to be challenged, 207-19

Manual on fathering *(cont.)*
  hurt to be expressed, 202-6
  independence from mother to
    be pushed, 157-70
  limit-setting, 185-86, 209
  open discussion, 152
  reality supersedes feelings, 152-
    53
  self-indulgence to be overcome
    by self-discipline, 194-201
  self-mothering to be taught,
    241-53
  self-restraint to be promoted,
    186-93
  teaching child to think, 220-29
  See also Father-daughter rela-
    tionship; Fathering; Father-
    son relationship
Margaret (story), 63-64
Marie (story), 76-77, 119-20
Marriage
  expectations in, 242
  as security, 45
Marshall, Thurgood, 83
Maryanne (story), 114-116, 117
Masculinity, 161, 165-66
Mastery of tasks
  and competence, 216-17
  praise for and help with, 192
  self-discipline required for, 258
Mays, Willie, 82
Meals, 214, 250. *See also* Food
"Me" generation, 193
Menendez brothers, 101
Mistakes. *See* Errors by father
Misunderstanding, of fathers by
  children, 54-55
Model(s), 90
  aggressive teenagers as, 188
  and black youngsters, 80-83, 89-
    90
  fathers as, 23-24, 38, 169-70
  Hunter as, 79, 89, 91

same gender parent as, 161
and self-restraint, 193
for sensitivity, 233
and values, 259, 261
Money
  child's management of, 191-92,
    218
  and self-indulgence, 197
  unrealistic views on, 217-18
Moral principles. *See also* Principles
Mother(s), 40, 43-44, 110, 157-59
  in alliance with child, 168-69
  alternative options available to,
    40, 127
  and claims of incompetence,
    212
  cocaine-addicted, 89
  as competing with fathers, 40
  contented and discontented, 44
  fathering by, 12, 19, 37-38, 222
  fathering rejected by, 165
  fears of projected on children,
    167
  need for independence from,
    159-62
  and new babies, 142-43, 146,
    147
  overpampering by, 167, 169
  and regressive behavior, 167-68
  as sole parent, 40-41 (*see also*
    One-parent families)
  and sons' relationships with
    women, 158-59
  in story of father-son reconcili-
    ation, 70
Mothering, 13, 24, 43-46, 241, 265
  of children during divorce, 98,
    101-2
  and child's thinking ability, 221-
    22
  and creation of male homo-
    sexual, 41, 122-23, 124, 126
  fathering seen as, 39

Mothering *(cont.)*
   and fathers, 46, 127-28, 200-
     201, 222
   harm in lack of, 45, 77, 121
   and parental division of labor,
     25
   and self-mothering, 169, 244 *(see
     also* Self-mothering)
   and shame, 210
   as soothing, 97
Mother's Day, telephone calls made
   on, 110
Mufti of Jerusalem, 264

Narcissism, 175, 180, 181
   Judeo-Christian attempts to
     control, 243
National Urban League, 88
"Natural Born Killers" (movie), 187
Newborns
   family centered on, 256-57
   fathers of, 141-47
Newton, Huey, 82
Nintendo, 31, 34-35. See also Video
   games
Nurturing, as outside fathering, 19,
   24

One-parent families, 11, 25, 40-41,
   222
Overidentification, 231-32, 240
Overprotectiveness, 203, 205-6, 232
   and well-to-do families, 245

Pain. *See* Hurt
Pampering, 167, 169
Panhandlers, 238
Parents
   division of labor by, 25
   divorced, 97-104, 169-70, 222
   reality conveyed by, 208

of same or opposite gender,
   117, 161
   See also Father; Mother
Parks, Rosa, 91
Passive-aggressive people, 180
Permissiveness, 12-13, 39
   by children of authoritarian par-
     ents, 60
   as harmful, 225, 258
   limits of, 209 *(see also* Limits,
     setting of)
Personal insults, 176-77
Physical closeness, and effects of
   mothering, 44
Physical needs, 250-51
Poitier, Sidney, 83
Political and social attitudes, and
   abuse of children, 64
Pouting, 50, 176
Powell, Colin, 83
Power
   appropriate use of, 52, 213
   new fathers' simulation of, 142
   parents' improper use of, 57, 64
   and the powerless, 64
Praise, 167, 192, 198, 245, 246
Pride, 246
   national or group, 261
Principles
   and "good heart," 231
   need to adhere to, 262
   vs. permissiveness, 258
   vs. style (Jefferson), 165
   See also Standards
Privileges, withholding of, 183, 200
Prostitution, in Marie's story, 76-
   77, 119
Protecting and providing, 19-20, 38
Protesters, political, 258
Protests by child, 63
   anger as, 171 *(see also* Anger of
     child)
   examination of, 174

Protests by child *(cont.)*
    expression of, 63, 176-77, 248
    loudness of, 176
    and self-pity or indignation, 177
    suppressed, 172
Public policy, errors in, 12
Punishment, 53
    by authoritarian father (ex-
        ample), 58
    for disdain, 183
    recommendations on, 62, 191,
        199
  • violence in, 61

Rage. *See* Anger of child; Feelings
Randy (story), 57-58, 60
Rationalizations, 53, 228
Reading to children, 253
Reagan, Nancy, 229
Reality
    vs. fantasy, 35
    fathers/parents as representa-
        tives of, 22-23, 208
    need to be guided by, 28, 51,
        152-53, 214, 216, 223-24
    and self-restraint, 186
Reasoning
    vs. arbitrariness, 248
    and explanations, 209
    vs. feelings, 225-26
    insistence on, 151, 164-65, 182-
        83
    as unique capacity, 221
    with young child, 27, 35
    See also Critical thinking;
        Thoughtfulness
Rebellious children, 181, 224-25
    and clothes, 248, 257
    sons, 39-40
    young children as, 22
Reconciliation between fathers and
    sons, 50, 69

example of absence of, 69-70
    in story of Bob, 70-73
Red-letter days, 260
Regression, 167-68
Rejection, 45
    by hurt child, 28
Relationships
    acts ruinous to, 50
    basis of, 153
Relaxation, 252-53
Respect
    for children, 153
    for father, 166, 183-84, 200
        and anger, 23-24, 175, 182
    lack of, 36
Responsibility
    black models of, 83
    and fathering authority, 194
    household assistance as basis
        for, 215
    lack of, 36
    need for, 156, 174-75
    promoting of, 256, 257
    rationality from, 175
    and rights, 218
Rewards, satisfaction vs. bribe as,
    27
Ridicule, 215
Rights of individual
    child's recognition of, 27
    emphasis on, 255
Roger (story), 94-96
Role model. *See* Model
Rules
    absence of idealized, 256
    father as making and enforcing,
        22
    and limits, 209 (*see also* Limits,
        setting of)
    and mother, 37

Saving face, by child, 184

Scorn. *See* Disdain
Seles, Monica, 12
Self-control, 201, 259
Self-determination, right of, 255
Self-discipline, 154, 196-97, 201
    and black youngsters, 81
    development of, 35
    difficulty in gaining, 50
    and fathering, 22, 41, 156, 196,
        201
    and hardships for others, 195
    and mastery, 258
    need for, 247
    and rules, 54
Self-esteem
    from doing tasks, 192
    and embarrassment, 210
    national or group pride in, 261
    from sensitivity, 231
    and shame, 210
Self-gratification, instant, 14
Self-indulgence, 40, 195-97, 200
    guidelines on combating, 198-
        201
    and self-mothering, 246
Self-love, 243
    excess of, 245
    guidelines on inculcating of,
        246-53
Self-mothering, 242-46
    insisting on, 169
    teaching of, 246-53
Self-observation, 226
Self-pity, 176, 177
Self-praise, 198, 246
Self-reliance, 196
Self-respect
    and hardships on others, 195
    and rules, 54
    and undisciplined lifestyle, 197
Self-restraint, 156, 186-90, 193
    difficulty in gaining, 50

early development of, 256
guidelines for development of,
    190-93, 247
Self-righteousness, 177, 181, 204
Self-scrutiny, 236
Self-sufficiency, 50
Sensitivity, 203, 230-31, 234-35
    to body messages, 250
    and objective observation, 236
    vs. overidentification, 231-32,
        239-40
    vs. phony hypersensitivity, 235-
        36
    and pride, 246
    teaching of, 232-33, 236-40
    toughness compatible with, 237
    See also Compassion
Sexual attack or abuse
    by fathers against daughters, 120
    fathers threatened with charges
        of, 101
Sexual fantasies, 158
Sexual revolution, 127
Shame, 62, 210-11, 215
    and authoritarian regimes, 60
    vs. embarrassment, 210
    and lifestyle choice, 128
    and use of force, 59
Shaw, Edward, 33
Shyness, 215, 251
Simpkins, Travis, 134-36
Single-parent families, 11, 25, 40-
    41, 222
Slavery, 83, 85-87
Spanking, 61
    in story of Jodie, 100
Spirituality, 261
Spock, Dr. Benjamin, 188
Spouse abuse, bitterness as source
    of, 235
Standards
    child's incorporation of, 201

Standards *(cont.)*
    explanation of, 191
    need for, 174-75
    See also Principles; Responsi-
      bility
Stinginess, vs. resource preserva-
    tion, 192
Structure, lack of in lives, 156
Stubbornness of children, 52, 213
Suicide, 45-47
    and mother-son relationship,
      169
    widespread concern about, 15
Survivalist themes, 177

Teachers
    children's demands on, 254-55
    harsh treatment from, 64-65,
      254
Teenage pregnancies, 88-89
Teenager(s)
    and crime, 33-34
    in gangs, 188
    and limits, 186
    materialist expectations of, 189-
      90
    sons after divorce, 169
    and spanking, 61
Temper tantrums, 48, 213, 214
Testing by children, 52
Thomas, Clarence, 83
Thoughtfulness, 220-21, 256
    developing of in child, 221-26,
      257, 259
    vs. feelings, 226-29
    and objective observation, 236
    See also Critical thinking; Rea-
      soning
Tom (story), 130-33
Traditions, family, 260-61
Truman, Harry, 237

T-shirts, 248
TV
    and budgeting of time, 218
    as distraction not relaxation,
      252
    and father's authority, 20-21
    limits on watching, 190, 238
    and self-mothering, 244
    thankfulness for, 249
Tyson, Mike, 81

Unholy alliance (mother-child), 168-
    69
Unjust fathering, 13, 46, 58-59
    harshness in, 52
    in story of Randy, 58

Vacations, 252-53
Values
    and child's adjustment to fam-
      ily, 257
    models in learning of, 23
    teaching of, 11, 13, 256, 259-62
Vegetarianism, 239
Victimization
    Black Power movement's claim
      of, 82
    by inadequate fathering, 29
Video games, 21, 187-88
    Nintendo, 31, 34-35
Vietnam years, 258
Violence, 61
    in ghettos, 187
    preoccupation with, 177
    against Seles and Kerrigan, 12-
      13
    See also Crime or criminality;
      Youth violence

Warhol, Andy, 82
Welfare state, 87-88
"Wilding" in Central Park, 31-32

Withdrawal, 153
    by child, 49, 50, 203-4, 250
    by father, 39, 54, 55
        and newborn baby, 143
Wright, David, 34, 35

Younger children, 22
    attempts at competence by, 215
    examples needed in teaching of,
        35
    and fathering pressure, 27-28,
        35
    identifying the needs of, 232
    impulsivity to be halted in, 256
    and limits, 186
    and mothering, 44
    and narcissism, 181
    and parental prohibitions, 209
    and reasoning, 27, 35
    responsibility to be developed
        in, 256
    as teachable, 28, 179, 189
Youth violence, 33
    from absence of self-restraint,
        187
    and fathering, 33, 34, 35
    fear of, 172
    and hate, 175
    See also Crime or criminality
Youth violence, examples of
    bus station kidnapping, 32-33
    Andrew DeYoung, 30-31, 34-
        35
    killing by "Z," 76
    Menendez brothers, 101
    rape, 33-34
    shooting of children, 90
    "wilding" in Central Park, 31-
        32
    David Wright, 34, 35

Z (story), 75-76, 77, 78-83, 90, 91

AN INVITATION TO THE READER

Readers are invited to send written questions about fathering their children and/or others for inclusion in a follow-up book to appear in 1996, in time for the Presidential election. *The Softening of the American Character* will describe what has happened as a result of the erosion of authority in permissive societies such as ours, not only in the family but also in public policy. One section of the book will consist of questions and answers about the process of fathering. The questions will be selected from those sent in by readers and chosen on the basis of having the widest interest and appeal. Each will be discussed fully.

You are invited to formulate a question that is of special concern to you *in no more than 100 words*. Please mail it to Fathering, Inc. Press at the following address, or fax it to (810) 355-9009. Since all questions will be promptly acknowledged, please be sure to include your full address. Also indicate whether you allow us to use your name, or whether you prefer to remain anonymous.

The authors of questions used will receive a leather-bound presentation copy of *The Softening of the American Character*, together with our many thanks.

• • •

Please type or print legibly and mail to: **Fathering, Inc. Press**
P.O. Box 725455
Berkley, MI 48072

Question _____

_____

_____

_____

Name _____
Address _____
City _____ State _____ Zip Code _____ Phone_____

Please mark <u>one</u> of the following:

☐ You have permission to use my name _____
                                          Signature

☐ I prefer to remain anonymous

**Additional copies of *Every Family Needs a C.E.O.*
are available at your favorite bookstore
or directly from the publisher**

ORDER FORM

For fastest service, phone or fax your credit card order to toll-free number:
1-800-6-FATHER (1-800-632-8437) or fax: **1-603-357-2073**
<u>We pay for shipping and handling when two or more books
are mailed to the same address.</u>

☐ Please send _____ copies of *Every Family Needs a C.E.O.*
($19.95 + $4.00 for shipping and handling)   _____

☐ Please send _____ copies of *Thinking in the Shadow*
of Feelings (<u>hardcover</u>) ($19.95 + $4.00 for
shipping and handling)   _____

☐ Please send _____ copies of *Thinking in the Shadow*
of Feelings (<u>softcover</u>) ($10.95 + $4.00 for shipping
and handling–limited availability)   _____

Express shipping and handling–$10.00: _____

Subtotal: _____

Michigan residents please add 6% sales tax on total order: _____

Total (U.S. funds only): _____

Method of Payment: Check / M.O. enclosed _____
VISA _____ MasterCard _____ Discover _____

Account number: _____ Expiration date: _____

Signature: _____

Name _____

Address _____

City _____ State _____ Zip Code _____ Phone _____
Please allow up to 2 weeks for regular delivery
or up to 3 days for express delivery

**Fax or mail: Fathering, Inc. Press
c/o Pathway Book Service, #509
Lower Village
Gilsum, New Hampshire 03448
USA**